How Did You Get to Be Mexican?

A White/Brown Man's Search for Identity

How Did You Get to Be Mexican?

A White/Brown Man's Search for Identity

Kevin R. Johnson

Temple University Press

Philadelphia

Temple University Press, Philadelphia 19122

Published 1999
Printed in the United States of America

The paper used in this publication meets the requirements of the American National Standard for Information Sciences—Permanence of Paper for Printed Library Materials, ANSI Z39.48–1984

Library of Congress Cataloging-in-Publication Data

Johnson, Kevin R.
How did you get to be Mexican? A white/brown man's search for identity / Kevin R. Johnson
p. cm.
Includes bibliographical references and index.
ISBN 1-56639-650-6 (cloth : alk. paper) —
ISBN 1-56639-651-4 (pbk. : alk. paper)
1. Johnson, Kevin R. 2. Mexican Americans—Biography. 3. Mexican Americans—Ethnic identity. 4. Racially mixed people—United States—Biography. 5. Racially mixed people—United States—Race identity. 6. United States—Race relations. I. Title.
E184.M5J58 1998
305.868'72073'092—dc21
[B] 98-11811
CIP

To Virginia Salazar and Teresa, Tomás,

And Elena Salazar Johnson

To My Parents, Angela and Kenneth

Contents

Preface ix

1 Introduction 1

2 A "Latino" Law Student? Law 4 Sale at Harvard Law School 10

3 My Mother: One Assimilation Story 52

4 My Father: Planting the Seeds of a Racial Consciousness 64

5 Growing Up White? 73

6 College: Beginning to Recognize Racial Complexities 89

A Family Gallery 101

7 A Corporate Lawyer: Happily Avoiding the Issue 109

8 A Latino Law Professor 121

9 My Family/Mi Familia 139

10 Lessons for Latino Assimilation 152

11 What Does It All Mean for Race Relations in the United States? 175

Notes 183

Bibliography 217

Index 235

Preface

Like other "mixed-race" people, I live in a unique place in U.S. society, a metaphorical borderlands between two worlds. The son of a Mexican American mother and an Anglo father, my identity was forged in an era of great change in racial sensibilities in the United States. In my lifetime, the study of civil rights expanded beyond simple black/white relations, multiculturalism rose (and fell?), affirmative action was invented and dismantled. The racial demographics of the U.S. population changed dramatically, in no small part due to immigration. And immigrants of color became the object of a ferocious nativism not seen in the United States since the 1920s.

Against this backdrop, slowly, sometimes painfully, I developed my Latino identity. Jerome McCristal Culp, Jr. tells his law school classes that he is the son of a poor coal miner. By so doing, he undermines the "homogeneity myth" that all African Americans are "the same with the same essential experience."[1] Like the African American community, the Latino community is not homogeneous. This book is my attempt to help make this clear. Though autobiographical in nature, it sheds light on issues of general significance to the Latino community as well as to the study of contemporary race relations.

But while this is my story, many people have helped to make this book happen. Richard Delgado initially approached me with the idea for the book and persuaded me that I could do it. I appreciate his support and encouragement at every step along the way.

Other support was more personal. Judge Stephen Reinhardt gave me my first job out of law school and taught me much about the law as well as about compassion. Many attorneys at my old firm of Heller Ehrman White & McAuliffe, especially Doug Schwab, Bob Venning, Charlie Freiberg, Bob Borton, Larry Keeshan, Scott Fink, Marie Fiala, and Charlie Clifford, made me a lawyer, for which I am deeply appreciative, and offered me many opportunities to do pro bono publico work. Friends like Carl Johnson, Robert Hawk, Sergio Garcia-Rodriguez, Melissa Katz, Jon Hayden, Amelia Craig, Meryl Macklin, Vanessa Wendenburg Vallarta, and Bruce MacMillan helped make work fun.

In the legal academy, Michael Olivas, the dean of Latino law professors, advised and encouraged me along the road to tenure and beyond. His support has had a profound impact on my academic career. I am lucky to call him a friend.

I also want to extend many thanks to my colleagues at the University of California at Davis School of Law, and to Dean Bruce Wolk and Associate Dean Rex Perschbacher, who became Dean in July 1998, for all the research and other support and friendship that they have given me over my years in academia. My friend Arturo Gándara served as a virtually endless source of ideas for this and many other projects. Ever since we joined the law faculty at U.C. Davis in 1989, he has acted as my sounding board and has given many more insights than I could ever hope to return. Joel Dobris talked with me about many of the issues touched on in this book and forwarded me a steady stream of research materials.

Diane Monheit, Glenda McGlashan, and Lisa Chance provided secretarial support with a smile. Peg Durkin, Susan Llano, and

Dolores Brown of the U.C. Davis Law Library responded quickly and tolerantly to my excessive requests for materials. Doris Braendel of Temple University Press committed herself to this project and enthusiastically pushed it (and me) along. Suzanne Wolk, my editor, did an excellent job of readying this book for publication.

Christopher David Ruiz Cameron and George A. Martínez talked me through various aspects of this project and encouraged me to plod forward. They served as my pillars of support throughout. Many people saw drafts of some or all of this book in one form or another. Thanks to Niko Pfund, Richard Delgado, Chris Cameron, George Martínez, Wendy Martínez, Joel Dobris, Eliot Dobris, Yxta Maya Murray, Arturo Gándara, Bill Piatt, Edwin Carlos Rocabado, Keith Aoki, Margaret Montoya, Sylvia Lazos, Leslie Espinoza, Bob Chang, Susan Gail Wilcox, and Marty West for taking the time and offering comments and encouragement. Dave Mackey gave me permission to use photographs from our law school years. Alice Levine, Rich Harroun, and Rosa helped me come up with the title of this book, for which I am appreciative. Melissa Corral, Christine Shen, and Jennifer Shih provided excellent research assistance.

I also am indebted to many law students who have made teaching worthwhile. Among them are Amagda Pérez, Rachel Shigekane, Cindy Kagiwada, Olga Sanchez, Dennise Willett, Lynn Martinez, Sergio O'Cadiz, Nipa Rahim, Joan Jackson, Joy Ramos, Aleem Raja, Saul Garcia, Ming Yuen Fong, Kerry Bader, Bob Orlowsky, Minty Siu Chung, Silva Darbinian, Gina Sirianni, Richard Egger, Sarah Orr, David Kornbluh, Lisa Duarte, Melissa Corral, Kathryn Gimple, Lynne Zellhart, Christine Shen, Dion Costa, Jennifer Shih, Frank Orozco, Miguel Valdovinos, Darcie Houck, Cecelia Wong, Sushil Narayanan, Erika Eichler, Reed Pruyn, Katy Filner, Darolyn Hamada, Michael Kopple, Meredith Linsky, and Michael Holmes. Thanks to all of my students for teaching me more than I could ever hope to teach them.

My parents, Angela and Kenneth, inculcated in me the need for a college education and many other values that have proven invaluable. A strong work ethic, intelligence, tolerance, and caring for others are but a few. My debt to them is immeasurable. I hope that nothing in the pages that follow will hurt them in any way. Dad read a draft and offered many important insights and pieces of information.

Last but not least, I want to thank Virginia Salazar, my wife, friend for life, and reality check. Calm and caring, she has been the foundation for any success that I have enjoyed in life and makes me want to be a better person. She also commented on a draft of the book. Along with Virginia, my children, Teresa, Tomás, and Elena, are the world to me. I have written this book knowing that they will read it, which made the project all the more daunting. I trust that it will teach them something about me and our family.

A version of parts of chapters 1, 3, and 10 were originally published in different form as "'Melting Pot' or 'Ring of Fire'?: Assimilation and the Mexican American Experience," in the *California Law Review* 85:1259 (1997) and published concurrently in *La Raza Law Journal* 10:173 (1998). Thanks to the *California Law* Review for giving me permission to publish this material and to the student editors of both journals who improved the article.

For a variety of reasons, I have not found it particularly easy to write this book. Parts of my life have been painful for me to relive, much less to describe for the world to see. I do not mean to suggest that my life was more difficult than that of Latinos with Spanish surnames or those with more indigenous phenotypes. I have been extremely fortunate. Still, my life experiences have been different from those of many Latinos, with different advantages and disadvantages. Many identity issues remain unresolved for me, just as many important questions involving race remain for U.S. society to address.

As in other autobiographical works,[2] errors no doubt have crept into this book. I wrote this book almost exclusively from memory, without the aid of journals or a diary. My memory has limits and, in various places, restricts the detail that I can share. At times, I have withheld information to protect the privacy of others, and sometimes my own, and to avoid hurting anyone's feelings. For similar reasons, I have changed some names in a few places.

Many who know me may think it odd that I wrote this very personal book. I am a private person. Nonetheless, writing this book has helped me to make some sense out of many seemingly disparate threads of my life. It has also allowed me to address constructively some nagging racial identity issues. More importantly, I hope to shed light on the experiences of an unexplored group of people and tell their untold stories. This book reveals some of the richness of race relations that makes the United States unique.

How Did You Get to Be Mexican?

A White/Brown Man's Search for Identity

Chapter 1

Introduction

Forty or so students looked up expectantly from their seats in a spartan classroom in Martin Luther King Hall. A hush came over the room as I entered and walked briskly to the lectern. It was my second year teaching at the U.C. Davis law school, but this was a new class and I was nervous. Five years in the litigation trenches had not fully prepared me for the butterflies that accompany looking out at all those young faces. "I am Kevin Johnson and this is Business Litigation," I blurted. As I took the class step by step through the syllabus, I began to relax. This isn't so bad, I thought. Now to wrap it all up. Thinking I had covered every conceivable issue, I asked if there were any questions. A hand appeared in the back row. "Have you ever tried a case?" a young woman asked skeptically. The class rustled, suspicion in the air. A challenge to my credentials before the course was even underway. Irritated, I reluctantly answered "yes" as my temperature rose and my brow dampened. Why had she asked? I wondered. Had she heard that I was a minority of some sort? Was it my youth?

This incident took place almost a decade ago. I am still a law professor and I still teach at the University of California at Davis School of Law, located in the Central Valley, an agricultural corridor that runs down the middle of the state. My work has been published in prestigious law journals and I have the security of tenure. My colleagues and students generally make me feel appreciated. Racial rumblings, however, regularly interrupt my peaceful life. I am still occasionally reminded that I might not have a job, or at least not such a good one, if I were not Mexican American.

My mother is Mexican American and my father is Anglo. They met and married young in Los Angeles, where I was born in 1958. Their story is unremarkable. Intermarriage between Anglos and Mexican Americans has occurred for centuries in the Southwest. For much of childhood and youth, I paid little attention to my mixed heritage.

Though I did not think much about it at the time, I have classified myself as Mexican American since adolescence. My eyes are brown and my hair dark brown, almost black. I am more comfortable in Mexican American than in Anglo culture. Over the years, the contrast between my name and self-identification has often been a source of curiosity to others and of occasional discomfort to me. The burning question always seems to be, "Am I a Latino?" This seemingly simple, straightforward question raises complex issues that go to the core of race relations in the modern United States. This book offers a glimpse into my life in the borderlands between the Anglo and Mexican worlds.

It is funny how a person's entire identity can be thrown into doubt in the space of a moment. Sitting in my cluttered office one day, I got a call from an old high school friend I had not seen for years. We chatted for a bit about mutual friends and reminisced about our wild youth. Eventually my friend came to the point. "I need some legal advice," he said. "I got a drunk driving arrest in Nevada. My attorney told me that it was a mandatory six months in jail, so I left the state." I understood his reluctance; who wouldn't try to avoid being locked up?

"I can't go to jail," he continued. "A white guy like me would get killed by the blacks and the Mexicans." My stomach tightened. Perhaps he heard my silence. Remembering that he was talking to a man whose wife's last name is Salazar, whose wedding featured mariachis, whose children are called Teresa, Tomás, and Elena, and whose mother was Mexican American, my friend quickly backpedaled. "No disrespect. I just meant Mexican *gang* members. That's what I should have said." Both angered and saddened, I gave him the legal advice he wanted. It would do no good to lecture.

I like to run. In December 1992, after months of training, I ran the California International Marathon with Steve Roscow, a college chum. The race started in the city of Folsom, a historic Gold Rush town located where the Sierra Nevada foothills begin their slow ascent. After a night of heavy rain, the skies had cleared and the sun was out. It was a magical moment when Bruce Springsteen's inspiring tune "Leap of Faith" came over the loudspeakers. "This is my day," I thought. About half an hour later, I was running through a downpour into a thirty-mile-per-hour headwind that dashed any hopes I had of qualifying for the Boston Marathon.

At the twenty-third mile, I was on J Street, approaching the State Capitol building in downtown Sacramento. Moving more and more slowly and caring less and less, I found myself on the wrong side of the red cones that marked the course as I approached a Safeway grocery store. A group of spectators braving the elements cheered for the back of the pack. A guy looked at me and yelled in a friendly tone, "Hey, *Ese*. *Ese*, there is a bus behind you. Watch out." Without thinking, I looked back to see a bus lurching behind me. I looked back at the guy, who looked Mexican American. It then struck me that he had called me *ese*, Spanish slang for dude or man. Did he see me as a Mexican American? Why? How? Did I look so obviously Mexican American? Or had he called me *ese* out of habit? Perhaps it had nothing to do with me or how I looked or ran. I pondered the question for the last three dreadful miles of the race and for a long time thereafter.

My mother-in-law, Mary Helen Salazar, a Mexican American from Los Angeles, was visiting our new house in Davis. We were sitting in the family room watching the television news. The program cut to a story about racism in the South. Listening intently, Mary Helen observed, "I would never survive there." I responded without thinking, "The real division there is between blacks and whites," to which she quickly replied, "Well, *you* don't have a Spanish surname."

In the spring of 1996, I was sitting in a bar off Pacific Coast Highway in Manhattan Beach, California, a white, upper-middle-class suburb of Los Angeles. Funeral services for my father's uncle, my great-uncle Kennard Johnson (known as "Brown-eyes" or "Brownie" to distinguish him from his blue-eyed twin), had just ended. I had time to kill with my father and step-brother while I waited for my return flight to Sacramento, and we were exchanging memories of Brown-eyes over a few beers. What a funny guy, I mused. "Remember on the way to Yosemite that year when he pulled up his car next to ours and, for a laugh, pulled out his false teeth?" But he sure was a worrier, which was no wonder given a lifetime of economic insecurity. He always worked hard at the bakery, where he was employed for as long as I can remember, but money must have been tight. I wondered what it had been like when he married Rosie and became one of the first in his family to marry a Mexican American woman. They had grown up together in a working-class neighborhood near downtown Los Angeles where Mexican Americans and Anglos lived side by side, and had spent fifty years there before moving to the desert to retire.

While I sat there thinking about Brown-eyes, a tall fellow sitting on the barstool next to us was rambling on to anyone who would listen about a recent trip to Texas,[1] interspersing his banter with a series of bad jokes. In retrospect, what happened next seemed inevitable.[2] I tuned in just in time to hear him ask, "How do you make sure nobody steals the stereo speakers in your car? You put a sign on them saying '*no habla español.*'" Nobody laughed. I wondered why I had to listen to this crap. Why couldn't I drink my beer and grieve without dealing with jokes that cut painfully to the core of my identity? Like a boxer in the late rounds of a fight or a weary runner near the end of a marathon, I was too tired from the travails of the long day—seeing mourning family, reliving the sad and happy memories, pondering my own mortality—to lash back at this insensitive Texan wannabe. "Please give me another," I asked the barmaid and emptied my glass.[3]

The guy got me thinking. On the flight back to Sacramento, I thought of the Spanish speakers I knew and found that I could not think of one who might steal a car stereo. I wondered what it would be like for my identity to be "transparent," a non-issue in my daily life, the way it is for many Anglos.[4]

These stories show how a few words may hurt and marginalize.[5] They also demonstrate the limits of assimilation for Latinos, even half-white ones like myself. Born in 1958 at the tail end of the so-called Baby Boom, I identify as a Latino,[6] specifically as a Mexican American or Chicano. My mother, whose maiden name was Angela (Angie) Gallardo, is a first- or second-generation Mexican American born a few miles north of the border in Brawley, California, a small farmtown in the Imperial Valley. My father, Kenneth

Johnson, is an Anglo who grew up in what was then a mixed Mexican-Anglo working-class neighborhood near Chavez Ravine, where the Los Angeles Dodgers play baseball today.

Through the experiences recounted in this book, I analyze some difficult but crucially important issues for Latinos in the modern United States. Though well aware that the use of autobiography in scholarship is suspect,[7] I believe that it offers a unique opportunity for bringing to the fore the stories of groups of people who have been invisible or ignored, and for offering general insights based on individual experiences.[8] "Mexican Americans need to tell their side of the story."[9] I am part of that story.

I specifically want to explore the assimilation of Latinos into dominant society, with a focus on the experience of Mexican Americans in the Southwest. In recent years, Latino intellectuals like Linda Chávez and Richard Rodriguez[10] have embraced the goal of Latino assimilation into the mainstream of American life. Chávez, for example, proclaims a "new theory" of assimilation, which argues that Latinos, like previous waves of white "ethnic" immigrants, should assimilate into mainstream American culture and are in fact doing so. Separate and unequal Latino enclaves in many cities, however, demonstrate that assimilation is far from complete. Moreover, the economic disparities show no signs of narrowing.[11] In addition, the current anti-immigrant backlash represents in no small part an attack on all persons, citizens as well as immigrants, of Mexican ancestry in the United States, including persons who trace their ancestry in this country back for centuries.[12]

In recent years a growing number of academic studies have looked at how and why some people voluntarily adopt a particular racial identity.[13] Because race is a social construction, people—some people, at least—decide to be Latino. Although physical features, surname, language, or accent make it difficult for some Latinos to pass as white, I could do so if I chose. For the most part, I was never forced to present myself as Mexican American. My brother, who as a youngster had sandy blond hair and blue eyes, never identified as Mexican American. Like him, I might have downplayed my background and hoped that nobody would remember, find out, or care. I could have shed my ethnicity and blended in, though I would have had to deny a family history that has grown increasingly central to my identity.

Because the Latino community is extremely diverse, the ability to choose an identity and assimilate varies widely. My own family history exemplifies Latino heterogeneity. I myself am multicultural.[14] I have my mother's dark brown hair and brown eyes, but I bear the last name Johnson and my height comes from my father's side of the family. My brother's blond hair and blue eyes come from my father's side of the family, though he is short in stature like my mother. My mother speaks Spanish, but she wanted her sons to assimilate and she never taught us the language.

My wife, Virginia Salazar, is from a tightly knit Mexican American family in La Puente, California, east of East Los Angeles. She has dark brown hair and brown eyes and a light complexion. Members of her mother's family generally have fair complexions and light brown hair; those in her father's family generally have dark skin and hair that is dark brown bordering on black. Although both her parents speak Spanish, she was not taught the language at home, either.

To our surprise, our first two children, Teresa and Tomás, have blond hair and blue eyes and fair complexions. By all appearances, they are "white." They are embraced by the family and occasionally have been referred to as *güeros*, Spanish slang for "white ones."[15] Such references hint at the value placed on whiteness in U.S. society. Our third child, Elena, looks more like us, with olive-colored skin and dark hair and eyes. Some have referred to her as our "Mexican" baby or *la morena* (the dark one).[16]

This diversity in physical appearance among a family of five Mexican Americans should make it clear that the Mexican American community is far from homogenous. If Mexican Americans are a diverse group, Latinos are even more so. Mixtures of race, national origin, immigration status, class, culture, education, political outlook, and many other characteristics abound.

As my story illustrates, one aspect of Latino diversity is the prevalence of persons of mixed Latino/Anglo background.[17] Latinos and Anglos intermarry frequently, adding to the population of mixed Latino/Anglo people in the United States. As Latino members increase, one can expect the number of intermarriages and mixed-race children to increase as well. But while poignant books by James McBride, Judy Scales-Trent, Greg Williams, and others[18] have documented the experiences of persons with one black and one white parent, the discussion of mixed-race people has not focused on Latinos of mixed parentage.

Changing demographics make the circumstances of mixed-race Latinos all the more important to consider. According to U.S. Census projections, by 2005 Latinos will be the largest minority group in the United States.[19] If current demographic trends continue, persons of mixed-race backgrounds will increase greatly as a proportion of the U.S. population.[20] Race relations and individual experiences of race are sure to change as a result.

As my own experiences show, American social, political, economic, and legal institutions attempt to force people into hard-and-fast categories, which accounts for some of the difficulties faced by mixed-race persons.[21] To take one small but important example, what box should a person check on the U.S. Census form when that person does not fit neatly into any of the enumerated racial or ethnic categories? What message does the absence of an appropriate box convey? The same questions apply to applications for admission to educational institutions and for employment. None of the recognized categories fully or accurately describes a mixed-race person. One hates to be in the position of denying one's background and appearing to be ashamed of one's heritage. At the same time, one fears being accused of claiming to be a minority—sometimes by members of the very minority group with which he or she has identified—simply to obtain a "special" preference in affirmative action programs.[22]

Ultimately, the assimilation experiences of Latinos tell us a great deal about race relations in the United States. Both Mexican Americans in the Southwest and Latinos throughout the country have been defined as different from and inferior to whites. Because they are different from the Anglo-Saxon "core" of the United States, Latinos are often viewed as "foreigners" to the nation, even if their families have lived in this country for generations.[23]

The stories in this book illustrate some oft-ignored facets of the assimilation process. My grandmother and mother were two of the most ardent Mexican American assimilationists you would ever want to meet. They never succeeded, and they suffered immensely in the effort. Whatever the world may think, their son and grandson—for all his Harvard education and cushy university job—has never been fully assimilated into the mainstream either.[24] The stories of my mother and maternal grandmother reflect the difficulties of assimilation for Latinas and are a sad metaphor for the story of the assimilation of Mexican Americans in the Southwest. My own experiences reflect the amorphousness of the concept of race, the difficulties resulting from racial ambiguity, and the complexities of racial mixture in a time of identity politics.

Chapter 2

A "Latino" Law Student? Law 4 Sale at Harvard Law School

I was groggy and disoriented after taking the red-eye from Los Angeles to New York and another flight from there to Boston. It was a muggy afternoon in August 1980 as I lugged an overstuffed backpack and two bags into my dorm room in Oliver Wendell Holmes Hall, the low-budget dorms aptly described as "Skinner boxes."[1] Where were the beautiful, ivy-draped dorms of classic New England architecture featured prominently in the movie *The Paper Chase*? A structure of cement slabs, Holmes Hall looked out on one side at an aluminum structure some might call art, known as the "World Tree." Not far away, a parking garage sported the spray-painted message "Law 4 Sale."

As I was unpacking my bags, I looked up to see a fresh-faced, athletic man standing in the doorway, squash racket under his arm. I walked over to an outstretched hand. "Steve Lawrence, Amherst," the stranger said. Who on earth would introduce himself like this? What was Amherst? It sure didn't have a major football team.

How had I ended up at Harvard Law School, anyway? My Mexican American grandmother often said, "The family needs an attorney." True, we regularly had legal problems, large and small, but Grandma's advice was much more than just a practical matter. Indeed, not a particularly practical person, she lived in her own upbeat world, which was no small feat given the hand life had dealt her. The family needed a professional, someone with status. Status was something that Grandma always wanted in life. Because most Mexicans in the United States lacked the kind of status she imagined for herself and her family, she denied her Mexican ancestry and defined herself as Spanish.

Never really questioning Grandma's choice of my career, I went to Harvard Law School, though my road to Cambridge was far from predestined. Indeed, I identified deeply with the experience of Supreme Court Justice Clarence Thomas, when he told the story during his Senate confirmation hearings of how he had once seen a busload of prisoners drive past and had thought, "there but for the grace of God." (Whether Thomas told the truth about this and other matters is an entirely different subject.) Not that I had any close relatives in prison. But I was the first university graduate in my immediate family, and there was not a single lawyer in my extended family, much less a Harvard-trained one.

After a slow start, I had earned good grades as an undergraduate at the University of California at Berkeley and was graduated Phi Beta Kappa with honors in economics. A high score on the Law School Aptitude Test (LSAT) assured my admission to an elite group of law schools: Harvard, Columbia, the University of California at Berkeley (Boalt Hall), and UCLA. I could not turn down Harvard, with its magical name and its promise of instant prestige. How could anyone? The Kennedys and Harvard were synonymous. During my childhood, an inexpensive portrait of President John F. Kennedy hung in the doorway to my Grandma's house, just as it hung in many Mexican American homes throughout the Southwest. Like nearly everyone else in the country, I know exactly where I was when JFK suddenly became a national martyr in November 1963—near that picture in Grandma's house, waiting to go to the afternoon session of kindergarten at Foothill Elementary School, watching a re-run of "I Love Lucy," the popular sitcom starring Lucille Ball, with Desi Arnaz as Ricky Ricardo, the stereotypical hot-tempered Latino.

Even with a solid undergraduate record and LSAT score, I wondered in the fall of 1980, as I do to this day, whether I would have been admitted to Harvard had it not been for a swift, perhaps even thoughtless, check of a box. In taking the LSAT and applying to law schools, I identified myself as Mexican American. I had done the same thing when I applied to college. When the Educational Testing Service sent my SAT results to the universities where I had applied, the words "Mexican American" were printed on the form in bold type that stood apart from everything else.

From the 1960s to the 1990s, nearly every major institution in the United States practiced affirmative action, and I knew that my Mexican American identity improved my chances for admission to law school. As most still do today, law schools required the submission of a personal statement highlighting the distinctive aspects of a prospective student's candidacy. My essay told of growing up on welfare with my mother and working my way through college as a dishwasher, busboy, janitor, doorman, leaflet distributor, and library clerk. Also prominently featured was my Mexican American background.

All of it was true, but I still wonder what might have happened, and where I might be now, if I had emphasized my father's credentials instead. Without affirmative action, would I have gone to Harvard Law School? Would I be a professor today?

Looking back, I am surprised that I did not immediately eliminate from consideration all the high-priced private law schools. But dreams and ambition—and I was full of both at the time—overrode monetary realities. When my father asked me how I planned to cover private school tuition, I had no idea, but I figured that something would work out.

In the 1980–81 academic year, Harvard's tuition was $5,000. That may not seem like much today, when private schools charge quadruple that amount and more, but at the time the figure seemed off the charts.[2] It dwarfed U.C. Berkeley's fees, which amounted to slightly over $600 my freshman year. Fortunately, Harvard promised me financial aid and loans, at least for my first year. Not only did the aid package allow me to attend Harvard Law School, but for the first time since high school I did not immediately have to take a paying job to support myself.

My legal education aside, the first year of law school scared the hell out of me. I was a California boy. Except for brief excursions across the border into Mexico and Nevada, I had never been outside California or east of Lake Tahoe, and New England struck me as incredibly foreign. Fruits and produce in plastic wrappers at the local market. Unintelligible eastern accents. Icy cold, endless winters with dirty snow and slick ice on the sidewalks for months on end.

My first trip to the grocery store highlighted for me just how different my new environment was from home. After searching aisle after aisle, I finally stumbled upon a *can* of tortillas. Tortillas in a can! What kind of place is this? I wondered. Applying my undergraduate training in economics, I reasoned that demand must not be that great or there would be *normal* tortillas on the shelves. Latinos must be few and far between in Cambridge, Massachusetts, I thought.

The absence of fresh tortillas in the stores symbolized the larger deprivation I felt. When I was growing up, tortillas were everywhere, a quick snack that could be heated over a burner on the stove or a reminder of the weekly tacos to come. They were food, not *Mexican* food. At Harvard, such pleasant little reminders of my old life were swept away, replaced by inhospitable, white-bread surroundings that were completely foreign to me.

Unlike the undergraduate dorms at U.C. Berkeley, the law school dorms lacked a meal plan, or at least one within my budget. A hot plate in my room allowed me to cook cheap, if not particularly tasty or nutritious, meals. Dinty Moore beef stew and Spam became staples. I could probably have eaten better on my budget, but I was tight on time as well as on cash. A mixture of canned corn and pork and beans filled me up. So did popcorn after a long night of studying. Cheese left on my windowsill in the winter stayed cold, often frozen. My one-cup coffee maker became a crucial study aid. My one weekly splurge was the Friday night double cheeseburger special at Charlie's on Massachusetts Avenue, a few short blocks from the law school (a definite advantage in the cold Boston winters). It cost around three dollars, though beer with friends added to the check. My Dad occasionally sent tortillas, enchiladas, tacos, and other Mexican food by airmail, an extra special treat.

After the initial excitement of being at Harvard wore off, homesickness hit me hard. It is difficult being on the East Coast during holiday seasons if you are a West Coast kid at heart, and budgetary constraints meant that I had to spend some holidays in Cambridge. During my second year, I stayed there over Christmas, as did Bill Hinchberger, a friend from high school and college who had an apartment across the Charles River in Boston. Bill invited me over for Christmas dinner with him and his roommate Araf, an exchange student from Ethiopia. As I walked through Harvard Square toward the Charles, a bank sign reported that the temperature was an even zero. As I crossed the bridge over the river, the wind chill made the cold downright painful. When I arrived at Bill's and we said our hellos, I asked where Araf was. "Well," said Bill, "he was invited by some neighbors to go out to the suburbs and he asked if I wouldn't mind if he went to a *real* American Christmas." So Bill and I ate Christmas dinner, two Californians stranded on the East Coast for an *un*real American Christmas.

Few graduates claim to have been happy at Harvard Law School, and many anguished accounts of life there have been written.[3] Then again, few law students admit enjoying law school anywhere. But while I found law school an unmitigated disaster socially, I enjoyed the challenge of the study of law. As it had since I was a boy, school and studying served as an escape from the unpleasantness of life. As a child, I read voraciously to forget family tensions. Graffiti in Moffitt Library, the undergraduate library at U.C. Berkeley where I had spent many a late night, proclaimed that "STUDYING IS FOR PEOPLE WHO CAN'T HANDLE REALITY." Intended as a joke, that fit me well.

Though alienation weighed heavily on many students at Harvard Law School, mine differed from the garden variety. It ran deeper, was more profound, and related to the fundamental core of Harvard Law School as an institution. Many of my Harvard classmates knew each other from prep schools, Ivy League colleges, and upper-crust social networks. When I arrived in Cambridge in 1980, I knew only a few people, and those not very well—a friend of the brother of a college friend, a teaching assistant from a political science class at Berkeley, and an acquaintance I ran into occasionally on the U.C. Berkeley campus. Harvard Law School was an intimidating place for making friends, especially if, like me, you are on the quiet side and need time to cultivate friendships.

Years later, as I leafed through the directory of the Class of 1983 published for my ten-year class reunion, many unpleasant memories came back. The arrogance of the Ivy Leaguers. The alienating wealth of many of my classmates. The resident Marxist intellectual who injected vaguely coherent rhetoric into any class discussion. The local libertarian who despised any government intervention in the free market, including anti-discrimination laws and remedial programs such as affirmative action. All were absolutely certain that they knew it all, but their ignorance of how real people lived astonished me.

From day one, the class differences between me and my Harvard classmates were all too apparent. Many were second- and third-generation Harvard. While I scraped by on financial aid (as I am sure others did too), the sons and daughters of privilege, though they must have felt pressure to succeed, lived well—extraordinarily well by my standards. Spring break in Jamaica. London for the weekend. Regular dinners at nice restaurants. More sophisticated and worldly than I would ever be, they walked the walk and talked the talk.

Stark economic disparities separated rich and poor at Harvard. During my second year, a fellow *Harvard Law Review* editor, now a partner at a high-powered, white-shoe corporate law firm on Wall Street, called me near the end of the summer to invite me to go to the beach. Sounded like fun away from the *Law Review* grind, I thought. We drove in his sports car to Cape Cod, known to locals as "the Cape." We stopped for clam chowder and "steamers" (steamed clams) at a roadside diner, and he borrowed five dollars to pay his part of the bill. Because he forgot to pay me back, I later reminded him of the debt, but he still did not pay up. Too embarrassed to ask again, I never was repaid. Five bucks was nothing to him. For me, it equaled a night on the town of burgers, fries, and beer at Charlie's, or perhaps some food for the week.

I must have seemed different, if not bizarre, to my classmates. Harvard distributes to first-year students a booklet known as the "Face Book," containing a picture of every student in the class along with his or her undergraduate college and hometown. This handy reference proved especially useful when trying to get the lowdown on a person who talked in class, particularly a rare contributor to class discussion, a nobody like me. The Face Book distilled my essence to a black-and-white snapshot and the words,

"U. of Cal.—Berkeley, Redondo Beach, CA," where my father lives. As a classmate pointed out to me, my picture in the Face Book made me look like I was fresh out of prison. But what kind of photograph do you expect from one of those picture booths at Woolworth's?

Marty Schenker, the friend of a college friend, said he had heard that I was "left of Abby Hoffman," the notorious 1960s radical, on the political spectrum. True, I was more progressive than my classmates on a range of political issues, especially issues of race. But part of the radical reputation had to do with my undergraduate degree from Berkeley. The standard Harvard lore pegged Californians as flakes and Californians from Berkeley as radicals.

I shaped my identity as an anti-Harvard type from the outset. Among a small circle of friends during my first year, I regularly spouted off that "this place sucks." Over beers, I disparaged Harvard and all it stood for. Young and unsophisticated, I undoubtedly shared these comments with too many of my classmates. I did not keep my politics to myself, and my self-packaging, or perhaps my lack of self-awareness, had an impact. I remember one classmate who had run across some reference in a court case to a Molotov cocktail. As the resident radical, he apparently reasoned, I must know how to make bombs. He asked me what a Molotov cocktail was and how to make it. I had no idea except for what I had read in the newspapers, which I passed along.

Despite its liberal reputation, conservatives dominated Harvard Law School. I remember watching on the dorm television the returns for the November 1980 elections, when California governor Ronald Reagan defeated the incumbent Jimmy Carter. The room roared with delight as the networks declared Reagan the winner in state after state. On a map of the country NBC, ironically, turned each state the color red as it fell to Reagan. "Reagan is about as far away from a 'red' as you can get," I lamented. Down in the dumps that night, I called my liberal Dad to lament what was happening to the country.

Sympathetic liberal friends agreed with my views on the evils of racism in America, but they did not want to dwell on it. "Who wants to be mad at the world all the time? It'll drive you nuts," one friend warned me. "I can't live like that." Race was just too exhausting to focus on for long. Lucky for him that he could avoid dealing with issues of race on a regular basis.

Hearing my complaints about the status of minorities in the United States, a well-meaning classmate from Oregon once asked me if I personally felt "oppressed." Well aware that I was privileged to be at Harvard, I pondered this thought-provoking question. I wasn't sure that I felt oppressed, but I certainly felt like an outsider. A dinner party with a few law school friends brought this home to me. As we ate supper, a hip liberal with a Yale degree probed my background as though I was part of a minstrel show. Cutting to the chase, she asked, "Are you one of those people whose high school friends are all dead from gangs and stuff?" I wasn't, but I had more in common with the dead gang members than with most of the folks at Harvard Law School.

I gravitated toward students who also felt alienated from the elite. A guy from a working-class family in Queens and a Polish American from the Ohio Rust Belt became friends. I felt most comfortable with these class outcasts during my first year at Harvard Law School. We socialized and enjoyed the little spare time we had. We complained of the elitism that permeated Harvard.

Harvard as an institution never paid much attention to tensions among the student body. Dean James Vorenberg's negative response to the protest of the lack of minority faculty at Harvard, and the concerns he voiced about affirmative action on the *Harvard Law Review,* were typical. His basic response never changed—race is a problem in our society but we must be careful what steps we take to integrate institutions. Let's not be too hasty, even if the goal is praiseworthy.

At the individual level, Harvard espoused the "sink or swim" approach to legal education. One Harvard professor personified the institution's insensitivity toward the individual. Holding court at a Chinese restaurant on Massachusetts Avenue where a group of us were having lunch, the distant, middle-aged professor, who fancied himself a radical theoretician, asked each student about his or her background. After several classmates had mentioned the professions of their parents, which included doctors, lawyers, and investment bankers, I proudly declared that I was the first person in my immediate family to complete college, much less attend law school. Radical Professor looked at me curiously, as if examining a specimen on display at a museum, and said, "That's risky. I hope your parents read a lot." I could have told them that they do, but I was silenced by his cold condescension.

My alienation, no doubt, was counterproductive. While more sophisticated students spent their three years at Harvard building networks for future social climbing, I kept mostly to myself. I failed to get to know any professors particularly well, which ultimately doomed any chance for a coveted clerkship with a Justice of the United States Supreme Court. The lack of a mentor also proved a hindrance when I later applied for a job teaching law. Having done nothing to build relationships with professors, I found it difficult to collect the recommendations necessary for a job in the lofty world of legal academia. Though this was partly my fault, Harvard did nothing to break down the barriers between a big, impersonal institution and outsiders like myself who were convinced that they did not belong.

My anxieties were not all that different from those of many first-year students. Many believed that they were admissions mistakes. The lack of feedback only increased our anxiety about whether we measured up; we were given only two grades the first semester (mine were good but not great). Almost all of our grades, including those in year-long courses like Civil Procedure and Contracts, were based solely on one final examination.

Being called on in class was the only feedback that most students got during the first year at Harvard Law School, and this brought its own anxieties. Using the much-feared Socratic method, a professor would question students about the assigned cases for the day. Though not without its flaws, this method of teaching at least ensured that first-year students were thoroughly prepared for class.

I was first called on in a class on property law taught by Professor Charles Haar, a humane man of liberal sensibilities who had served in the administration of President Lyndon Johnson. Rumor had it that Professor Haar never tested on water law, so my preparation that day was not what it would have been otherwise. When we came to the water law assignment, I was daydreaming. After posing a lengthy hypothetical question about one landowner sucking up the water from under his neighbor's land, which just happened to be the home of a brewery, Professor Haar broke into my thoughts with, "Now, what would you tell your client, Mr. Johnson?" My weak reply slowly emerged from my mouth: "I would like to pass." "Are we playing bridge? Come on, this is your biggest client," Professor Haar replied politely yet firmly. "Well, could you repeat the hypothetical?" He did and I responded as best I could.

In the spring, as we were taking our seats for Professor Arthur Miller's civil procedure class, a classmate and I joked that I would be called on in the case of *Garcia v. Hilton Hotels*.[4] Not a minute later, Miller queried, "Mr. Johnson, can you tell us about *Garcia v. Hilton Hotels*?" The decision, involving a defamation suit brought by a Puerto Rican hotel employee against Hilton Hotels, taught some rudimentary procedural niceties about dismissing a lawsuit. Hilton Hotels fired the employee for allegedly procuring prostitutes, and he sued them for it. One of the few cases with a Spanish surname in the law school's entire first-year readings thus reinforced prevailing Latino stereotypes. Although Professor Miller, famous for his legal commentary on television as well as for his civil procedure scholarship, probably had no idea that I was Latino, the irony of the coincidence made me laugh. How likely was it that a professor would call on a Latino with an Anglo surname to discuss the *Garcia* case?

Given my dubious record of classroom performance, my grades came as a great surprise and a profound relief. I earned an A+ in both Civil Procedure and Property, coincidentally the two courses in which I had less than stellar classroom experiences, and did well in my other classes. Affirmative action might have helped me get to Harvard, but I was as good a student as most of my peers, and better than most. Why, then, all the self-doubt?

During my law school years, family at home tugged at my emotions. On welfare back in California, my mother and half-brother lived on the economic and psychological brink. Talking like a whirlwind one moment, my mother would be depressed, uncommunicative, and sullen the next. Twelve years old when I left for Cambridge, my kid brother Robby had to navigate the difficult high school years with my mother's topsy-turvy mental state. I worried. I studied to distract myself. Once I received a hysterical telephone call in the middle of the night from Robby after my mother was in a car accident. He had overreacted—my mother was okay—but his fear was real. Whatever her frailties, she was the only one there for him. As I studied at Harvard, I often waited for bad news from home, feeling guilty that I was not there. To this day, I always expect bad news when the telephone rings. The guilt lingers as well. I often wake up nights wondering what I should have done differently.

As a gift, I bought my mother a small Harvard Law School

plaque, which she hung proudly on the wall of her apartment. Located across from the Azusa Drive-in, where families on welfare lived, her apartment must have been the only one with a Harvard insignia engraved with the motto *Veritas,* "truth" in Latin, on the wall. On Christmas day, I took the bus from my father's house in Redondo Beach to my mom's, for Christmas dinner under the Harvard plaque. My mother literally could barely hold her head up at the dinner table. As I looked into her glassy eyes, I could tell that she was in a never-never land, a more pleasant place than the one she inhabited on earth. I thought that day about dropping out of law school to stay with her and my brother. But selfish as I was, I would not give up the dream of Harvard for anything. This Christmas dinner comes to mind every Christmas.

My Latino Identity

In my desire to stress my difference from the Harvard norm, I was not reluctant to advertise my Mexican American heritage to my classmates. This self-designation began with my rebellion against my mother's and grandmother's denial of their Mexican ancestry and was encouraged by my studies at U.C. Berkeley. But I knew that my simple proclamation that I was Mexican American was not the end of the story. Others could, and did, question my identity. Consequently, I was never sure where I belonged.

My acceptance by Latinos at Harvard was far from automatic, and most of the friends I made at Harvard Law School were white. I opted for this kind of safety and avoided Latino militants who might reject me, reasoning that no white person in his or her right mind would challenge my Latino credentials, whereas other Latinos might. How many Latinos do you know named Kevin Johnson? Latinos wondered who I was, whether I was authentic, or simply a "check-the-box" Mexican attempting to cash in on affirmative action benefits. All of this made me extremely self-conscious about my identity. Was I Latino or not? I worried about how people would react if I showed up at a meeting of *La Alianza* (The Alliance), the umbrella Latino student organization at Harvard. Out of deference to my conservative mother, I identified myself as Mexican American, as opposed to the more radical term Chicano. How would they react to this choice? My racial identity seemed to rest on shifting sands. Open to attack on all fronts, I could find no firm ground on which to stand.

Despite my self-consciousness, I did become friendly with a number of Latinos at Harvard. I spent a considerable amount of time with fellow students from the Southwest, especially California, including a number of Mexican Americans. I had more in common with them than with my Eastern classmates, who tended to stereotype Californians as flaky, dope-smoking hippies. Dan Torres, a Mexican American from Southern California whom I had seen around the Berkeley campus, became a friend. Vic Sotomayor, a fellow Berkeley graduate, lived across the hall from me in the dorms. A New Mexican, Jim Anaya, now a law professor at the University of Iowa, roomed with me in an apartment in the Berkeley Hills with a stunning view of the San Francisco Bay during the summer of 1982, when we both worked at law firms in San Francisco. During my first year, I often talked sports with Rosanna Marquez while watching events on the dorm television. One thing all of these Latinos had in common was that they were not radicals.

The Harvard student body reflected the diversity of the Latino experience. Harvard exposed me for the first time to a significant population of Cuban Americans, many of whom were extremely conservative politically and came from well-to-do backgrounds. I quickly learned not to say a word to any Cuban about Fidel Castro unless I was willing to spend hours listening to a spirited anti-communist lecture. Most of the Cubans at Harvard were fair-complexioned. Foreign students from Mexico, Guatemala, and other Latin American nations also attended Harvard Law School. From all appearances, they were from their countries' elites—highly educated, fair-complexioned, and financially well-off.

To confuse my burgeoning Latino identity, a number of Harvard students thought I was Asian. An Asian American classmate from California whom I dated at Harvard told me that she had initially thought I was half-Filipino. A socially conscious person who has devoted her legal career to public interest work, Mari Mayeda was active in racial politics at Harvard. That the U.S. government put her parents in internment camps during World War II no doubt contributed to her social consciousness. A devoted political activist as an undergraduate, Mari continued her activism in law school, fighting the administration's opposition to the Third World Coalition's efforts to diversify the faculty and advocating for the poor in the Harvard Legal Aid Bureau, a clinical program that allows law students to develop skills by helping low-income people with legal problems.

One odd episode concerning my phantom Asian identity occurred when the hiring partner of Irell & Manella, a prominent West Los Angeles law firm, invited me to dinner. The firm invited me to bring friends, so I brought Mari, knowing that she would be more comfortable than I in a fancy Boston restaurant. The evening went well, and the hiring partner complimented me on my nice friend. Invited to fly out to Los Angeles to interview with more attorneys, I was taken to dinner by a young, up-and-coming Asian American partner (of which there were very few—probably only one at this firm—at the time). After we had talked for a while, he asked me politely whether I was Asian. I politely told him "no" and explained my heritage. He emphasized that he meant no offense, which I accepted at face value.

This innocuous mistake was more amusing than a similar problem of mistaken racial identity. One night after a long night of studying, my friend Dave Mackey and I were having a beer in a working-class bar named Studley's in Somerville, a predominantly white, working-class town next to Cambridge. As Dave and I sat there enjoying our beers, an obviously drunk woman approached us. She told us how her brother had been killed in Vietnam, which is where she thought I was from. Though we tried to ignore her, this woman refused to be ignored. I began to fear for my safety, more from the locals who might get riled about the death of this woman's brother than from the crazy woman herself. We quickly finished our beers and left.

Despite a significant Latino student body, Latino perspectives were largely left out of the law school classroom.[5] *Garcia v. Hilton Hotels,* the case in which the Puerto Rican hotel worker sued Hilton Hotels for defamation, was the only case I can remember during my first year that dealt with Latinos. Similarly, I cannot name one legal issue of special significance to the Latino community discussed during my three years of study at Harvard. Bilingual education and English-only laws simply never came up. At the time, the Harvard curriculum lacked a class in immigration law, which logically would have required study of the long history of Mexican migration to the United States. Not coincidentally, the Harvard faculty failed to include a single Latino professor.

In fact, Harvard has never had a full-time, tenure-track Latino professor.[6] It reportedly once made an offer to Gerry Lopez, now a professor at UCLA, but he went to Stanford instead. In the spring of 1997, a Latina student working with a minority coalition to pressure the administration to diversify the faculty called me and asked me to send her my resume. She was collecting the resumes of Latino law professors to show the Harvard administration that qualified Latinos were available. Not wanting to be too discouraging, I told her that the fight to diversify the Harvard faculty had been going on for many years. When I hung up the phone, I thought, "fat chance." Harvard hire a Latino law professor? Me? Yeah, sure!

Alienation among Latinos at Harvard was rampant. One memorable student in the class behind me epitomized this phenomenon. A Chicano from San Jose, Mike Medina rebelled by living the antithesis of the model Harvard law student life. He partied often, studied minimally, and disdained most of the student body. I liked him. With hair down to the middle of his back and a weathered black trenchcoat, Mike's striking appearance showed all who cared to see just how out of place he was. He drew hilarious cartoons that he periodically packaged in comic books for sale. His "Rat Race" comic strip, in which all the characters were rats, poked fun at the law school, its students, and the firms where most of them eventually ended up. Mike could often be found at the law school's beer bar, called a pub in classic Harvard doublespeak, which was named "The Back Bench" after the last row in a classroom, where a student could sit to avoid being called on by professors.

It may seem odd that Harvard Law School had its very own bar. Alcohol use, a coping mechanism for some lost souls, seemed high among Latinos at Harvard. The use of alcohol was high among the student body generally, no doubt because of the high stress level of the Harvard Law School environment. The law school sponsored a "TG" (short for "TGIF" or "Thank God It's Friday"), where cheap beer and drinks flowed freely every Friday afternoon in the Back Bench Pub in Harkness Commons. The TGs generated a never-ending stream of stories about some poor student getting drunk and saying or doing something embarrassing. The stories were grist for the law school rumor mill. "Did you see so and so? He (or she) was so drunk," the stock story went.

One of my few pastimes in law school had a racial dimension. Since childhood, I had loved to watch boxing. When I was growing up, boxing was one of the few sports venues where Latinos were common. My father had taken me as a boy to see one of Bobby Chacon's first fights at the Forum in Los Angeles. Chacon, later known for his no-holds-barred style, became a hero among Mexican Americans in Los Angeles and later Sacramento, though he ultimately ended up destitute and psychologically disabled. I also rooted for Roberto Duran, a Panamanian, in his fights with African American Sugar Ray Leonard. The most memorable of these was the match in which Duran stopped the fight by saying "*no más*" (no more), but the best was the first fight, when he won a decision by mugging Leonard.

A law school friend from Ohio once invited a group of us over to watch a Youngstown hero, Ray "Boom Boom" Mancini (who had previously killed the Korean fighter Duk Soo Kim in the ring), fight Alexis Arguello, an excellent boxer from Nicaragua. Like a surgeon, Arguello took Mancini apart and knocked him out in the middle rounds. The amazing energy of this event stuck with me for days afterwards. That fight and the famous 1981 match between Tommy Hearns and Sugar Ray Leonard were high points of my three years at Harvard.

Affirmative Action

Like almost every other major educational institution of that era, Harvard Law School employed affirmative action in student admissions, undoubtedly because of the school's poor record of admitting minorities and women. Before 1950, Harvard had never admitted a woman to the Law School, and before 1963 it often admitted only one African American student per year in a class of over 500 students.[7]

Though institutionalized throughout U.S. society beginning in the 1960s, most Harvard Law students considered affirmative action suspect, though much of their discontent was submerged, deemed inappropriate for polite conversation. Perhaps because most students assumed that I was white, I regularly heard complaints about how affirmative action unfairly benefitted minorities in admissions decisions. Classmates talked about how few African Americans were really "qualified" to attend Harvard Law School and how those who made it in could not have done so without affirmative action programs.

I was struck, in discussions about affirmative action, by the myopic focus on race to the exclusion of other arbitrary criteria used in the Harvard admissions process. Besides the solid core of Ivy League graduates, admissions officials weighed geographic diversity, boasting that an incoming class had at least one student from every state of the Union. Harvard Law School evidently pursued the same quest for diversity that Harvard College did as described in the famous Supreme Court decision endorsing affirmative action, *Regents of the University of California v. Bakke.*[8] In addition, famous last names could be found in the class, including the great-great-grandson of Teddy Roosevelt. Persons with recognizable names from publishing houses and other well-known businesses filled the class.

There were others besides myself who feared that they were mistakes of the admissions process. In fact, the entire class could legitimately have had the same concern. Did my classmates from Missouri and North Dakota get in because of their ability or because they offered some sort of diversity? To my mind, they were as qualified as anybody else there. Did young Roosevelt get in because he was a Roosevelt or because he was one of the top 540 law students in the country? We all could wonder whether we truly deserved to be at Harvard Law School. The geographic diversity folks may have figured that they were fortunate enough to be in the right place at the right time. The elite Ivy Leaguers, however, never seemed to doubt that they belonged there. As a rule, white students spoke quietly about African Americans as the unworthy beneficiaries of affirmative action. Only the qualifications of blacks, and to a lesser degree of other racial minorities, were seriously questioned by the student body of Harvard Law School.

Mixed (Up?) Anglo/Latinos at Harvard Law School

Other Harvard classmates had mixed Latino backgrounds similar to mine, though each formulated a different identity. One classmate was from a mixed background with Mexican American and Anglo parents. Her surname might have been Spanish. Her physical appearance was indeterminate. She might have fit in with either Latina or Anglo women. Despite a fine undergraduate record, law schools rejected her application. When she re-applied, this time "checking the box" as a Mexican American, Harvard admitted her into the class of 1983. But she did not publicly identify herself as Mexican American, and she kept her distance from La Alianza, the Latino law students' organization.

Another classmate, a native of New Mexico, lived in the pretentiously named low-rent dormitories. His mother was Mexican American and his father Anglo. With his fair complexion and light brown hair, I would not have guessed from his physical appearance that he was Mexican American. We shared our longing for *menudo,* a spicy Mexican soup, which many find disgusting because it contains tripe. Like myself, he was not active in *La Alianza*. More than a decade after law school, he ran unsuccessfully for Congress as a gay candidate. His liberal credentials and gay identity were given prominence in his campaign, but not a word was said about his Mexican ancestry—a revealing comment on California's racially polarized politics in the 1990s.

Another student in my class also had a Mexican mother and Anglo father. Though fair-skinned, she had dark hair. She acknowledged her background but did not focus excessively on it and, as far as I know, she was not involved in any La Alianza activities.

A fellow *Law Review* editor, Chris Cameron, came from a background similar to my own. His mother, whose maiden name was Sylvia Ruiz, is Mexican American and his father Anglo. Growing up with his mother in southern California, Chris spent a lot of time with his maternal grandparents. For years, he never "checked the box" or otherwise officially identified himself as a Mexican American. In no small part, this was due to his light complexion and red hair. During law school, Chris's grandmother regularly sent packages of Mexican food that was impossible to find in Cambridge. Thanks to her, we enjoyed weekend breakfasts of *chorizo,* a spicy Mexican sausage, cooked with eggs or potatoes, fresh tortillas, and home-cooked refried beans. Her care packages were a small taste of home and a welcome escape from the everyday tensions of life at Harvard Law School.

This group had some things in common. None of us was certain where we belonged in Harvard Law School's racial politics. A politicized organization, *La Alianza* did not appear particularly hospitable to us. Were we Latino? I know I worried, and I am sure others did, that "real" Latinos might reject us, perhaps in humiliating fashion. Already feeling alienated enough at Harvard Law School, I had no desire to seek out new venues for rejection. Such worries may have been more a figment of my imagination than an accurate perception of reality, but the uncertainty about belonging and the fear of rejection were all too real to me.

This group of mixed Latinos was an assimilated bunch. We were not political activists bucking the administration but tended for the most part to be quiet, middle-of-the-road people. Little Spanish came from our mouths. Fairer in complexion than many Latinos, not one of the mixed Latinos I have described had anything resembling an indigenous appearance. Physically, we looked "white" and, if we wanted, could easily adopt a white identity. To varying degrees, we all did.

Latinos of mixed background were not the only assimilationists at Harvard Law School. Latinos at Harvard hardly seemed representative of the broad diversity of Latinos but were "whiter" than the average Latino, mostly conservative in life style, and generally middle class or better. A number of my Mexican American classmates butchered their grand Spanish surnames, just as my mother had.

At the other extreme some students, like Margaret Montoya (now a law professor), who attended Harvard a few years before I did,[9] embraced their Mexican American heritage. Similarly, some La Alianza members were militant in this way, radicalized like some of the Chicano Studies students I knew at U.C. Berkeley.

The mixed Anglo/Latinos at Harvard experienced some degree of identity choice. Most identified as Latino for affirmative action purposes. Socially, a person of a mixed background might or might not identify as Latino. To the extent that affirmative action attempts to attract minorities who in fact identify with and plan to contribute to the minority community or to serve as role models for other minorities, persons of mixed heritage must be considered individually.[10] Box checkers fail to serve any conceivable goal that affirmative action seeks to further. They neither act as role models nor go on to serve minority communities.

Harvard as an institution benefitted by the self-identification of the mixed Latinos. The more who identify as minorities, the better it is for the institution, which often complains that there simply are not enough "qualified minorities" to choose from in admissions decisions. Minority identification of mixed-background persons thus helped Harvard Law School as well as the individuals.[11] The law school found it easier to claim to students, alumni, and the wider world that it had a diverse student body. Harvard had no interest in interrogating any Latino's identity, even if that person was not fully representative of the Latino community. We were at some level used by the institution, though we personally were rewarded as well. But again, it may not have done much for the Latino community that affirmative action programs ostensibly serve when a mixed Latino at Harvard sheds any minority background after "checking the box."

Those who chose not to identify publicly as Latinos clearly perceived the advantages of being "white." Race is not an issue for those who have assumed a white identity; it simply is not a complicating factor in one's life. If I had a dime for every person who interrogated me about my background, I would be very rich indeed. But what costs did denial impose? One can only guess about the psychic toll that denial of one's heritage has on a person.

After graduation, Harvard tried one last time to capitalize on my quasi-minority status. The admissions office asked me to contact a recently admitted Chicana from U.C. Berkeley. I was living in Berkeley at the time and had breakfast with this pleasant woman, giving her what I thought was a fair, evenhanded picture of Harvard. Maybe it was too neutral, or maybe too negative. In any event, she went to Yale. The Harvard admissions office has never again asked for my assistance.

Racism Boston Style

Life at Harvard exposed me to some harsh racial realities. Latinos at the time seemed invisible, but due to the poor race relations in the greater Boston area, with its history of school desegregation through court-ordered bussing,[12] a subtle—and sometimes not so subtle—undercurrent of racism was directed specifically toward African Americans. One African American friend, Cecil McNab, told me how he was walking down the street not far from the law school when someone in a passing automobile threw chicken bones at him. Law students generally were more civilized than that, and simply categorized African Americans as undeserving products of affirmative action.

A night on the town demonstrated the dangers of racial hostility to me. A group of us hoping to blow off some steam went to The Channel, a rock club near South Boston, to listen to a soon-to-be forgotten rock band called the Plasmatics. We were a racially mixed group, not a great idea in that area, as we discovered when a drunk white man at the concert screamed at our African American friend, "What are you doing here, nigger?" Rather than escort the unruly drunk out of the club, the bouncers asked the tall, thoughtful African American law student from Texas, to leave with his friends. My friend Mike Ermer, scarcely more than five feet tall, yelled at the top of his lungs that these racists made him sick.

Unable to get a cab, we walked slowly and carefully out of the neighborhood, watching every car that drove by for any sign of trouble. Robbed of his dignity, our friend wondered aloud what he should have done. "I should have fought him," he said with tears in his eyes. Nobody knew what to say.

Even though this man was a student at Harvard Law School, he remained black in a society where African Americans are severely disadvantaged. Not surprisingly, that night was not his first brush with racism. During his freshman year at Baylor in conservative Waco, Texas, a white student yelled to him from a tower, "Hey, nigger, what are you doing here?" He later transferred to the University of Texas. But his experiences in "conservative" Texas unfortunately followed him to "liberal" Boston.

Harvard's Racial Politics and the Third World Coalition

A racially charged event at Harvard Law School received national attention during my last days in Cambridge. During my third year the Third World Coalition, an alliance of minority student organizations, organized a boycott of a civil rights course taught by Jack

Greenberg, the famous white civil rights litigator for the NAACP Legal Defense and Education Fund, Inc., and J. LeVonne Chambers, the African American president of the Fund.[13] The Third World Coalition demanded that a minority scholar, preferably a full-time faculty member, be hired to teach the course and protested that there were only two African American professors then on the Harvard faculty, Derrick Bell and Chris Edley. Bell, a prominent African American professor, later left Harvard in protest of its refusal to to hire an African American woman.[14] Only in the spring of 1998 did Harvard announce that it had appointed a tenure-track African American woman—Lani Guinier, who was made famous when President Clinton withdrew her nomination for a top-level civil rights post in the face of conservative opposition.

Dean James Vorenberg made clear his displeasure about the boycott of Greenberg's civil rights class, writing to alumni,

> I believe that the boycott discouraged many students who would have otherwise enrolled. . . . I believe that in an educational institution this kind of pressure on students' choices raises serious questions. I was also struck by the irony of seeking to advance the cause of racial justice by refraining—and urging others to refrain—from taking a course designed to teach the principles and strategy of applying law to the fight against discrimination.[15]

The boycott dramatically affected enrollment in the three-week winter-quarter course in January 1983. All forty-three students who took the course were white.[16] According to a referendum voted on by law students, 79 percent of those who voted, or slightly over one-half of the school's 1,500 students, agreed that the school "should be in the forefront of affirmative action in legal education" and that the underrepresentation of women and minorities deprived students of their "talents and contributions and unique perspective."[17]

For students interested in civil rights who honored the boycott of Greenberg's course, the Third World Coalition organized an alternative Civil Rights course and invited minority speakers to lecture on issues of race.[18] Kimberlé Crenshaw, a student who later became a pathbreaking law professor herself, helped organize a series of lectures by prominent minority law professors. The illustrious group included Richard Delgado, Neil Gotanda, Linda Greene, Charles Lawrence, and Mari Matsuda (then a graduate law student at Harvard), among others. These scholars later formed the backbone of an exciting intellectual movement known as Critical Race Theory, which holds that race is of central importance to the study of law in U.S. society.[19]

Since I supported the goals of the organizers, I did not take Greenberg's class, but I did not take the Third World Coalition's alternative civil rights course, either. I opted instead for a course in the Legal Process taught by Norman Dorsen, a visiting professor from New York University who was then president of the American Civil Liberties Union. Distracted by my work on the *Law Review* and a couple of other jobs, I was far removed from the boycott, though I had friends among the organizers. I was simply too burned out to have anything more to do with Harvard Law School. As had become customary, I shied away from racial politics. My confused identity and uncertain minority credentials made participation in this arena uncomfortable. My experiences on the periphery of such issues in my work on the *Harvard Law Review*, particularly the divisive debate about affirmative action that I discuss below, made me all the more skittish. With no idea where I belonged, I was not sure that there was even a place for me in the racial identity politics of the day. As writer and poet Cherríe Moraga wrote in explaining her own distance from the Chicano movement of the 1960s, "I was a closeted, light-skinned mixed-blood Mexican American, disguised in my father's English last name.

Since I seldom opened my mouth, few people questioned my Anglo credentials."[20] The Kevin Johnson who was graduated by Harvard Law School in 1983 felt much the same way.

Law 4 Sale

As others have observed, Harvard is a factory that produces lawyers to work in law firms.[21] The law school helps prepare its students for the extravagance of working in a plush, high-priced corporate firm, and that kind of life seems only natural to most graduates.

The summer after my first year, I worked in the Los Angeles office of a now defunct New York City law firm, Donovan Leisure Newton & Irvine. Firms had been my economic salvation during law school. Besides funding my education, the law firm dole—if I scheduled interviews carefully—covered the costs of trips home for the Thanksgiving and Christmas holidays.

As a first-year law student, I knew almost nothing about how law firms were structured, what their attorneys did, or how the social hierarchy worked, and I often asked inane questions at interviews. I once asked a tax lawyer, whose job it was to offer tax advice to businesses, what it was like to litigate a case. Nor did I have any idea of the difference between an associate, basically an employee of the law firm, and a partner, in effect one of the firm's owners.

The summer of 1981 exposed me to a new world. On my first day of work at Donovan Leisure, a high-powered partner took me to lunch at the California Club, an exclusive club that I later learned barred women and minorities from membership and from eating lunch in the main dining room. Because I was permitted to eat with the elite, I guess that neither the partner nor the club's management viewed me as a minority. It did strike me as odd that there were no women in the dining room, and that the only people of color in the vicinity were bussing tables.

The annual summer extravaganza at a Long Island resort forever sticks in my mind as an instance of capitalism gone hog wild. We all stayed at the Grand Hyatt in New York City and were issued a "credit card" and told to charge whatever we wanted. We did, staying at the hotel bar until late into the night. The day of high-priced partying featured waitresses dressed in preppie outfits serving cocktails on the beach. People spent the day on the tennis courts of a sprawling country club and lounging on the beach. The hiring partner drove summer clerks from the beach in his classic red cadillac with huge fins. The group congregated in the evening for a grand dinner, which concluded with a toast to General "Wild" Bill Donovan, a founding partner of the firm who also established the Office of Strategic Services, the predecessor to the Central Intelligence Agency, in the 1940s. "To the General" resounded through the room as everyone lifted a glass. The resources devoted to this textbook example of conspicuous consumption astounded me. Much more was spent that night, I am sure, than my mother lived on during an entire decade. I had never seen such things, a black-tie dinner followed by cigars and high class partying late into the night.

Although my summer salary bolstered my bank account, Harvard responded by reducing my financial aid package for my second year to near nothing. Election to serve on the *Harvard Law Review,* a prestigious capstone to my first-year success, made it impossible for me to take a job to help relieve the financial strain. My tuition and expenses made it necessary to take out non-federally subsidized student loans at high interest rates. The story repeated itself during my third year, but by then finances had become so tight that I was forced to hold several jobs to make ends meet. Among other things, I taught a legal writing class for first-year law students and did legal research for a civil rights law firm and a law professor.

The Harvard Law Review

New arrivals at the law school are inundated with lore surrounding the famous *Harvard Law Review.* Before my arrival, I knew nothing about this institution or its significance in the legal world, but not long after classes began, every Harvard law student, it seemed, dreamed of being on "the review." An aura surrounded the editors of this illustrious law journal. I later learned firsthand that editors of the *Harvard Law Review* were in fact "special," though not always in a positive way.

In the summer of 1981, I received a telephone call that literally changed my life. Mark Helm, president of the *Harvard Law Review* (a glorified title for editor-in-chief), called me in my comfortable office in downtown Los Angeles from what was undoubtedly an equally posh office in Washington, D.C. Helm told me cheerfully that because of my first year grades I was invited to become an editor. In my heart of hearts, I truly never expected that call. My hands trembled as I hung up the phone.

The buzz about the newly-elected editors grew as word quickly circulated from firm to firm. A classmate who also had a summer job in Los Angeles called; this was a person who had told me many times during our first year that I worked too hard and that it didn't really matter in the end because we would all end up with the same grades. I had not heard from him all summer. We chatted about work and friends for a bit before he asked in a mocking tone, "So did you get your call from the *Law Review*? I hear that Jerry Roth made it." Expecting me to be saddened by the abrupt notification, he was speechless when I told him, "Yeah, I made it."

At the time, half of the editors of the *Harvard Law Review* were invited on the basis of their first-year grades and joined the *Review* in early August, several weeks before school started. Harvard divided its first-year class into four sections of about 140 students each, but we all took the same basic courses—Civil Procedure, Contracts, Criminal Law, Property, and Torts. The *Review* invited the five students with the highest grades from each section to join the *Review*.

Should I have been shocked by earning the grades necessary for editorship? Not really. I had worked like a dog during that first year, harder than just about anyone I knew. After a full day of classes and studying, I drank several cups of industrial-strength coffee and headed off each evening for a 7:00 P.M. to midnight shift at Langdell Library. A friend from New Mexico dubbed me *la maquina* (the machine) for my long hours. My goal was not to excel—far from it—but simply to avoid failure. I was sure I was a fraud, convinced that I was not as "qualified" as my Harvard classmates. An affirmative action admit. A person destined for mediocrity, perhaps even failure.

Even as an editor of the *Harvard Law Review,* perhaps the most prestigious student legal publication in the country, my feelings of being an uninvited guest to the law school party never changed. The editors constituted a small club of students, primarily from Harvard, Yale, Princeton, and other Ivy League schools. Housed on the edge of the law school campus in a white, two-story building called Gannett House (but dubbed by some editors Granite House), it represented the crême de la crême of the student body, as some of the editors liked to say. Without exception the editors were bright and talented, just like everyone else at Harvard Law School. Because the top corporate law firms in the country scrambled to hire *Harvard Law Review* editors, membership on the *Review* meant instant, guaranteed jobs. California law firms were more than willing in the early 1980s to fly editors out to the West coast, where they were put up in fine hotels, wined and dined, and offered jobs. I took a number of fly-outs to California for interviews, often combining the business trip with a visit to family and friends. My grandfather, a lifelong Democrat, told his friends that I was "living like a Republican." Once a *Law Review* friend told me on the spur of the moment that Munger Tolles & Olson, a prestigious Los Angeles firm where he had spent the summer, was on campus and wanted to interview me if I was interested. "I don't have time to go home and change," I said, wearing faded blue jeans and snow boots, but he said they would still talk with me. After my interview in snow boots, the firm offered me a job.

Despite the perks, the *Review* was a demanding taskmaster. Besides the time-consuming grunt work, such as checking citations for lengthy articles on arcane subjects written by law professors, the centerpiece of the second-year experience was a short paper of about twenty pages called a "note." Based on research I had done at the Los Angeles law firm over the summer, my note, entitled "In Defense of Tribal Sovereign Immunity," defended the longstanding immunity of Indian tribes from lawsuits, on the grounds that the tribes deserved the same treatment accorded sovereign nations.[22]

Despite the importance of Indian law, Harvard failed to offer the class as a regular part of the curriculum. I was fortunate enough to be there when Ralph Johnson, a prominent Indian law scholar from the University of Washington, was a visiting professor. A warm, friendly man (he was the only professor I ever saw in the weight room at Hemingway Gym during my three years at Harvard), Johnson was not the least bit like the average Harvard Law professor. He read and offered helpful comments on my paper. I compared his thoughtful help to the more typical response of another professor, later dean at another Ivy League law school, who offered vague, unhelpful responses that revealed only a cursory reading of the paper.

Though a number of editors expressed a distinct lack of enthusiasm for my Indian law topic, the *Review* ultimately published my note. In defending the immunity of tribes from suit in the hope of preserving tribal assets and political autonomy, my argument fell within the mainstream and conceded that Congress had plenary power over the Indian tribes. A more far-reaching position would have been that Congress lacked power over the tribes because they were independent sovereign nations. Given the conventional nature of my note, I was not surprised, though I was disappointed, when my classmate Glenn Morris, an American Indian activist whom I greatly respect, was less than enthusiastic about my argument.

As my writing topics illustrate, issues of race were important to me. While every other editor wrote one comment on the latest decision of the U.S. Supreme Court, I wrote two comments on decisions dealing with civil rights, one involving decisions under Title VII of the Civil Rights Act of 1964[23] and the other involving a challenge to a local electoral scheme in Burke County, Georgia under the Equal Protection Clause of the Fourteenth Amendment.[24] The decisions all dealt with claims of discrimination against African Americans. I concluded that the Court, with conservative Chief Justice Warren Burger at the helm, had correctly decided two of the three cases.

When I joined in August 1981, the *Harvard Law Review* did not have a single minority editor. Years later, I heard that up until the mid-1980s only a handful of Latinos had ever been on the *Review* in more than 100 years of its existence. In short, the *Harvard Law Review* editors did not much "look like America," to use a phrase popularized by President Bill Clinton in 1992. Indeed, it was one of the slowest institutions in U.S. society to integrate in any significant degree. In 1977, Susan Estrich, later a law professor who directed the unsuccessful 1988 presidential campaign of Massachusetts governor Michael Dukakis, became the first woman elected to the prestigious position of president of the *Law Review*, a stepping stone to a coveted Supreme Court clerkship. Not until 1990 did a mixed-race black student, Barack Obama, born in Hawaii and the son of a Kenyan government minister and a white anthropologist, become president of the *Review*.[25] The previous year, the first Asian American, Peter Yu, served as president.

The *Harvard Law Review* was a difficult place, and by some accounts became even more of a political battlefield in the 1990s.[26] The *Review* was even less diverse in terms of race and class than the law school generally and was an even more exclusive Ivy League enclave. True friends were few and far between. I did my work and left. Hard, tedious work, few friends among the editors, and alienation beyond belief made me want to throw in the towel more than once. Out of sync with the general student body, I was even more alienated from the crême de la crême. In my second year, I nearly quit.

Easily the most controversial topic during my tenure on the *Harvard Law Review* was affirmative action. During my second year, the editors considered a proposal that the *Review* adopt an affirmative action plan in an attempt to diversify its membership. The proposal ignited controversy and attracted national attention. Editors expressed radically different views of the plan. Opponents leveled the tried and true arguments against affirmative action; it undermined merit, it might stigmatize minorities, and so on.[27] Proponents emphasized the need for diversity and a corrective to past discrimination.

Chris Cameron later remembered the affirmative action plan for selecting student editors as "egalitarian."[28] Others remember it less fondly. John McGinnis, for example, an editor who is now a law professor, wrote that

> The "first" that occurred during Volume 96 was that, for the first time in its history, the *Review* used racial classifications, however covert, in selection of editors. This departure from an almost 100-year tradition of selection solely on the basis of individual accomplishment (whether through grades or writing competition) must disturb anyone who believes that the enterprise of scholarship fares best when decisions are based on merit alone.[29]

Many of the *Law Review* editors would find this recollection more apt:

> The burning issue for Volume 95 was the institution of an "affirmative action" plan for the *Law Review*. The editors were nearly evenly divided on this issue: on the one hand, the disproportionately low participation of minorities on the *Review* was of great concern; on the other hand, many were reluctant to tamper with the "blind" selection criteria of grades and performance in the writing competition and were hesitant to introduce a selection system that might stigmatize any minority participant on the *Review*. After lengthy meetings and debates, and innumerable late-night discussions at Gannett House, a final meeting and vote was held. The vote came out in favor of affirmative action, by a very narrow margin.[30]

In reporting the adoption of the plan to the alumni, Dean Vorenberg emphasized that the faculty formally "took no action with respect to that plan" out of respect for the *Law Review*'s independence, but mentioned that many letters from alumni and others "reflected a wide range of views, though most of the writers opposed any affirmative action in the selection process."[31] William T. Coleman, a famous African American attorney who had been an editor, weighed in against affirmative action on the *Review*.[32] At the other extreme, some minority student leaders charged that the program did not go far enough and suggested that *Law Review* editorship should be voluntary.[33] According to Chris Cameron's notes, I sided with a handful of editors who voted for a proposal allowing anyone who wanted to join to be a *Law Review* editor at one of the meetings. This politically unfeasible proposal went nowhere.

The editors met many times to debate the affirmative action proposal. Before one meeting, a handful of affirmative action supporters from the second year-class organized by Peter Enrich, now a law professor at Northeastern, got together at a building on the Harvard campus built with money from Eastman Kodak (from the air, the building looks like a Kodak camera), to strategize about building political support for the plan. The proposal listed a number of minority groups, including African Americans, Asian Americans, Native Americans, and "Hispanics," as eligible for affirmative action consideration. I raised the issue whether the term "Hispanics" should be changed to "Latinos." Some Latinos considered the term "Hispanics," a creation of the U.S. Census Bureau, equivalent to the outdated term "Negro" for African Americans, a teminological debate that continues to this day. Enrich later raised this issue—I was too nervous and self-conscious to voice my opinions—at one of the affirmative action forums for the editors. An affirmative action opponent pounced on this minor suggestion. "What would the *Review* do if Eskimos did not like being called Eskimos?," he queried. Anti-affirmative action editors argued that every group would want to be identified in a "special" way.

After much acrimony, the editors adopted an affirmative action plan. It required that each applicant submit a "personal statement" that would allow a committee to consider membership in an underrepresented group and "economic, societal or educational obstacles that have been successfully overcome."[34] The *New York Times* reported that the year *Review* editors adopted the plan, ten women and no minorities were among the eighty-four editors, even though 32 percent of the student body were women and

14 percent were minorities.[35] The *Times* apparently did not count me as a minority.

In the spring of 1982, the president of the *Harvard Law Review,* Jim Feldman, appointed me to the committee that would implement the first affirmative action plan for *Law Review* membership. Thus began a history of service on committees as a "minority" representative of sorts. One or two editors had lobbied on my behalf, though I did not ask them for their help. I have no idea whether I was invited because of my racial background, which was known to those who knew me well, or because I was dating an Asian American woman and was thought (perhaps erroneously) to have some good will with the minority community.

The committee first met with the various minority organizations at Harvard to request their input. When we met with the president of *La Alianza,* he mentioned his concern about Latinos who "check the box" to get admitted and then disappear from the Latino community. Perhaps overly self-conscious, I felt that he was directly challenging my credentials. "Maybe he is right. Maybe I am a fraud. Am I Latino?" were the thoughts that streamed through my mind. Uncomfortable as I was, however, I did not respond to his comments.

In the summer of 1982, the committee met by conference call to select a number of minority members based on their personal statements. After a businesslike discussion, we agreed to add a handful of minority members to the editorship, and in the fall of 1982 a more racially diverse group of student editors joined the *Harvard Law Review* than it had ever seen before. Indeed, the *New York Times* reported that the *Review* admitted a record number of minorities, including two blacks (and the first black woman ever) and four Asian Americans out of the fifty-one students selected.[36]

Although the selection procedures have been changed since adoption of the first affirmative action plan in 1982, the *Harvard*

Law Review remains one of the most prestigious student-run legal publications in the country. Among legal academics, to have an article published by the *Review* remains a high honor.

The Harvard Law Revue

One of the most gala events at Harvard Law School is the annual *Harvard Law Review* banquet, held each spring at the Harvard Club in downtown Boston. As one admiring writer put it,

> what made [the banquet] such a distinguished event was that over the years some of the most esteemed and distinguished members of the bench, the bar, Congress, business, and even the media have attended or addressed the banquet: most came from the roster of the *Review*'s former members. Therefore it was not unusual to see or hear at the banquet Supreme Court justices, federal appeals judges, congressmen, senators, diplomats, writers, and entertainers.[37]

An elegant black-tie affair, the banquet marks the end of the year and, for third-year editors, the end of an illustrious term with the *Harvard Law Review.*

It is a Harvard Law tradition that each year a couple of *Law Review* editors get together and write a parody of the *Review* called the *Harvard Law Revue.* A copy is left at each place setting at the annual banquet, which is where most editors see it for the first time. Published in a format similar to that of the actual *Review,* it pokes fun at the authors, articles, and editors of that year.

Because the banquet was one of my last rites of passage before leaving Harvard, I felt good as I walked into the Harvard Club that night in the spring of 1983. I sat down at a table with Chris Cameron and Rob Noblin, opened the *Revue,* and almost fell out of my chair. To my horrified surprise, it was full of references to me, almost all of them negative. Besides suggesting that I was an alcohol[38] and substance abuser, the *Revue* reported that I had authored a book entitled, *I Hate Whites.*[39] In a more innocuous barb, fictitious "television listings" had me starring in a show in which a "disgruntled law student (Kevin Johnson) abandons his studies to work with native Americans," a reference to my student note on federal Indian law.[40] What had I done? Why did I deserve this? I had worked so hard. I had done everything that had been asked of me. My thoughts were scrambled. Nothing made sense.

Sitting there in shame, I did not know whom to lash out at. I still do not know who put the *Revue* together and I don't really care. They would just say that I was "too sensitive." Too upset to listen to the speeches, I walked out to the lobby and sat sullenly in an over-stuffed chair. I exchanged pleasantries with a friendly partner from a Los Angeles law firm whom I had met on the recruiting circuit. But I wanted to be alone as I sipped a drink to calm my nerves and boost my spirits.

The 1983 issue of the *Harvard Law Revue* made fun of others, but not in such hurtful ways. No other editor was subjected to such racially tinged mockery. As I moped in the lobby, it struck me just how racist this was. What better way to marginalize one who feels strongly about civil rights than to suggest that he "hates" white people? Such charges are often leveled against committed minority leaders, whether it be Louis Farrakhan or César Chávez. And how many times have we heard conservatives charge that a feminist like Gloria Steinem or Catherine MacKinnon—or even anyone who believes that men and women should have equal rights—"hates men"? I am neither important nor famous but the marginalizing impact was no different. Labeled a hater of whites, my views on issues of race, even those middle-of-the-road ones printed in the pages of the *Harvard Law Review,* did not have to be taken seriously.

I most definitely do not hate white people. To paraphrase the proverbial claim of the racist in denial, some of my best friends are white. So is my father, whom I love dearly. My desire for racial justice has nothing to do with hatred of whites. I do hate some of the things that white society has done, such as enslaving African Americans, exterminating the Indian tribes, and engaging in violence and discrimination against Asian Americans and Latinos, to name a few. But such practices are not the exclusive preserve of whites, and my condemnation of them does not translate into racial hatred.

As for the jokes about substance abuse, what better way to discount a person's ideas than to suggest that they are the product of a drug- or alcohol-induced stupor? Of course I enjoyed some good times as a law student, as did many of my classmates. I had a rebellious, irreverent streak that I did not try to hide. But my ideas, beliefs, and actions were carefully considered and tended to err on the side of caution, far from the rantings of an alcoholic or lunatic fringe.

Fifteen years later, the *Revue* issue that robbed me of what should have been a happy event still haunts me. I wonder whether such pointed "jokes" would have been made about an African American, Asian American, or Latino with a Spanish surname. I occupied a never-never land of racial identity, a borderland between two very different worlds. I was the invisible man, perhaps a metaphor for all Latinos in the United States, a quasi-minority that could be attacked with impunity in an era when society frowned on public displays of racism and an anti-black joke was thought to be in poor taste. Perhaps I was singled out because I dated an Asian American woman. Or maybe it was because I dressed poorly, had long hair (by Harvard standards), and refused to wear a shirt with an alligator on it, or the shirts with button-down collars that are so popular among the children of privilege. (I once gave a fellow student so much grief about the alligator on his shirt that he tore it off and gave it to me.) Yes, I cultivated an anti-Harvard image. But I did not deserve the harmful, racist grief that came through in the *Revue*'s spoof of my very existence.

Beyond causing me emotional turmoil, the statements in the *Revue* threatened my legal career. The power structure at the law school and the many *Law Review* alumni who attended the banquet all got copies. Dean Vorenberg made the opening remarks that night, Professor Paul Bator was the toastmaster, and the speaker was the Honorable John Minor Wisdom, an appeals court judge of national renown. Who knows what they thought as they read the *Revue* that evening?

The *Harvard Law Revue* tarnished an already sick experience for me at Harvard Law School. I worked as hard as anybody during my two years in Gannett House. I had published two case comments for the prestigious Supreme Court issue when every other contributor had published one, served on the affirmative action committee, helped with the time-consuming writing competition for *Law Review* editorship, and much more. Why was I the subject of this scathing humor? Was it an attempt to devalue my contribution? Reminiscent of the adolescent cruelties of high school, the event demonstrated to me the limits to my ever being fully assimilated into the mainstream. My law school accomplishments had been belittled in one swift kick in the teeth, and the public nature of the forum made the humiliation even worse. That I had earned my way onto the *Law Review* by making good grades, that I had taught legal writing to first-year students, that I had judged moot court, that I had obtained a prestigious clerkship with a famous court of appeals judge—all of these accomplishments were forever tainted that evening.

Nobody seemed to notice, much less care, when some half-breed was maligned in the *Harvard Law Revue*. One well-meaning editor told me that the references were "mean," and that was about it.

In fairness, I was not the only victim of the cruelty and poor taste of the *Law Revue*. When the famous feminist law professor Mary Jo Frug was brutally murdered in 1991 not far from Harvard Law School, the *Revue* featured a disgusting parody of an article she wrote that was published posthumously in the *Harvard Law Review*, and made a chilling reference to her as the "Rigor Mortis Professor of Law." This sick spoof rightly provoked a national controversy.[41] The slights I suffered in 1983 paled in comparison with the hurt ruthlessly inflicted on poor Mary Jo Frug's family and friends and with the disgrace to her memory. Different in degree, both experiences reveal the serious racial and gender tensions at the *Harvard Law Review*, and the meanness and arrogance of some of its editors. Today, most of those same people are leaders of the legal profession.

The grand Harvard graduation ceremony was the icing on the cake of three years of alienation. The law school held its graduation about a month after final examinations ended, with all the other schools of Harvard University. A fellow Harvard alum cynically tells me that Harvard times the event to keep the riff-raff—the poor and working class unlikely ever to contribute to the huge Harvard endowment—from attending. As my new job with a federal judge did not begin until the end of June, I had arranged to work at a California law firm for the month between exams and graduation. Desperately needing the money—emergency loans from the law school had just barely carried me to the end of my law school career—I returned to California a bitter man. I did not really care that I was unable to attend the graduation ceremony; still, nobody wants to feel excluded. I told friends that I would return to Cambridge in a tank as part of an invading force. As I got into the cab bound for Logan Airport, I was glad to be leaving Harvard Law School behind.

When I told all who would listen that "this place sucks" during my first year at Harvard Law School, I was as right as I have been about anything in my life. My sense is that things have not changed much. There still are no Latinos, and until 1998 Harvard never had an African American woman on the faculty.

My bitterness about Harvard Law School has faded over the years. Today I am more ambivalent than angry. But Harvard left a bittersweet taste in my mouth that persists even now. When I showed my wife-to-be, Virginia, around the law school campus four years after I graduated, an eery feeling crept over me. We stopped at Gannett House and saw my black-and-white picture on the wall among the photographs of the other editors of volumes 95 and 96 of the *Harvard Law Review*. Looking at those pictures, my years there seemed a distant, melancholy, almost dreamlike memory. For a fleeting moment, I wondered whether I had ever really been there.

Perhaps more than college, law school helped transform my identity. The Harvard experience reinforced and heightened my interest in issues of civil rights and social justice. Ironically, the *Harvard Law Revue*, not my law school courses, may have had the most profound impact on my future studies as an academic.

At Harvard, I reveled in the difference of my background and life experiences. I was proud, not ashamed, of my Mexican and class background. My mother's experiences had been much different. She grew up in a different world.

Chapter 3

My Mother: One Assimilation Story

In the spring of 1996, Refugio Rochin, director of the Julian Samora Research Institute at Michigan State University, invited me to lecture on immigration and civil rights issues. While in Lansing, I met with a group of community activists. At an informal dinner in a community center in the Mexican part of town, I sat next to a member of the Lansing City Council, a warm, congenial Mexican American with whom I immediately felt comfortable. We talked politics and family, and I told him, among other things, that my mother was Mexican American. After we had talked for a while, he delightedly told me, "Your mother got your heart." He told me how his own daughter, who had married an Anglo, made sure that her children took pride in their Mexican American heritage. His simple observation spoke volumes about the genesis of my racial identity.

According to family lore, my maternal grandmother was born in El Paso, Texas, though circumstances suggest to me that she might have been born in Mexico. Her mother, my great-grandmother Josephine Gonzales, was definitely born in Mexico in 1900, and she lived there for most of her life. About my maternal grandfather, Charles Daniel Swalez, I was told only that an automobile accident took his life when my mother was a child. A sprinkling of family still lives in the small town near the U.S.-Mexico border where my mother was born, though my mother lost touch with them long ago, something not uncommon for Latinos from rural communities.[1]

My mother, baptized Angela Gallardo, was born in 1938 in Brawley, California, an agricultural town an hour from San Diego in the Imperial Valley. She grew up in downtown Los Angeles. With olive-colored skin and black hair that has now gone gray (she always emphasized that it was "dark brown"), she stands under five feet tall. As a young woman, she was an inveterate talker, though she speaks only intermittently now. Her preferred nickname, Angie, reflects the assimilationist tendencies she inherited from my grandmother. A diligent, hard-working student, she was the first in her family to graduate from high school, and she went on from there to Los Angeles City College, where she met my father. Her education was quite an accomplishment for a Mexican American woman in 1950s Los Angeles. Every once in a while, my mother still talks of her dream of becoming a dental technician, though less frequently as the years go by.

Married in a Catholic ceremony in 1957, my parents were young newlyweds, my mother just nineteen. The duality running through her life is reflected in the guest lists to her four wedding showers in her "Our Wedding Memories" book. Guessing from surnames, three were primarily Anglo and one was predominately Mexican American. I was born almost a year after the wedding in Culver City, where my father worked for the *Culver City Star News*. Not long after my brother Michael's birth three years later, my parents separated and eventually divorced.

Divorce was not as simple in the 1960s as it is today. Theirs was acrimonious, requiring trial separations, numerous court appearances, and findings of fault. All of this took time, and put a lot of stress on each member of the disintegrating family. After the divorce, my mother moved to Azusa, a suburb east of downtown Los Angeles in the San Gabriel Valley where my grandmother lived. Not to be confused with Los Angeles's San Fernando Valley and its upscale, shopping-mall culture, the San Gabriel Valley of that era was a mostly blue-collar area of middle- and working-class whites and Mexican Americans.[2]

My mother lived by a strict moral code that was especially rigid for women.[3] Her strait-laced nature stood in stark contrast to my happy-go-lucky grandmother. Julia, as my grandmother called herself (Hortense was her name by birth), enjoyed life. She told me many a story as I grew up, fantastic tales that were upbeat, funny, and uplifting.[4] My brother and I looked forward to riding our bikes to her house. She loved her daughters (my mother had two half-sisters), taught me how to make guacamole (I still follow her recipe), and would make me a quesadilla or a hamburger whenever I showed up and asked for one, day or night. She would do anything for family. In her youth, she had lived in faraway San Francisco, a distant, foreign place in my young eyes. It was unclear what she did there, though there were murmurs of a wild lifestyle. A picture of her and my mother in fur coats documents that era.

Grandma fancied herself a writer and in fact spoke of a book called *Beauty Was My Downfall,* which she often mentioned when I was a child. I would have liked to see the manuscript. Whenever she came into a little money, and sometimes when she didn't, Grandma was lavish with her children and grandchildren. When she took us shopping, she often charged to her credit limit and beyond. When her daughters became interested in boys, she threw small "wing dings," as she called them, with snacks, cokes, and rock 'n' roll music.

Grandma was a complex person and there was more to her than

met the eye. Her apparent zest for life hid much sorrow, and masked a life of hard work and a lot of moving around—from San Francisco to East Los Angeles to Valencia Street in downtown Los Angeles. She had never married my mother's father, and she refused to talk about him. My mother would say only that he had hurt my grandmother deeply. The story of his death in a car accident may have been more figurative than literal.

My grandmother was still an attractive young woman when she married an Anglo man, just as her three daughters would do later. This marriage produced my mother's two half-sisters, Cathy and Josie. Neither, as far as I can tell, identifies as Mexican American, though both share an Anglo father and Mexican American mother. Both married Anglo men in their teens only to have these marriages fail. Both ended up re-marrying men of color, one a Mexican American and the other an American Indian. My seven cousins run the gamut of physical appearances but, to my knowledge, none identifies as a Mexican American.

My step-grandfather was an angry, irritable man who abused Grandma both psychologically and physically. During my youth, I visited her only during the day, when he was not around. I could not stand to witness the verbal and physical assaults that she suffered when he came home at 4:15 each afternoon. Although the neighbors must have heard some of the yelling, battered women had few options in the 1960s. I have a vivid memory of a bent-up fork flying through the air, hitting the wall, and landing at my feet. I was but six or seven years old at the time. Grandma's escape was cheap Olympia beer, which she stashed in a brown paper bag in the back of a kitchen cabinet.

Despite their Mexican roots, my mother and grandmother were ardently assimilationist in outlook. Marrying Anglo men was part and parcel of the assimilationist strategy. They also both claimed that they were not Mexican, but Spanish. Always the storyteller, my grandmother had a favorite tale that explained her mixed "Spanish-French" background, with particular emphasis on the Spanish.[5] This fictional background made its way into many of her stories. My mother emphasized her Spanish ancestry as well.[6]

As I grew older, I began to realize that this magical Spanish ancestry was very much an exaggeration. My grandmother, with her indigenous features, and my mother with her olive-colored skin looked no different from the other Mexican Americans in the San Gabriel Valley. We went to school with Mexican American kids. We socialized with Mexican American families. My great-grandmother, Josephine Gonzales, by contrast, never mentioned her Spanish ancestry in my presence; she was apparently more comfortable with her Mexican citizenship and identity. All of our relatives in the Imperial Valley, only a few miles from the U.S.-Mexico border, were Mexican American. "Where are the Spaniards?" I could only wonder.

The myth of Spanish heritage is not uncommon among Latinos, and indeed is still embraced by some Latinos in today's anti-immigrant, not infrequently anti-Mexican climate. Mexican identity was seen as even less desirable, especially in the Southwest, before the civil rights movement of the 1960s.[7] Latinos have attempted to "pass" as Spanish, and therefore as white, just as some light-skinned African Americans and other minorities have. Many Anglos consider "Spanish" origins, with their European aura, more acceptable than Latin American origins.[8] My mother and grandmother were well aware of the racial hierarchy that existed in southern California, and their response was that they had better convince people that they were not Mexicans.

The Spanish mythology was fully consonant with my mother's assimilationist leanings.[9] To this day, rather than pronounce her maiden name Gallardo in proper Spanish, which requires a special "ll" sound similar to "y," she uses the English pronunciation, as in the word "fallen." Consequently, the word "lard," with all its connotations, sticks out right in the middle. My wife Virginia and I chuckle about this, but efforts to assimilate into the mainstream served a critical purpose for my mother and many others of her generation. The Anglicization of Spanish surnames was one way for Mexican Americans to attempt to pass as white.

In no small part because of her assimilationist convictions, my mother deliberately avoided teaching her children Spanish.[10] She spoke Spanish herself, but like many of her generation she considered Spanish an educational impediment to assimilation. When my mother was growing up, it was not unheard of for teachers in the public schools to punish students for speaking Spanish.[11] She and others like her believed that we would only succeed in school and in life if we mastered English, which somehow, this thinking went, would be impossible if we knew Spanish. Some Latinos still hold this view today, even in a society with a growing number of Spanish-speaking people. When I was growing up, my mother and grandmother spoke Spanish only when they wanted to have a private conversation in our presence. My mother would become irritable, which she did not do easily, when my brother and I teased her for speaking "Mexican." "It is *Spanish*," she would emphasize. "There is no *Mexican* language."

While my mother and grandmother lived in a state of denial, the Anglo men in their lives often emphasized their Mexican ancestry, though in dramatically different ways. When my grandmother talked about her Spanish background, my step-grandfather would respond sarcastically, "Get off it. You're a Mexican like the rest of them." Weakly protesting that he did not know anything and laughing uncomfortably, Grandma was visibly wounded. My own father, by contrast, emphasized the positive side of my mother's

Mexican background. He used to tell me that the mixture of his "Swedish" (another exaggeration) and my mother's Mexican bloodlines were good and would make me strong.

My mother's and grandmother's assimilationism also meant that they adopted the dominant society's racial attitudes.[12] Long before I was old enough to date, my grandmother warned me never to bring home an African American girlfriend. "Don't bring home anyone who wants pork chops," she would joke. We sometimes ate pork chops, but I knew what she meant. Although my mother never said such things, I sensed her agreement. My mother embraced one white girlfriend in particular, a woman I dated in college. Later, when I brought an Asian American friend to meet her, she inappropriately—and very uncharacteristically—asked over dinner how my old flame was doing. Mom wanted me to "marry white," as she had.

My mother and grandmother also considered immigrants from Mexico as lessers, referring to them in supposed jest as "wetbacks" or "Julios." Years later, my poor Grandma was killed by a car as she was going to the store to buy her granddaughter some milk for dinner. As one family member later informed me, Grandma was run over "by some Mexican wetbacks."

My mother never fully recovered from the break-up of her first marriage. For many years, I sensed that she wanted to get back together with my father. She made regular inquiries about him, and reminded me that she made better tacos than he did. Today, she talks relatively little of my father, perhaps because the memories are too painful.

Part of my mother's inability to cope with divorce had to do with her Catholic upbringing and the moral code that the Church imposed on her life. In the Catholic Church, it is expected that you marry once and for life. Many Catholics today understand that this is both unreasonable and unrealistic. But my mother was an old-fashioned Catholic and she was devastated when her marriage fell apart. Because her identity was in large part defined by her husband, the divorce disrupted her entire life.

She tried hard after the divorce to get a good job, but that wasn't easy for a Mexican American woman in the 1960s. She went to the local unemployment office every day, but nothing came of it. For a short time she cleaned houses, but with two children to raise, she could not keep it up for long. My father dutifully paid child support, but that was not enough to keep us off welfare and food stamps.

After the divorce, my mother fought depression, but her mental state gradually worsened. Listless and nearly speechless, she would sit in a sad, distant trance when in the depths of a depression, a sharp contrast with her normal mile-a-minute talking. The divorce began a downward spiral; a pattern emerged of hospitalization followed by heavy medication and improvement. But it took further trauma to permanently disable my mother.

In the late 1960s, my mother met another Anglo man, got pregnant, had a baby, and got married, in that order. Years later, she told me with fierce pride that the welfare doctors told her that having the baby would jeopardize her life and advised her to have an abortion. On Catholic principle, she refused and instead took her chances with childbirth, which fortunately did not take her life.

The second marriage was delayed because her new husband-to-be refused to have my brother and me become part of his new family. My mother would not give up her two sons and he eventually relented. With a new breadwinner, we got off welfare, and for a few years lived together as a family. Like my grandmother's Anglo husband, my new stepfather made jokes about "spics" and "taco benders," reminding my mother of her Mexican ancestry and her sons of their dubious heritage.

When I was in junior high school, my stepfather contacted my father and told him that my mother was an unfit mother, instigating a custody battle that my father eventually won. Losing two of her sons drove my mother into the depths of her worst depression ever. She was diagnosed with schizophrenia, medicated, and hospitalized. We did not hear from her for months, though it seemed like years to her young sons. A colorfully wrapped Christmas present that we bought for her sat on the shelf of my bedroom closet for months after the holidays.

Over the years, my mother's mental condition worsened. Her mood swung dramatically from good to bad and back again. Her second husband unceremoniously left her and she returned with my half-brother Robby to the very same apartment—apartment 26 of the Rockvale Apartments in Azusa, California—where we had lived between her two marriages. Faced with the threat of losing custody of her remaining son, she gave up any interest in the modest home they had bought in exchange for sole custody of Robby.

As the years passed, my mother's depressions became increasingly lengthy. In manic spells, she fantasized of a joyful life in which she had a boyfriend. She became extremely angry when one of her sons tried to bring her back down to earth. She would shut down when depression hit and walk with her hands held out in front of her as though trying to defend herself from the world. Eventually she would return to the hospital in a state of total despondency. Now receiving disability benefits, my mother lives in a group house with other mentally disabled persons.

As my mother approaches senior citizenship, the Spanish myth that dominated her early adult life has faded from her mind. She rarely if ever brings up the issue. She gets along very well with my wife's family, especially Grandma Lupe. And she has my children call her "Nana," a version of "grandma" common in Mexican American families. The persistence of her assimilationism, however, had a profound impact on her and our family. My mother's illness aged my grandmother and two aunts, who steadfastly watched over her. My mother's sons grew up too fast. I worried about her, my half-brother, and my family. I wonder what might have happened if my mother and grandmother had survived the assimilation process intact.

Many Latinos have been much more successful at integrating themselves into the Anglo mainstream. Assimilation, however, involves pain and suffering, and my mother was one of its casualties. Though it is impossible to sort out all the contributing factors, I am convinced that my mother's psychological traumas were inextricably linked to her assimilation experience and her efforts to be "white."[13] As researchers concluded in one important study of schizophrenia,

> it seems to us that *without exception* the experience that gets labeled schizophrenic is *a special strategy that a person invents in order to live in an unlivable situation.* In his life situation the person has come to feel he is in an untenable position. He cannot make a move . . . without being beset by contradictory and paradoxical pushes and demands, pushes and pulls, both internally from himself, and externally from those around him. He is, as it were, in a position of checkmate.[14]

In short, my mother faced an "unliveable" situation in which assimilation pressures placed her needs and desires in permanent contradiction. Caught between two worlds, the Mexican American one she was born into and the white one she strived to join, my mother could not cope with the internal strife and endless contradictions that resulted.

This became all too apparent as I was in the middle of writing this book. As she descended into another schizophrenic moment, my mother said on the telephone, "I love you, *mijo*" (short for *mi hijo,* "my son," in Spanish). I was thirty-eight years old, and that was the very first time in my life that she had called me *mijo*, with all the love that it connotes. Walking a tightrope between two worlds, only as madness took hold could she speak the Spanish taught her by her Mexican American mother.

Though hers is an extreme case, racial minorities suffer a disproportionate number of mental health problems in this country. The dominant culture demands that we assimilate but places distinct limits on our opportunities to do so. As a society, we should not kid ourselves about this, or ignore both the costs and the limits of assimilation.

It was not only her attempts to assimilate that made Angela Gallardo's life unlivable. The fact that she was a woman contributed, as did the fact that she was poor.[15] At the intersection of three subordinated worlds—brown, poor, and a woman—my mother didn't have much of a chance.[16] Serious health problems over the years made her life physically as well as psychologically painful. I vividly remember her torture as she lay on the couch with kidney stones when I was a child. Long, nasty-looking scars mark her body from many surgeries. I sometimes wonder how much of the pain and scarring resulted from the fact that state-funded health care cut corners. Later it was diabetes and cataracts that troubled her, and she always worried that Medi-Cal would not cover the costs of her treatment. But it was the travails of the assimilation process that started my mother on her downward spiral.

The "melting pot" or "tossed salad" metaphor for immigrant assimilation fails to capture fully the experiences of racial minorities in the United States. Rather than a melting pot, racial minorities find themselves in a "ring of fire." Survival is possible only if one remains near the middle of the figurative ring. The fire is hot and even those fortunate enough to survive get burned. All Latinos in the United States, even those who successfully navigate their way through the flames, are scarred. Many are not so lucky, however, but suffer immense pain, perhaps even self-destruction, as they get too close or even touch the ring and are burned, sometimes beyond recognition. Like my mother and grandmother, they are unidentified, nameless casualties of the "ring of fire" known as the assimilation process.

My mother is a Mexican American woman. I take pride in her ancestry. When I look into my olive-skinned daughter Elena's eyes, I see my mother, just as when I look at Teresa and Tomás, I see my father. My mother desperately wanted to avoid being seen as a Mexican. She tried to deny her heritage and embraced a mythical, ancient tie with Spain as part of her effort to assimilate. She shielded her sons from Spanish and the disadvantages that it brought her generation; but she could not escape. Her denial of her ancestry is a sad but revealing indication of a more general phenomenon among Latinos in the United States.

I love my mother, but I grow angry with her at times. Why did she try so hard to assimilate and rob me of the Mexican American culture that she shed? Why did she "give up" and let her illness win? I should not blame her, but I sometimes do. It helps me to cope with a deep sense of guilt. I dreaded the visits home from college and law school to see my mother, poor and not "all there." What would she be like today if things had worked out? Why had I survived? Maybe I should have stayed home and helped her. Perhaps she would be better off if I had.

Chapter 4

My Father: Planting the Seeds of a Racial Consciousness

On May 24, 1991, my wife Virginia gave birth to our first child, Teresa Salazar Johnson. Happy as we had ever been, we looked at baby Teresa with awe and delight. Like all new parents everywhere we said, "What a beautiful baby," and she will always be our beautiful baby. But we were as shocked as we could be when we first saw her. She was very, very white! Blond hair, blue eyes, pink skin. Beautiful in every way—but not at all what we expected. Parents-to-be visualize their soon-to-be-born children. Will it be a boy or a girl? Who will the baby look like, mother or father? I thought, in our excitement, that we had covered all the bases. Our baby had to look *something* like her parents. We had some relatives with darker skin and more indigenous features. Maybe she would look like them. Perhaps she would be lighter and look like us. But blond hair and blue eyes simply never crossed our minds. How could the child of two brown-eyed, dark-haired parents have a child with bright baby-blue eyes and blond fuzz on her bald head? Later I thought to myself, this is my white father's revenge on his Mexican American son.

An Anglo with blond hair and blue eyes, my father as a young man towered over my mother, who is not even five feet tall. If I got my

Mexican American identity from my mother, my tolerance of racial difference unquestionably came from my father.

Ken Johnson grew up near downtown Los Angeles in a working-class neighborhood sandwiched between Chavez Ravine, home to the Los Angeles Dodgers, and the Los Angeles River, a free-flowing waterway when he grew up. Then called Little Valley or "Frogtown," because frogs from the river invaded the neighborhood every spring, the extended Johnson clan initially settled here. As a kid, Dad often got into trouble for swimming in the river. He was easily caught because he would return home covered with the oil that the railroads dumped into the river in those days. Years later, when the family visited my great-grandma Murrill, I caught tadpoles in that river, which by that time had been cemented over as part of Los Angeles's giant flood control system.

Family lore tells of ancestors who immigrated from Sweden. My grandfather Raymond, from whom I inherited my middle name, came to California with his family of eleven brothers and sisters from Nebraska in the 1920s. His mother died carrying her twelfth child and his father was hit by a car in a crosswalk; both are buried in Evergreen Cemetery in East Los Angeles. A politically progressive man, Ray Johnson championed the working man and the Democratic party. He had a tough exterior, no doubt the result of his own family's hardships. He never finished high school; only one of his siblings did. My father recalls his father complimenting him twice in his life, once for a tackle in a high school football game and once to a union organizer trying to organize my father's newspaper. As was common among his generation, racism coexisted with his politically enlightened views. He didn't believe in intermarriage and thought that the "races"—particularly blacks and whites—should stick to their own kind. In college, I came to think of him as a modern Tom Watson, a Southern populist who fought to organize poor farmers during Reconstruction but was moved by political realities to support the rise of Jim Crow.[1] But

Grandpa's views of race were apparently complex. My dad tells me that Grandpa's best friends were two Mexican Americans and an African American, and that they often visited his home.

My father's mother, Mary, who tragically died of cancer when I was a toddler, also traced her roots to the Midwest. My dad was closer to his mom, whom he found easier to talk to. My mother, to this day, speaks fondly of Mary Johnson, who treated her with kindness and respect. Grandma Johnson was not preoccupied with race. At the same time, my dad says that she was shocked and surprised, though not angered, when an African American college friend of his, Ken Jones, now a local television newscaster in Los Angeles, attended a birthday party for my mom. Grandma Johnson and Aunt Gladys stayed in the kitchen during the party.

Though I don't recall meeting Grandma Johnson, her memory remains with us. She gave me a child's rocking chair when I was a baby. Though passed around the family for many years, I eventually tracked down that sturdy wooden chair. Virginia refinished it and I have enjoyed seeing my children rocking in that chair.

Ray and Mary Johnson were salt-of-the earth people. They both came from large families, and they treasured family. Many of my father's family lived in Little Valley. His uncle Brown-Eyes and aunt Rosie lived there through the 1980s. His maternal grandmother Murrill died there when I was in high school. Never forgetting his roots, Dad regularly returned with his own sons to mow Grandma Murrill's lawn. He showed us the "temporary" housing where his family had lived, little more than a plywood shack in her backyard, built immediately after World War II. Though money had been tight, the family always stayed together. When I was young, the extended Johnson family vacationed each summer in the campgrounds of Yosemite National Park.

Little Valley was a mixed neighborhood with both working-class white and Mexican American families. In discussing California's anti-immigrant Proposition 187 years later, Dad explained how difficult it was for him to understand the hatred directed toward Mexican immigrants during that tumultuous campaign. They worked hard, they treasured their families, they didn't ask for hand-outs. As far as he could tell, the Mexican Americans with whom he grew up were no different from his own family.

Times were tough for the Johnson family during the Great Depression of the 1930s; jobs were few and far between. But if prosperity eluded them, the family still managed to make ends meet. My grandfather ultimately found financial security later in life working for Sylvania, which made electrical products like light bulbs and flash bulbs for cameras, first as a laborer and member of the Teamsters' Union and later as an administrator. Like my Grandma on my mother's side, he was full of stories. As a boy, I was always amazed by his ability to turn a mundane event into a good yarn. Once, on a family vacation to Yosemite, he entertained us with a story about our adventures when the battery of his car died on the trip. Until he told the story, I had not known that I had been part of such a grand adventure.

In many ways Ray Johnson was a pessimist, one of the many characteristics that we share. The Depression no doubt shaped his brand of pessimism, and also made him appreciate the virtues of frugality. "Don't be afraid to ask for a doggie bag," he once told me in a restaurant. When law firms would fly me home for interviews and holidays with family, Grandpa told all within earshot that I was "living like a Republican." In that vein, he complained when Los Angeles County gave my father a car to do his job. "Why should we pay for that car?" he wanted to know.

Though I deeply respected Grandpa's class sensibilities and grew to appreciate them even more in college, his racial views were far from enlightened. I heard stories about how he threatened not to attend my parents' wedding because my mother was Mexican

American and the ceremony was to be held in a Catholic church. His family had left the Catholic Church, so the combination upset him all the more. As my Dad put it years later, "When your Mom and I planned to marry in a Catholic church, he became distant and I became stubborn. He said he wouldn't come; I said I didn't care. Neither of us was telling the truth." Part of my grandfather's racism—especially against blacks—may have resulted from his father's having been killed in an automobile accident with an African American man.

One of his younger brothers, my uncle Brown-Eyes, could often be found with Grandpa. While Grandpa tended to have a gloom-and-doom outlook on life, Brown-Eyes was always brightness and sunshine, a mirror image of his brother. He married a Mexican American woman, Rosie, but I never figured out her ancestry until I was over thirty years old. Rosie is not light- or dark-skinned. She has a country sort of accent, probably acquired from being around the Johnsons for too many years. Rosie's mother lived with Rosie and Brown-Eyes until she died. As I look back, I can see that Rosie's mother (whose surname was Moreno) "looked" Mexican, but it was not until we were vacationing in Yosemite in 1992 that it dawned on me. Around the campfire, Brown-eyes's son Richard and his wife were talking with Virginia and me. Richard's wife made some reference to Richard's being half-Mexican. Suddenly it all clicked, and I understood the special affinity between Rosie and my mother, two Mexican American women of the same generation. To this day, Rosie always asks how my mother is doing. My dad describes Rosie and Brown-Eyes as super-patriotic, always flying the American flag. They were most ardent assimilationists, which is consistent with Rosie's downplaying her Mexican ancestry.

As it had been for my mother, attending Los Angeles City College represented quite an achievement for my dad, who was the first in his family to attend college. He could not afford to attend UCLA, though no doubt he would have excelled there as well. Class issues no doubt affected his life as well as mine. Perhaps because of his lack of guidance about the importance—or even the possibility—of getting a college degree, Dad did not pursue a bachelor's degree. Measured against his peers, he was a superachiever for attending college at all.

Unlike my mother, my father recovered from the collapse of his first marriage and went on to see the most prosperous years of his life. A hard worker with good political sense, he was successful first as a journalist for a variety of local newspapers and later in a career devoted to public service for the county of Los Angeles. As a journalist, he started off working at places like the *East Side Journal* in East Los Angeles, where he could see men lining up for *menudo,* known as a hangover cure, on Saturday morning. He rose to the position of news editor of the *South Bay Daily Breeze,* a newspaper serving the beach cities south of downtown Los Angeles. A Los Angeles County supervisor appointed him press deputy in the late 1960s and later chief deputy. Because a five-member Board of Supervisors runs the sprawling Los Angeles County, his post was a politically powerful one. He later became Deputy Director of the Los Angeles County Department of Beaches. Along the way, he was the local Chamber of Commerce Young Man of the Year and later Man of the Year, wrote a book about the history of Redondo Beach, worked on numerous political campaigns, and served on a hospital's publicly elected board of directors.

After the divorce, my father had court-ordered visitation rights to see his two sons every other weekend and every Wednesday night. Despite a busy schedule, he rarely missed a visit, even though he had to drive about fifty miles from Torrance to Azusa in the San Gabriel Valley to pick us up. My brother and I looked forward to his visits with great anticipation. We had fun whatever we did, whether it was a drive in the San Gabriel mountains near my mother's house, a day at the beach, or a trip to the miniature golf course. He always gave me sound advice, including the maxim "everyone makes mistakes," which he told me when I was a young boy and I passed on to my children.

The thing that my father emphasized most in my childhood was that a college education was essential to my future. This idea became so deeply ingrained in me that I *never* for a moment doubted that I would go to college.

Ironically, it was my father, not my mother, who encouraged me to take pride in my Mexican heritage. Unlike my Mom, who felt that her Mexican ancestry was a liability, he emphasized my roots from my earliest days. His encouragement was consistent with his racial attitudes generally. My father has a tolerance for difference when it come to racial minorities that many people, including his own father, lack.

Because of my father, I became conscious of racial issues at a young age. In elementary school I won an award for a paper about the dramatic black power salute of Tommie Smith and John Carlos at the 1968 Olympic Games in Mexico City.[2] I argued that while some people claimed that the two track stars were unpatriotic, there were many in this country, especially blacks, who believed that their salute showed pride in their community. I studied the civil rights movement and the history of the despicable treatment of blacks in the South.

It was my father's influence that awakened my perception early in life that African Americans were horribly mistreated in this country. We talked about the 1965 riots in South Central Los Angeles, then known as Watts. It was my father who scolded others who, in the presence of his children, used the "n-word" and other racial epithets. Indeed, he liked to make a scene out of it, an opportunity to show his own rebellious, contrarian streak. One fellow once left our home in a huff in the middle of watching a football game after Dad told him not to attack African Americans in front of his sons.

I cannot say where he got his sensibilities, but not everyone in his family shared them. His tolerance of others who were different, and his willingness to be "in your face" if you crossed the line into racism, distinguished him from most of the adults I encountered growing up.

My father also taught me how to argue, an important skill for law school and for life generally. He enjoyed a good, combative argument over important issues of the day, and he would sometimes deliberately goad me in order to provoke one. He supported the goals of affirmative action, for example, but sometimes played devil's advocate, teasing that "affirmative action is bad because a bunch of unqualified people get jobs," in order to get a rise out of me. Although his love of argument not infrequently created tension, it sharpened my mind.

As I grew older, I reflected on the contrast between my father's respect for my Mexican heritage and my mother's and grandmother's denial of their own backgrounds. In some ways, it was easier for him to appreciate my heritage; being white, he had privileges, advantages, and freedoms in the dominant white culture that they did not. He had not suffered the disadvantages of being perceived as Mexican. Throughout his life, my father enjoyed Mexican culture, Mexican food, and fishing trips to Mexico, and he spoke some Spanish when necessary to order food and drink. Class issues were more salient to his own experience. This was also true for his sister Marilyn, who is an educator and has always been close to my family. For years Aunt Marilyn taught in a poor, African American and Latino school in South Central Los Angeles and turned down offers to teach in "nicer" schools. She spent her afterhours taking her students to L.A. Dodgers games and Disneyland.

Her avowed interest has always been in helping low-income kids, be they white, black, Latino, or Asian. At the same time, she thinks immigrants should assimilate, learn and speak English, and "be American." In this she echoes the conventional wisdom in this country. She moved from Monterey Park, once a mixed Mexican American/Anglo suburb of Los Angeles, when the influx of Asian immigrants changed the flavor of the community.

When I look back on my early years, I see how deeply my father's racial sensitivities shaped my own. They undoubtedly influenced my brothers as well. Michael married a Filipino woman. My half-brother Eric married a woman who is half African American.

Despite my upbringing, I remember my silence in high school when classmates disparaged African Americans. A quiet child trying to fit in—to assimilate as my mother had tried to do—I was not as ready or willing to stand up to the racism of others. I was not as brave as my father.

Chapter 5

Growing Up White?

When I was living with my Mom, my Dad would drive twice a month to Azusa from Torrance to pick his two sons up for the weekend. During this hour-long drive, we went from a racially mixed area of whites and Mexican Americans to affluent white suburbs near the beach. I peered curiously out the window of the car and watched the change in scenery. The dusty heat of the San Gabriel Valley contrasted sharply with the windblown coolness of the beach communities. I lived in two very different worlds, not sure where I belonged.

My younger brother Michael was born in 1961. As a child, he looked much like my blond-haired, blue-eyed father and was shorter and stockier than I am. He never identified himself as Mexican American, though he would acknowledge that part of his ancestry when pressed. Though we moved around quite a bit growing up, Mike and I lived together until I went off to college. In the shadow of an older brother who excelled in school, Mike was not much interested in education and spent his youth rebelling. He eventually enlisted in the Navy and has served the United States for nearly two decades now. While based in the Philippines, he met and married a Filipino woman and has two beautiful children, both of whom look more like their mother than father. The racial mixture of his family—Filipino, Mexican American, and Anglo—will be the book of the future.

I also have two half-brothers. Born in 1967 with brown hair and brown eyes, Robby was my mother's son by her second Anglo husband. When he was young and we lived in Azusa, I called him Roberto or Berto, though I have no idea why. We grew up together in Azusa before Mike and I went to live with our father when I was in seventh grade. Like my brother Mike, Robby acknowledges his mixed ancestry without embracing it. He also joined the Navy after high school and later married. My other half-brother, Eric, is tall, blond, and blue-eyed, just like our father. A graduate of UCLA, where he was a member of a fraternity, he now works in the advertising business. Married to a woman of a mixed black/white marriage, Eric has evidently addressed racial issues constructively.

One of my earliest childhood memories is of sitting on my parents' bed in our home on January Drive in Torrance, California, staring in a daze at the faded yellow shade on the bedroom window. My father had just explained to me that he was moving out, and I had a painful lump in my throat and was speechless with shock.

In retrospect, I can see that the divorce was predictable, perhaps inevitable. For one thing, my parents married very young—she at nineteen and he at twenty—though in those days that was not uncommon. More importantly, they were very different people who grew in different directions. As was characteristic of women from her generation, my mother wanted to be a homemaker. My father was more ambitious.

After the divorce, my mother, Mike, and I moved to Azusa in the San Gabriel Valley, near my grandmother. In the late 1960s, Azusa was a quiet town of poor and working-class whites and Mexican

Americans. The older part of town surrounding City Hall was predominantly Mexican American; the newer part was more Anglo, though these lines were not rigid. We moved into an apartment complex that was home to a good many single mothers. Some had jobs, while others lived on welfare. The Rockvale Apartments, like my own place in the world, was on the line between the old Mexican and the newer white part of town. We lived on the border between the two parts of Azusa.

Mike and I went to school at the Charles H. Lee Elementary School, where Orlando Lopez, Frankie Ramirez, Nancy Landeros, and Jimmy Benitez were among my were fourth-grade classmates, as were Geraldine Plumer, Eddie Hart, and Phil Cartwright. I played baseball with Orlando Lopez. Frankie Ramirez grew into a local tough with his black, slicked-back hair, though I never found him threatening. I had my first crush on Nancy Landeros, with her long, black hair and fair complexion. On Valentine's Day, she gave me a card that boldly declared, "I LOVE YOU." She giggled and pointed out that it featured a picture of a skunk. Jimmy Benitez was the first classmate who ever gave me a Christmas card. I cannot remember ever classifying any of these kids as "different" because they were Mexican American, but subtle distinctions did exist in my mind.

Mexican American culture was certainly an influence on our lives. I loved my mother's *chorizo* and potatoes (still one of my favorite dishes), tacos, and *menudo,* the spicy soup made with tripe. We went to holiday gatherings with friends, eating turkey and molé, a chocolate and chili sauce that tastes much better than it sounds. Near the Catholic church where I attended Catechism, Mike and I would always ask our mother for money to spend at the "little Mexican store," a weathered old building with faded white paint, where I bought candies and *pan dulce* (Mexican sweet bread). I remain to this day on the lookout for good *pan dulce,* and in Mexico or Mexican American neighborhoods in the United States, I always try to find the local *panadería.*

I hated going to church, except for the few times we went to the movies after Mass, and have vivid memories of the St. Francis of Rome Church on Foothill Boulevard, where I took my first communion. In those days the priest conducted mass in Latin. I did not and still do not speak Latin and I understood little, as I suspect was the case for most of the parishioners of that predominantly Mexican American church. In one of the few sermons I remember, the priest railed against the godless communists in Vietnam torturing U.S. soldiers.

Every few summers, my mother, brother, grandmother, step-grandfather, and aunts would take a trip down to Mexicali, just across the border in Mexico, to visit my great-grandmother. (I have no idea how we all fit into one car!) Mexicali was only a few miles away from Brawley, the small Imperial Valley town where my mother was born. We traveled in a white Chevrolet Impala popular during that era and still fashionable today with "low riders" in southern California. Because the car had no air conditioning, the trip was long and hot. We often stopped to visit relatives, including Aunt Carmen and Uncle Tommy Gallardo in Westmoreland, a small farm town near the border.

On these trips, we crossed the border from Calexico on the California side to Mexicali in Mexico. The border was a much less formidable barrier then than the militarized zone it has become. Years later, I returned to these borderlands as an attorney to see the military build-up and a prison full of Central American refugees in El Centro.

My great-grandmother, Josephine Gonzales, and her husband Alfonso lived in a relatively well-to-do part of Mexicali, just across the border from its sister city Calexico. It was a different world, but comfortable. A street vendor made his daily rounds, pushing a cart loaded with fresh fruit for sale. Our family relaxed, talking the day away in the coolness of the indoors.

The Welfare State and Our Lives

Because my mother could not get a decent job, we lived on a combination of welfare and child support provided by my father. President Lyndon Johnson's "war on poverty" exposed me to the welfare bureaucracy. When we needed a doctor, we walked to the Medi-Cal center, a joint state-federal program that provides basic medical assistance to the poor. In this drab building on Azusa Avenue, I lost my first wristwatch, a Mickey Mouse watch with a thin red leather wristband.

Being on welfare during the 1960s meant that a social worker made regular visits to our home. The social worker, who remains faceless in my memory, would ask Mike and me in our mother's presence, "Does anyone else live in the apartment? Have any men been spending the night?" The idea was to make sure that we were not welfare cheats with a stash of hidden income in our spare one-bedroom apartment, or using welfare money to support no-account men. A shy, private person who *never* talks about such personal matters, my mother must have found the interrogations humiliating.

Food stamps were another constant reminder of our socioeconomic status. As many people know, whether they have ever had to use them or not, the Department of Agriculture issues these dollar bill-size stamps for food purchases only. Not every store will accept food stamps as substitutes for cash, and in poor neighborhoods some storefront windows hold signs proclaiming, "no food stamps." I sometimes did the shopping for my Mom, and everyone else in the checkout line could see that I paid with food stamps. I had repressed this embarrassing memory until years later, while on vacation, I was waiting in line in a grocery store behind a young boy who had a note from his mother giving him permission to use food stamps.

In the mid-1960s, after we had lived in Azusa for a few years, my mother met the man who became her second husband. As was the case for so many single mothers, this was her way off welfare. The marriage was not a foregone conclusion even after my mother became pregnant, because she steadfastly refused to give up custody of me and Mike in spite of my stepfather's demands. It was only after much discussion that they finally married after Robby was born. My stepfather was a racist who was oblivious about filling the heads of two young, impressionable children with ugly remarks about African Americans and racial epithets like "boon" and "coon." He also poked fun at my Mom as a "spic" or "taco bender." Too young to find these remarks offensive, I actually thought them funny at the time.

My mother's second marriage was far from perfect, economically or otherwise. She did her best to economize, driving a series of cheap old American cars, including the quickly discontinued Corvair, a Plymouth with big fins and a push-button transmission, and similarly wondrous vehicles. For years before her marriage, she had gone without a car and walked everywhere—to the shopping center, church, the movies, and anywhere else we had to go. We shopped at thrift shops (I remember AmVets in particular), bought day-old (and older) bread at the bakery, and patronized discount stores of all types. To pay for my lunch at school, I washed dishes in the cafeteria.

But money could be stretched only so far, and one weekend we ran out of food. Mike and I made a big deal of this, moping indoors all day during that bleak, overcast weekend. "I wish I was dead," I heartlessly told my mother. She must have felt guilty as only a mother could. My step-grandfather described our family as "destitute," a word I had to look up in the dictionary. To this day, I *never* express financial worries around my children, let alone say things like "we are broke," which I heard regularly from Mom while growing up.

One night I left the house despondent because our telephone had been disconnected and walked to the local shopping center to call my father on a pay phone. I was young, sad, and crying. My father was not home. I was dejectedly heading home, hands in my pockets and eyes glued to the ground, when a police cruiser stopped me. I was so mad at the world that when the police officer questioned me, I yelled, "What, do you want to know my life story?" He tried to scare me by threatening to arrest me for the crime of insolence but eventually let me go home.

As a child, I did well in school thanks to both natural ability and hard work. Though I was genuinely curious and interested in my studies, my schoolwork was primarily a refuge, an escape from things I wanted to avoid. Indeed, family stress helped me excel in school. In the fifth and sixth grades, I devoured biographies of famous people like George Washington, Andrew Jackson, and Abraham Lincoln. Struck by how "normal" these famous peoples' lives were, I sometimes read a biography a day. The rockier things became in my family life, the more I read. This pattern began in elementary school, when I would check dozens of science and history books out of the Azusa public library. I well remember the long walk home carrying a heavy stack of books. In fourth grade, I once skipped school and spent the afternoon reading in the library.

In addition to reading and schoolwork, basketball became a favorite pastime. Tall and lanky, I spent many hours playing on the blacktop courts at William Drendel School, where I attended fifth and sixth grades. I had some talent and was in fact one of the best playground players. I also became a fairly good fighter during these years. In informal rankings, I was in the top five or so fighters in the school, known for an emotional streak and for losing my temper.

When I was in seventh grade at Foothill Junior High, my mother's second marriage fell apart. Though I was shielded from the details, vague rumors circulated in the family about another woman, drugs, and the like. I did at least know by then that my stepfather was capable of great psychological cruelty. When the court awarded my father custody of my brother and me, the judge told my mother in open court to get away from this man who had hurt her so deeply.

I continued to be confused about my identity during my adolescence. My father had instilled in me a fierce pride in my Mexican and Swedish ancestry. As a youngster in search of an identity, I wrote Kevin "Swede" Johnson in the inside cover of one of my school textbooks. During my youth I went back and forth between my parents' separate homes, which only confused me racially and economically. My father's economic circumstances improved considerably while my mother's remained constant. On weekends with my father, my brother and I saw how the middle class lived; we went to sporting events and saw the Dodgers, Lakers, and UCLA play. During the week, we witnessed the lives of people on welfare. My mother, who did her very best for her sons, was unquestionably haunted by this contrast.

Over the years, the income disparities widened. During high school and college, I visited my mother and little brother in her small apartment. The claustrophobia of poverty always drove me away after a day or two. With no money and nothing to do, we spent the time in conversation, but there were not too many pleasant memories to talk about.

When I was in seventh grade, my brother and I moved in with my father, who had married a woman with two children from a previous marriage. Adolescence is a difficult period in anyone's life, but the many disruptions and upheavals in mine made it seem especially hard. We moved from the poor and working-class, racially mixed town of inland Azusa to an upper-middle-class, predominantly white part of Long Beach and later West Torrance, near the beaches of Los Angeles. My school teachers' names changed from Diaz and Casellas to Gold and Stanford, and the student population reflected a similar homogeneity.

In Long Beach, we lived in a nice tract home. The fence behind our house was literally the border between Long Beach and Hawaiian Gardens, an ineptly named poor community where many Mexican Americans live and which is plagued by gang violence today. This border divided the white world where I now lived and the brown world from which I had come. On the other side of our fence the Mexican American kids went to one school, and on our side the white kids—and I—went to another. Once our family was surprised to see a pregnant, Mexican American teenager come trick-or-treating at our door on Halloween. "She must be from Hawaiian Gardens," someone said.

Racial tension was much more apparent in the Long Beach area than it had been in the San Gabriel Valley. Like many southern California cities, Long Beach was divided into a white and a black part of town. I played on a basketball team in a league organized by the local parks, and in the championship game our all-white El Dorado Park team played a predominantly black team. The referees were white, and at one point one of them became very angry at a black ballplayer. It seemed clear to me that the referee would not have become so upset with a white player.

Our family soon moved to West Torrance, part of the "white flight" from Los Angeles communities like Inglewood, Gardena, and Hawthorne, which were being "invaded" by African Americans and today are largely populated by minorities. The South Bay area became the suburban home to many families who benefitted handsomely from the booming defense industry that buoyed the southern California economy. Many of them worked for McDonnell Douglas and Hughes Aircraft near Los Angeles International Airport during the defense buildup of the 1970s and 1980s. At that time, the only minorities to be seen in these beach cities were those fishing off the piers in Redondo Beach, Hermosa Beach, and Manhattan Beach. Few African Americans lived in West Torrance. As one would expect among "white flighters," the most virulent form of racism was reserved for blacks, who were held responsible for crime, declining property values, and any other sign of decay.

I did not fit neatly into the black/white classification scheme, nor had I had never lived in an environment with such overt racial animosities. There was racism in Azusa but it had, for the most part, remained in the background. I had heard racist chants in the schoolyard like "fight, fight, nigger and a white," and "Daniel Boone was a man, yes a big man, but the bear was bigger so he ran like a nigger up a tree." A subtle, almost unconscious anti-black sentiment pervaded life in the suburban Los Angeles communities where I lived. The usually unspoken assumption was that blacks were inherently inferior and it was proper to look down on and even despise them. All of this seemed normal and natural, and it generally went unquestioned and unexamined. A grade school friend once told me that a fellow student was 99 percent "American." Today I have no idea what that means. At the time, however, it made such perfect sense that it did not warrant further inquiry.

Only when I moved in with my father did the racial issues become overt and unavoidable. It was in West Torrance that I first heard anti-Mexican slurs on a regular basis, though I did not take them personally. Some of the students at my new school mistook me for Asian, and I remember being called "Rickshaw" after someone saw me high-stepping on the football field. Another guy told me in class that he had heard I was a karate expert.

In West Torrance, Mexicans (often referred to as "Meskins" and "wetbacks") were disparaged, but less so than African Americans. Trying to fit in made it difficult to respond to such comments. They were wrong and they hurt, but I was confused as well. Was I Spanish, as my mother and grandmother pretended? Was I Mexican American? Was I half Anglo/half Mexican American? And what was that? Mexican stereotypes, considered racist only in hindsight, permeated popular culture during this era and added to my confusion. For example, the popular 1950s television show "Father Knows Best," which was rerun daily during my high school days, featured an episode in which a nice, hard-working Mexican gardener with a thick accent changed his Spanish name to "Frank Smith" to get more business. I laughed, but the gardener was right about the significance of the social perception of a name.

Every high school student experiences angst in finding an identity. As the product of three divorces, a mixed background, and many different schools, I certainly did. In an attempt to fit in, I adopted a carefree attitude toward life and did a lot of partying—a stark contrast to the carefully controlled nature of my life today.

I spent my years at West High School in Torrance, then a predominantly white school with a small handful of Asian Americans, a few Mexican Americans, and virtually no African Americans, adrift in a sea of confusion and low self-esteem. I spent far too much time trying to fit in with the other kids—to assimilate with whites as my mother had spent her life trying to do.

I took a fair amount of abuse for doing well in school from the group of underachievers with whom I hung out. I had always been made fun of by other students for excelling in school, but this bothered me more deeply in high school, where the abuse seemed harsher than ever before. Often called names like Poindexter, I reacted by setting out to prove that I did not give a damn about school. I showed up late, skipped classes, and some days did not go to school at all.

My interactions with my high-school classmates, including jokes and puns about the way I looked, exacerbated my identity confusion. I was not the blond, blue-eyed ideal of southern California beach cities, and I was regularly reminded of my difference. I did not bother to explain my background to my Anglo classmates, some of whom I even grew fond of. Indeed, I emulated them and wanted to be accepted. I got a surfboard and hung out at the beach, though I was never much of a surfer. Walking to the beach with friends from Torrance through Redondo Beach, we passed a series of streets with Spanish women's names, like Juanita, Irena, Maria, Elena, and Lucia, and the reminder of my roots made me feel uneasy about betraying my heritage, though of course I kept this to myself.

My high school chums' derision of African Americans, Mexicans, and to a lesser extent Asians nagged at me. Some of the guys knew of my Mexican ancestry and gave me grief for it. With or without a Spanish surname, I was different from them and they knew it. My thoughts often wander back to those days. During one sleepless night in the 1990s, I concluded that racial animosity had fueled some of the mean-spiritedness I experienced in my youth.

As one might expect, this environment warped my own racial sensibilities. Once when my father and I were returning from a Father's Day family reunion, a guy who I assumed was a Mexican immigrant driving an old Chevrolet rear-ended my father's sports car. For all I knew, he was a Mexican American citizen or not even of Mexican ancestry at all. I loudly complained about the "damn wetback" who had dented the car. My father correctly scolded me. I had adopted the anti-Mexican rhetoric of my high school classmates. At the same time, I never directed such animosity toward African Americans, which to my mind was unquestionably wrong. I had learned too much about the oppression and mistreatment of African Americans, both from my father and from my reading about the civil rights movement, to make that mistake. I would have done well to learn about how Mexican immigrants and Mexican American citizens have suffered in the United States.

In spite of all the pressures I felt, I never did completely forsake my Mexican American heritage. Finding the subject more relevant than my other studies, I took four years of Spanish in high school and worked diligently at it, even dropping out of calculus my senior year in order to take a fourth year of Spanish. Unlike math, the language proved useful in my everyday life. I enjoyed speaking Spanish with my mother and grandmother, who seemed by then to have retreated a little from their denial of their Mexican ancestry. Besides talking with my family, I conversed with Spanish speakers at a job I held during high school. I even read Hemingway in Spanish.

Although West Torrance was predominantly white in the 1970s, north and downtown Torrance had a Mexican American community. I ran cross country and track in high school against some Mexican American runners. Tomás Rodriguez, a boisterous, happy-go-lucky sort, was the best cross-country runner at Torrance High School during my sophomore year. Always joking and laughing, Rodriguez told many stories, and I listened intently to tales of his exploits. A guy named Guerra, a quiet, intense miler from North High, was the best local cross-country runner at the time. Their running exploits were more interesting to me then than their Spanish surnames or Mexican ancestry.

Another high school friend and I shared a mixed background. His mother was Mexican American and his father was of Italian ancestry. As far as I could tell, this family was one of the most ardently racist around. When African Americans began moving into the neighborhood, they fled to nearby Torrance. My friend rarely mentioned that his mother was Mexican American and simply did not recognize or identify with that background. Indeed, he referred to Mexican immigrants as "wetbacks," told plenty of anti-Mexican jokes, and frequently poked fun at the Mexican immigrants with whom he worked in restaurants.

High school in West Torrance was difficult for any Chicano, not just those like me who were confused about their identity. One fellow student did his best to mix in with the surfer crowd at West High School, but underwent a gradual transformation from surfer to "home boy," a transition that is clearer to me in retrospect than it was at the time. He got a tattoo and began spending more time with the Chicanos in another part of Torrance known by whites as "Tortilla Flats." I went on a van trip with him to "the Pike" in Long Beach, a run-down old amusement park frequented by transients, so that another friend could get a tattoo. In those days, it was difficult to find a tattoo parlor because only gangsters and ex-cons got tattoos. On the way back, we stopped at a liquor store. While another friend and I waited in the van, he grabbed a case of beer, ran out of the store, jumped in the van, and we took off. From what I have heard, his activities in this vein have escalated.

My high school years also exposed me to the immigration laws. As a fry cook at Fishpeddlers on the waterfront in Redondo Beach, I worked with a number of undocumented Mexican immigrants. José Serrano, my supervisor, was one of them.[1] Supporting a family in Mexico, he lived frugally with a number of other men in a small apartment complex on a street of run-down apartments just off the busy Pacific Coast Highway. Our employer considered José the most reliable and responsible employee and always had a job waiting for him. Of all the employees at Fishpeddlers, the owner trusted only Serrano with the secret recipe for the restaurant's best-selling clam chowder.

I occasionally shared a beer with José and his friends after work, and I soon learned how deeply they feared "La Migra," the Immigration and Naturalization Service, which periodically raided and emptied the apartment building. José was deported several times to Mexico but always returned. We spoke a mixture of English and Spanish. His English was pretty good; my far from elegant Spanish got the job done.

I often joked with José about his immigration status. I jokingly called him "espalda mojada," which literally translated means "wetback." He never laughed. I had no idea how insensitive this was. I did not make jokes about his nationality, which would have been offensive to me, but about his immigration status. I had been taught that "they" had violated the laws to get to this country, that "they" were "illegal aliens." To my mind, it was permissible to slight José by joking about his immigration status, something I very much regret today.

I respected José and his devotion to work and family. My colleague Jim Smith has told me that everyone has a José Serrano story. Professor Bill Ong Hing has written similarly about Rodolfo Martinez Padilla as "mi cliente y amigo" (my client and friend).[2] Unfortunately, we hear much too little about these good people in the modern debate about immigration.

I had a number of other undocumented friends. Blas, for example, washed dishes at Fishpeddlers. Less serious than José, he enjoyed a busy social life. An attractive young man, he was out the door for a new adventure at the end of the day. My wife Virginia has had similar experiences in a variety of restaurant jobs. The hard-working Mexican immigrants she worked with treated her with respect. Virginia did know one immigrant who committed marriage fraud, but she was from England. Popular stereotypes often fail to square with our experiences in working with undocumented people.

For me, high school was a kind of free fall. As far as I am concerned, West High should have been called Waste High. Though it was relatively easy to keep my grades up, I was troubled. I gave up high school track and cross country running, for which I had talent, to pursue what I thought was a good social life. Always trying to fit in, I pointlessly got into trouble, as when I was caught smoking in the boys' room even though I did not smoke.

I felt alone in those years, confused about my identity and uncertain where I fit in. The people of mixed background I knew growing up ignored or denied their family's past. They considered their Mexican ancestry an impediment to the persona they needed to live in a white suburb. Just as one can voluntarily adopt a racial identity, one can deny one's background. Whatever I wanted to be, I could not fully assimilate. The way I looked, the way I was raised, and my memories were impediments to the assimilation process—if assimilation meant forgetting your family history, accepting racial hatred as a norm, and disregarding what you knew was right and true.

Chapter 6

College: Beginning to Recognize Racial Complexities

An affable law student named Sergio O'Cadiz, a miler as an undergraduate at UCLA, asked me if I wanted to go for a run with a couple of other students. Runners talk and as we ran, we chatted, and the subject soon turned to our backgrounds. One student had his father's Spanish surname, though his mother was of German ancestry. I had always thought of him as Mexican American. The other student, with an Anglo surname, mentioned that his mother was Mexican American. I had always classified him as white. Three mixed Latinos, similar but different, reflect some of the complexities of being Latino in the United States, complexities that I first began to grasp as a student at U.C. Berkeley.

In recent years, conservative (and even some liberal) forces have mounted an attack on the programs that ensured the racial and ethnic diversity so important to my intellectual and social development at Berkeley. In 1996, the Regents of the University of California eliminated affirmative action in student admissions and California voters passed the California "Civil Rights" Initiative, which eliminates the use of virtually any "racial preference" by the state. These measures together threaten one of the greatest strengths of the University of California, the respect for racial and ethnic diversity that changed my life.

In filling out the standardized college admission test forms, I never seriously doubted that I would give my identity as Mexican American. My willingness to do so, at least in this painless way, might have been the result of my high school alienation. But it might also have been rebellion against my mother's and grandmother's denial of their own Mexican heritage. Or maybe I was deliberately distancing myself from my anti-Mexican high school friends—or responding to my father's encouragement. Though I did not know it at the time, my identity choice would greatly affect my educational and career path.

Before college, my general view of affirmative action came from a high school teacher named Mike Kellogg, a former professional football player who preached to his class of young, impressionable students that racial classifications could only be used for discriminatory purposes and that affirmative action amounted to unlawful racial discrimination. Why I continued to identify as a Mexican American for purposes of standardized testing, I cannot explain.[1] As with many complex choices made during that period in my life, I simply did not pay much attention to the ramifications of my actions. But did I consciously or unconsciously seek an advantage by "checking the box"?[2] One of my father's African American friends, who occasionally referred to me as "Mex," encouraged me to identify myself as a Mexican American for college admissions purposes. An opportunistic man who later became a state court judge, he told me that this would improve my admission chances.

Both of my parents had impressed upon me the need for a college education, and the only question in my mind was which college I would attend. Because of my test scores and, presumably, my Mexican American identification, I received promotional materials from schools all over the country. Some were from excellent colleges such as Haverford, which I failed to appreciate until years later. Flattered that any school at all was interested in me, I idly pondered attending West Point or the Naval Academy, though I had no real interest in serving in the military. The family preference, especially my father's, was that I go to UCLA, a school close to home that he had dreamed of attending as a young man.

I found the prospect of staying in the Los Angeles area, however, distinctly unattractive. High school had been difficult, my relationship with my family was tense at times, and my mother's life depressed me deeply. Leaving Los Angeles became even more important to me than any education I might receive.

I applied to and was accepted by the University of California at Berkeley. I knew surprisingly little about U.C. Berkeley, except that it was notoriously "radical." My grandmother had reputedly lived a wild life in San Francisco, and northern California seemed a good place to escape to. After I was admitted, my father and I drove up for a visit. Suitably impressed as we drove across the Bay Bridge connecting San Francisco and Oakland, and hearing that Patty Hearst had been convicted of bank robbery, I found the Bay Area tremendously exciting.

Berkeley was wildly different from anywhere I had ever been. Vendors sold trinkets and tie-dyed t-shirts on Telegraph Avenue. Colorful street people abounded, including such characters as the Bubble Lady (a poet named Julia who walked the streets blowing soap bubbles) and the "Hate Man," who stood on his street corner in a shabby skirt and yelled "I hate you" at every passerby. (He later shouted that he hated me in Harvard Square; when I asked what he was doing there, he replied that he spent the summer in Cambridge and the winter in Berkeley.) I discovered new kinds of food, espresso, and cappucino. Having grown up in the relative, bland safety of suburban Los Angeles, I found it exciting to be in a place where freshmen worried about whether they could walk the streets at night.

In retrospect, I sometimes wonder whether I would have been

admitted to one of the elite Ivy League schools that so many of my classmates at Harvard Law School attended. For financial reasons, I never seriously considered applying to the Ivy League, nor did I know anyone who had gone to Harvard, Yale, or Princeton. None of my high school teachers had pushed me in that direction, either. The only person who had completed a university education in my mother's or father's families was my father's sister, Aunt Marilyn, who studied physical education in the California State University system.

Berkeley represented an opportunity to leave the Los Angeles area, my family, and my problems behind. In the fall of 1976, Dad drove me up to Berkeley, moved me into a dorm room on the eighth floor of Ehrman Hall, and tearfully left his firstborn behind.

U.C. Berkeley was an eye-opener from the beginning. With more than 30,000 students, the university offered a diversity beyond anything I had imagined possible. I had always lived in suburbs where urban life was non-existent or neatly packaged, sanitized for mass consumption. Berkeley exposed me to an entirely new world.

Before college, I had never had to work especially hard to do well in school. At Berkeley, weekly papers in English 1A proved difficult because I was a poor writer. Despite much hard work, my freshman grades were little better than average. By my sophomore year, however, I had gotten the hang of things and, more importantly, I was truly enjoying my studies. Lights flashed on for me as I gained a better understanding of myself and the world. I learned that it was a good thing to be academically engaged, the warped values of my high school crowd notwithstanding. My classmates at Berkeley respected diligent study and valued intellectual curiosity.

Curious about how the economy worked, I majored in economics. Supply and demand curves, the link between inflation and unemployment, how macroeconomics influenced major events in U.S. history, such as the Great Depression, the New Deal, and the rise of labor unionism, intuitively made sense to me. History and political science courses supplemented my economics training. Fascinated by psychology, I immersed myself in my psych courses and for a while toyed with the idea of a double major in economics and psychology. But I also enjoyed math and science courses, especially human physiology and molecular biology. Trite as it may sound, I thrived intellectually at Berkeley. Though I held paying jobs throughout college, I devoting most of my waking hours to academic study and found it gratifying.

I evolved politically as well. Cary Zeitlin, a college friend, called me a Marxist of sorts, though I would never have classified myself that way. At the same time, I spouted some radical political rhetoric, some but not all learned from my professors. I talked politics with Cary, Steve Roscow, and Leo O'Farrell, all of whom I still see regularly.

U.C. Berkeley offered a racial diversity that I had never imagined existed. The Asian American community in southern California, at least where I grew up, was relatively small at the time. The large number of Asian American students at Berkeley surprised me. Because of the established Asian American community in the greater San Francisco Bay area, Asians constituted a significant portion of the student body. I had an Asian American roommate, Paul Fong, in the dorms. A transfer student from a junior college in San Francisco who dreamed of becoming a dentist, Paul introduced me to San Francisco's Chinatown. Like me, Paul had a spotty academic past, and he impressed on me just how hard we needed to work in order to succeed at Berkeley. I remember lamenting that I worked so much harder than classmates who did just as well (perhaps a mistaken perception). Paul's response was to the point: "An A is an A on the transcript."

I made a number of Asian American friends at Berkeley. Friendly, unassuming Mary Yoneda, from the San Jose area, lived next door to me freshman year. Jeff Oki and I studied in Moffitt Library as we sweated our way through the economics curriculum. The fifth floor of Moffitt was known among students as the place where Asian American students studied, and that is where I met Jeff. I was a serious student and I wanted to be around other serious students. It was quiet on the fifth floor, and every night, coffee thermos in hand, that is where I could be found.

Although I checked the box on my college application and standardized test, I cannot recall ever being contacted during my four years at U.C. Berkeley, or in the years after graduation, by any Latino student organization. Uncertain where I belonged, I never learned how to penetrate the Chicano student organization barrier and was uncertain how I would be treated if I tried. I never visited the Joaquín Murieta[3] house, home to a number of Chicano students, and cannot even tell you where it is. Less than confident in my racial identity, I was perplexed about how a half-Mexican American guy with an Anglo surname should present himself. I would almost inevitably be regarded with suspicion by strident Chicano activists. Was I a "check-the-box" Mexican hoping to gain from affirmative action? Or was I a bona fide Mexican American—whatever that might be?

Only later did I learn that my experience was not so unusual. After I joined the faculty at U.C. Davis, a number of my students with mixed Latino/Anglo backgrounds who had attended U.C. Berkeley told me that they had felt less than accepted there by fellow Chicano students. We shared a self-consciousness about our precarious identity and Latino credentials. Over the years, several students of mixed heritage became chairs of La Raza Law Students Association, the U.C. Davis law school's Latino student organization. For example, one student with an Anglo mother and Mexican American father led the organization. His Spanish surname ensured that few questions were asked about his identity. Another mixed Latino worked on an unsuccessful attempt to establish a La Raza Journal of Law and Policy at U.C. Davis, though she later withdrew from organized Latino activities because of political infighting.

Perhaps I was oversensitive, my self-consciousness unwarranted. But identity politics among Latinos on college campuses across the country often occasion heated debate. Consider Ruben Navarette's description, in his book *A Darker Shade of Crimson,* of the "game" he saw played by Mexican American undergraduates at Harvard:

> The rules of the game were simple. The contestants might be two Harvard Chicanos, similar yet different. The difference is noted. It might be a difference in skin color, Spanish-speaking ability, religion, even political affiliation. At first glance, it appears unlikely that both people can be authentic. The difference dictates that one must be a real Mexican, the other a fraud. The objective of the game becomes for the contestants to each assert his or her own legitimacy by attacking the ethnic credibility of their opponent. *More ethnic than thou.* The weapons are whispers. A pointed finger. A giggle. A condescending remark from one to another.[4]

I counted a number of Latinos as friends at Berkeley. I never asked my Ehrman Hall next-door neighbor, Anne Fernandez, about her heritage, though I assumed that she was Latina. I worked in the library with a former member of the Berkeley boxing team named Antonio and enjoyed speaking with him in Spanish, though mine had gotten rusty. During the first week of my sophomore year, I met a freshman Chicana named Jenny who came from Whittier, a Mexican American enclave east of downtown Los Angeles not far from where I had spent much of my childhood. Though excited about being at Berkeley, she found it difficult to adjust to a new, Anglo-dominated environment. Sensitive to anti-Mexican comments made by students in the dorms, Jenny soon became despondent. Increasingly unkempt, she would talk slowly and stare off into the distance as if in a trance. After a while, Jenny began spending time at the Joaquín Murieta house and dated a nice Chicano student. But she still did not feel that she fit into the Berkeley scene. I was told that she put a cigarette out on a Chicana student's head. The Anglo who told me this story had grown up in an affluent Bay Area suburb. He had dated a Mexican American student himself—a personable, attractive woman who also spent time at the Joaquín Murieta house. Though he went out with this woman for several years, he always hinted that she was less than ideal. My sense, though I could be dead wrong, was that her Mexican blood stood in the way of their relationship.

Though I shied away from organized Latino activities, my studies awakened me to issues of race and class in the United States. Classes with Harry Edwards, the prominent African American sociologist, Mario Barrera, a respected Chicano Studies professor, and David Montejano, now at the University of Texas,[5] opened my eyes to many things and built on the racial sensitivity that my father had taught me. A physically imposing man who lectured in a loud, booming voice to nearly a thousand students without benefit of a microphone, Edwards was interested in how organized sports exploit African Americans. Barrera, author of an influential book on the subject,[6] lectured on the racial and class stratification of Chicanos in the Southwest and the ways in which Mexican immigrants served as a source of cheap labor. Montejano's upper division sociology class motivated me to write a paper on the role of nationalism in the brutal race riots between black and white during World War II in Detroit and Beaumont, Texas, as well as the "zoot suit" riots in Los Angeles, where Chicanos wearing stylish "zoot suits" were attacked by white mobs.

These and other classes at U.C. Berkeley opened my eyes to the history of Latinos in the United States and ultimately contributed to the construction of my identity as a Mexican American. As many studies have shown, individuals can experience great flux in ethnic identification when they leave home.[7] Though critics may claim that I was brainwashed by radical professors, I prefer to think that my education provided me with a better understanding of my racial identity. My college courses spanned the intellectual and ideological spectrum, and included a series of market-oriented economics courses and an anthropology course taught by a controversial professor who argued that intelligence was linked to race. Of course I didn't believe everything I heard in the classrooms of U.C. Berkeley.

I worked at various jobs to help pay expenses during my college years. During the summers I worked as a parking lot attendant at Dockweiler Beach at the end of Imperial Highway, a main thoroughfare into what was then a predominantly black South Central Los Angeles. With the unenviable job of collecting two dollars from each parking car, I occasionally experienced hostility from the African American beachgoers. Some called me "whitey" and "honky." "But I ain't white!" I thought to myself, "I'm Mexican." Once I got into a fender-bender with a couple of African American men on a motorcycle in the Dockweiler parking lot. A Los Angeles police officer came to sort things out. Siding with me, the officer refused to make out a report. After he left, I paid the guys $20 to settle the dispute. Later, a Salvadoran co-worker said to me, "Isn't it good that the police sided with you because you were white?" What saddened me was that José, who knew of my background, may well have been right.

At Dockweiler Beach, I once saw some lifeguards treating some African Americans rudely as they were closing the parking lot for the night. It seemed clear to me that race had something to do with their rudeness, and I mentioned the incident to my father, a higher-up in the Department of Beaches, who saw that the lifeguards were questioned about it. They never spoke to me again.

Though it did not compare to Harvard in this respect, U.C. Berkeley had its own children of privilege, many of whom lived in the fraternities and sororities on the eastern edge of campus where the Berkeley Hills begin. An incoming freshman who lived down the hall from me drove home how alienating it could be to come from a "lesser" class. He was from a working-class section of San Francisco's Sunset District and liked to race souped-up cars on the Great Highway, along the Pacific Ocean, on weekends. Uncertain where he belonged at Berkeley and very conscious of his class background, he became depressed. One weekend, the head resident assistant knocked on my door to ask if I knew where my friend was. The RA opened the door to his room, two doors down from mine, to find the tile floor covered with a pool of blood. We later learned that he had spent the day methodically slashing his arms and then walked to the campus hospital and saved his life. Not long afterwards, he dropped out.

My own class anxieties were dwarfed in comparison. Though my father helped me out some financially, especially during my freshman year, I worked my way through college at a variety of odd jobs. I washed dishes in the dormitories, distributed flyers on Telegraph Avenue for a copying shop, washed the windows of a sprawling house in the Berkeley Hills for an elderly woman, and worked as a janitor and later as a doorman at the Berkeley City Club, a retirement home for the affluent in a beautiful building designed by the famous architect Julia Morgan.

I was supervised in my dishwashing job by a warm, gentle African American man named Odie. We exchanged jokes and stories, and I learned that he had lived a tough life. Every Monday I would tell him about the weekend parties in the dorms, making things sound infinitely more exciting than they actually were. "Johnson," Odie would say, "you gotta straighten up. You'll learn." At the

Berkeley City Club, an elderly co-worker once praised me as much more dependable than another worker he called the "Chinaman."

I worked throughout the summers as well, as parking lot attendant, busboy, and at similar menial jobs. In this way I was able to avoid borrowing money to fund my undergraduate education, in part because U.C. Berkeley's student fees were so low at the time—less than $215 a quarter when I started in the fall of 1976.

During vacations, I visited my father and his side of the family, which was pleasant enough. Visits with my mother and Robby, in contrast, tore me up. Money was always tight, and Christmases were usually depressing. In time my mother began her drift in and out of depression; sometimes she was sullen and morose, at other times manic with energy. I never knew what to expect. As I did later at law school, I wondered during my college years whether I should leave school and stay with her and Robby. But I did not want to end up in Azusa forever; I could not go back there. Perhaps there was nothing I could have done, but I still wake up nights thinking about those days and feeling guilty and remorseful.

Because my mother could not afford to have attended, I skipped my graduation from U.C. Berkeley. This was unfair to my father, and years later I felt guilty when he mentioned in passing that he would have liked to have attended the graduation ceremony. But my mother would have been devastated if she had missed my graduation while I and other family members attended. When I attend the graduation ceremonies of my students each May and see the joy in their parents' faces, I wish that I had found a way to bring my mother to my graduation at U.C. Berkeley.

My years at Berkeley were a revelation to me. I lived in the thick of a challenging and racially diverse group of people, even if I was

unsure where I fit into the racial mosaic. Little more than a sympathetic observer of the organized Chicano student organizations, I began to study the history of Mexican Americans in the United States, a study that continued well into my adult life. I became increasingly sensitive to the struggles of racial minorities—and a little more confident about who I was.

Mother and Grandmother (sometime during WWII)

Mom and Dad's
Wedding,
Los Angeles, CA 1957

Mom and Dad

Mom, Dad, and me on Easter Sunday

My brother Michael and me

My brother Michael and me, Torrance, CA.

My 5th Birthday Party, Torrance, CA,—Michael, my brother, is sitting. I am second from right.

Harvard Law School 1983, Spring (photographer: David Mackey)

Gannett House, Harvard Law School, home of the Harvard Law Review, my friend Mike Ermer and me at the right (photographer: David Mackey)

Harvard Law School 1983, Spring (photographer: David Mackey)

Robbie's Wedding 1988, Virginia, me, Mom, Grandma, Aunt Josie, Aunt Cathy

Christmas 1997,
Teresa—six years,
Tomás—five years,
Elena—2 years

Chapter 7

A Corporate Lawyer: Happily Avoiding the Issue

In the summer of 1995, I returned to Los Angeles to attend the funeral of the best man at my wedding. Killed by AIDS at the tender age of 37, Ed left behind a wife and two young children. Another high school friend picked me up at an airport and at my suggestion we stopped at La Villa, a Mexican restaurant along Pacific Coast Highway in Redondo Beach, where I treated him to lunch. Funeral services were held at a church down the street from West High School, where we had graduated in 1976. It was mid-afternoon, and children were walking home from school. My friend looked at them with disgust and said, "Look at that, not a white face among them." I must have looked as shocked as I felt. He began to talk in racial code about all the "gang members" who now frequent the Jack-in-the Box on Torrance Boulevard, where we hung out on Friday nights during high school. Thoroughly drained by Ed's death and dismayed by the diatribe, I sat numbly in silence.

After graduating from Harvard Law School, I returned to Los Angeles to serve as law clerk to the Honorable Stephen Reinhardt, a federal appeals judge and ardent liberal who had been active in the California and national Democratic parties before becoming a judge.[1] Deval Patrick, later the U.S. Assistant Attorney General in charge of civil rights (nominated to the post after President Clinton abandoned the nomination of his law school classmate Lani Guinier),[2] helped me land the job. Deval, whom I knew from Harvard, clerked for Judge Reinhardt the year before I did. Though Judge Reinhardt, whose work habits are legendary, kept me extremely busy during this year, I reacquainted myself with Los Angeles, family, and old friends after a seven-year absence.

Judge Reinhardt taught me much about hard work, careful craftsmanship, political acumen, and sympathy for the underdog. During my tenure with him, I met Carlos Manual Vazquez, a Cuban American who now teaches law at Georgetown and also clerked for Judge Reinhardt. Though Judge Reinhardt probably never thought of it in these terms, he had two Latino law clerks, one with a Spanish surname, one without.

For most of that year, I rode a bus from my father's apartment in Redondo Beach to downtown Los Angeles. I saw a lot of the city during the hour-and-a-half bus ride through South Central Los Angeles, past the Los Angeles Coliseum, and around the outskirts of downtown. This Los Angeles was a city that I had never really known.

I had stayed in contact with few friends from high school, though my wife Virginia later wondered why. We had grown up together and shared some common experiences that forever bound us together. But I returned to Los Angeles in 1983 a different person. Most of my old acquaintances had lived the workaday life for close to a decade, while I had spent those years in universities. My views on a wide range of subjects had developed considerably and I looked forward to a brand new, exciting life.

During my clerkship, I tried unsuccessfully to land a teaching job. In response to a letter soliciting candidates, especially minorities, Judge Reinhardt sent a letter of recommendation on my behalf to Hastings College of the Law in San Francisco. His letter, curiously, explained that he was not sure I was a minority but my mother was Mexican American, which must have confused the appointments committee at Hastings.

After I had finished my clerkship, I studied diligently for the California Bar exam in a small basement apartment in a large house in the Berkeley Hills. Once that formidable exam was out of the way, my friend Ed (the best man at my wedding who later died of AIDS) and I set off for a little holiday in Baja California, south of San Diego and across the Mexican border. It was a beautiful drive along the coast, with breathtaking views of the Pacific Ocean, and we ended up in Enseñada, a beach town with great, inexpensive seafood. Ed, who spoke virtually no Spanish, was much more apprehensive than I about the trip into Mexico. He decided to take a stroll before turning in for the night, and was followed by a local police officer back to the hotel room. Afraid of being arrested and jailed in a foreign country, Ed sat in the corner of the hotel room while I negotiated with the officer, who was reasonable though not completely on the up-and-up. Ed got a little education in what it is like to be a foreigner in a country where you cannot speak the language.

I received offers from a number of private law firms but was more tempted by an offer from the civil rights division of the U.S. Department of Justice. Civil rights work was what I really wanted to do, but the political climate in 1984 proved a formidable barrier to meaningful work of this type. Under President Ronald Reagan, the federal government's enforcement of civil rights laws had ground to an abrupt halt, and I did not want to serve as window dressing in a Republican-dominated Justice Department with no real interest in civil rights. More or less by default, I accepted a job at the San Francisco law firm of Heller Ehrman White & McAuliffe, where I had clerked one summer during law school.

A reputedly liberal law firm, Heller Ehrman was formed in 1890 as the first San Francisco firm to hire Jewish and Irish Catholic attorneys.[3] Many of the attorneys were active in Democratic politics, among them Charlie Clifford, a former president of the California State Bar who helped run the unsuccessful campaign of Yvonne Braithwaite Burke, an African American woman from Los Angeles, for California attorney general in 1978.

I spent five years at Heller Ehrman as a litigator. During this time, my mixed ancestry was not an issue; indeed, it was invisible. Free to deal with issues of race on my own terms, I generally chose to avoid them. I kept to myself and worked hard. Securities litigation and accountants' liability, areas in which I had no experience whatsoever as a law student, were intellectually challenging. I threw myself into my work, billing in the neighborhood of 3,000 hours per year (about 60 hours a week) on paying client and *pro bono* cases.

The *pro bono publico* work I did at Heller Ehrman (volunteer work in the public interest), was more satisfying and enjoyable to me than the billable cases I was assigned. I learned a great deal about poverty law from my legal work for the poor. Poor people, as I knew from my mother's experience, have many problems, most of them beyond the reach of lawyers to solve. One of the most important lessons I learned from doing *pro bono* work is that the best way to help the poor is to help them help themselves.[4]

I took my first deposition in a case involving the sale of a defective automobile. The client was a feisty, African American single mother trying to raise a family on one income, and was suing a used car dealer for selling her a lemon. When the car began spewing smoke soon after she bought it, the dealer refused either to take the car back or to repair it, in spite of the expensive service agreement she had purchased, which the dealer now claimed covered just about everything but the problem in question. Irritated by having his deposition taken in the case, the dealer gave me a tongue-lashing for wasting his time; but he eventually settled the suit with my client on satisfactory terms.

I represented another African American woman who paid exorbitant rent—it was much higher than my own—for an apartment in ill repair. When she refused to pay the rent until repairs were made, her landlord brought an eviction suit. We aggressively defended the action as only a big law firm could do. The landlord hired an immigration attorney who did not fully understand civil litigation. We sent a request for admission by the landlord that the apartment was "uninhabitable." We never received a response, which under California law meant that it was deemed admitted; as a result, we were able to secure a rent-free year for the lucky client.

My most memorable work, which greatly influenced my subsequent academic career, involved immigrants and refugees. In 1984, when I was still new at Heller Ehrman, Bob Borton, a partner committed to *pro bono* work, offered me a case in which Central Americans who had fled violent civil wars in El Salvador and Guatemala were in effect being coerced by the Immigration and Naturalization Service (INS) to leave the United States "voluntarily." The INS, within hours, would send refugees who had been arrested in the San Francisco Bay Area (where an organized bar provided free legal services to help them achieve political asylum), to faraway locations in El Centro, California and Florence, Arizona, where few or no attorneys were available to provide free legal services and friends and family were too far away to help. Many desperate applicants for asylum had no choice but to abandon their claims and grudgingly return to their native countries. As summarized in the conclusion of our brief,

> Assistance of counsel in the asylum process is essential to refugees from El Salvador and Guatemala who, if deported, may face the ultimate loss of life and liberty in the form of political persecution. By instituting and maintaining a policy under which indigent Salvadorans and Guatemalans are transferred from the San Francisco

> District, where counsel is guaranteed, to remote detention camps, where counsel is unavailable, the INS has demonstrated a cold indifference toward the plight, and the rights, of these frightened refugees.
>
> By constructing a high volume, fast moving system of transferring class members before they can even talk to a lawyer, combined with tactics that both intimidate and frighten, the INS has acted in a way that encourages genuine refugees to abandon their legal rights and makes it impossible for them to fairly present their asylum claims. Those actions, which are contrary to every notion of fairness in our Constitution, cannot be tolerated.[5]

This case engaged me deeply, and it also took me back to my childhood. El Centro, California, where one of the INS detention centers in question is located, is just a few miles from where my mother was born. Visiting El Centro for depositions of INS and immigration court employees, I drove through my mother's birthplace of Brawley. I had visited the Imperial Valley as a child, and it felt vaguely comforting and familiar to me.

The Imperial Valley is an isolated area, and we found it difficult to find either an appropriate place to take depositions or a court reporter to transcribe them. The depositions ultimately took place in a recreation room next to the pool at the Best Western Motel in El Centro. After many telephone calls, we were able to find a court reporter, a friendly woman who was enthusiastic about the work. After exchanging cards with her, I gave her the name of the case so that she could include it in the deposition transcript. When she saw that the INS was a defendant, she asked politely whether this was the case "about all the wetbacks."[6] This offensive term—based on the stereotypical Mexican swimming across the Rio Grande—had not been used in polite conversation for years, but the court reporter obviously had no idea that present company might be offended. I was sorely tempted to give her a lecture or even fire her on the spot. But I was wearing my litigator's hat, and I had learned that court reporters enjoy a good deal of discretion in what they transcribe, from whether each "uh" is included to how coherently the questions and answers are transcribed. As she was the only available court reporter in the vicinity and we had gone to some trouble to find her, I bit my lip and described the case to her as sympathetically as I could. "No, this case involves refugees fleeing political persecution in El Salvador and Guatemala," I explained.

The court reporter's comment, however, told me a lot about life in the borderlands. She used the term "wetbacks" descriptively, as though it carried no racist overtone. No doubt many Anglos in the region, and perhaps some Mexican Americans, characterized undocumented Mexicans as "wetbacks," and the court reporter clearly thought it appropriate to use the term with me—a big city lawyer in a suit who was certainly not a "Mexican wetback." We shared an unstated racial allegiance, as far as she could tell.

After a trial, the judge ruled against our poor Central American clients.[7] The experience demonstrated to me how much discretion a judge—whether conservative or liberal—has in a case. Our facts were good, and the law was even better. But we had a judge, the late John Vukasin, a Reagan appointee and an old crony of Attorney General Ed Meese, who clearly did not care about the plight of these refugees *or* the fine points of the law. In the trenches, the political views of judges matter, as I learned from other cases as well. During the appeal of another political asylum case, I described in oral argument how my client and his wife had been tortured with chemicals by the Guatemalan security forces. A well-known conservative jurist interrupted me, "Isn't this just another case of an illegal alien jumping into the trunk of a car for a better life?" Not surprisingly, I lost the appeal.

Over the next few years, I represented a number of persons fleeing political violence in Central America. I was drawn to these cases and felt an affinity for the clients.[8] To my mind, this work was particularly worthwhile and I built ties with the tight-knit group of immigrant and refugee rights advocates in the San Francisco Bay area. In 1987, I visited El Salvador as part of a delegation of attorneys studying the Salvadoran justice system and its response to human rights abuses. We met many people, including Francisco José Guerrero, President of the Supreme Court,[9] and Herbert Anaya, the head of a non-governmental human rights commission investigating human rights atrocities,[10] both of whom were later killed in the political violence that gripped the country. We met with a Jesuit priest, Jon Sobrino, whose six Jesuit colleagues were later executed by the Salvadoran military.[11] The law in El Salvador did little to deter or redress such flagrant human rights violations.

In El Salvador, the Catholic Church served as one of the few positive influences on society. The church provided land and food to the people of a poor, war-ravaged country. Issues such as abortion and birth control, for which the Catholic Church is frequently criticized in the United States, were largely irrelevant to the situation in El Salvador in the 1980s, where poverty and violence dominated people's lives. My view of the Catholic Church was softened by my exposure to liberation theology, a movement within the Catholic Church embraced by many priests in Central America and advocates that the church play an active role in the war against poverty and oppression.

My rusty high school Spanish proved useful in El Salvador and improved with use. I also had a general understanding of the culture, language, and history of the people, partly because of my friendship with a Salvadoran family in Southern California. I also dated a Salvadoran woman one summer in college, who liked me better when she thought I was a rich white boy than when she found out I was a mixed white/Mexican without much money.

I loved and learned from the *pro bono* work I was able to do at Heller Ehrman, but I never felt completely at home with the culture of the firm itself, nor with its racial politics. Heller Ehrman, despite its liberal reputation, had a long way to go in terms of diversity. While major corporations tended to embrace affirmative action (at least up to a point), law firms responded much more slowly. Like many elite law firms, Heller Ehrman focused its hiring efforts on graduates of the elite schools, Harvard, Yale, Stanford, and U.C. Berkeley (Boalt Hall). It emphasized traditional credentials such as membership in the Order of the Coif (designating the top 10 percent of the graduating class), law review membership, and judicial clerkships.

A small number of minorities worked as summer clerks at Heller Ehrman, but most turned down offers of permanent employment. The few who came generally left after a few years. Like many law firms, Heller Ehrman had a revolving door for minority associates; when one would leave, another would come in. Few remained to become partners. There were no Latino partners at Heller Ehrman when I was there. Sergio Garcia-Rodriguez, hired a few years after I was, became a friend and later a partner at the firm, though he later left to take a job with a subsidiary of the Chrysler corporation. Maria Ontiveros, now a law professor like myself, was there for a time. Arturo Gándara joined the firm near the end of my tenure there and left to join the U.C. Davis faculty when I did in 1989. The Latino summer clerks who filtered through Heller Ehrman were first rate. Ian Haney López and Rey Valencia both spent summers there before going on to teach law. But competition was fierce for the few Latinos who met the traditional hiring criteria, and it was difficult to land and keep Latino attorneys.

A well-meaning partner at Heller Ehrman described the firm's commitment to affirmative action when he said that an individual's minority status was a "plus factor," a tie-breaker of sorts if the applicant met traditional hiring criteria and all else was equal. Other firms treated affirmative action in the same manner. The end result was that many prestigious law firms competed for a small number of "qualified" minorities. Some partners cautioned against deviating from "merit," which traditional hiring criteria were supposed to measure. The firm hired a Mexican American attorney, for example, when it was opening its Los Angeles office. An enthusiastic, energetic, and genuinely nice man, he lacked the paper credentials so cherished by Heller Ehrman. The decision to hire him in spite of this perceived deficiency may have created a self-fulfilling prophesy; in any case, the attorney did not work out. Some attorneys at the firm used this poor guy as an example of the risks of hiring minorities who lacked the traditional credentials.

In many ways, a large law firm was a welcome relief from the racial politics that dominated my existence at Harvard Law School. Few people at Heller Ehrman knew of my Mexican American background, and with a presumably transparent racial identity, I was treated as white.

Racial issues did come up occasionally, however. A friend with whom I had shared my background thought it was funny to refer to me as "bean" and asked if my middle initial stood for "Raimundo" or "Reynaldo." One associate with a mixed background (her mother was a Mexican citizen, her father Jewish), once asked me why I was so interested in immigration issues. We had become friends through our work and she pressed until I told her what she apparently had sensed or heard—that I was half-Mexican and that my family history probably contributed to my interest in immigration.

My quasi-minority status led to some odd episodes. At a litigation department retreat, a well-meaning African American associate preparing to make a presentation on diversity in hiring asked me whether I wanted to be classified as a minority when he reported the number of minority of attorneys at the firm. He hoped not, because the lower the numbers, the stronger his argument that the firm should take aggressive affirmative action measures. Without giving it much thought, I acquiesced in his desire that I not "check the box."

Near the end of my stint at Heller Ehrman, minority associates organized a series of meetings aimed at increasing the number of minority attorneys at the firm. At the time, the major San Francisco law firms were considering affirmative action hiring goals for lesbians and gay men as well as for racial minorities.[12] I received a memorandum notifying me of a meeting of interested attorneys and shared it with a friend with whom I had never discussed my Mexican American heritage. Looking at the list, he saw that it included gay and lesbian as well as racial minority associates. He said with a gleam in his eye, "You'd better find out why you are on that list." Heller Ehrman, along with some other San Francisco firms, eventually embraced minority hiring goals.[13]

As affirmative action politics finally filtered into Heller Ehrman, I found myself in an environment reminiscent of Harvard Law School. I heard secondhand that the head of the litigation department and one of the leading partners of Heller Ehrman had announced at a "a state of the firm" speech that minorities were doing well at the firm, and he offered me as an example. When I was hired, however, few if any knew anything about my racial background. As has been my experience in other large institutions, Heller Ehrman had trouble classifying me in terms of race, and I enjoyed a great deal of choice in defining my identity. Few knew or cared about my background, and I felt no compulsion to "admit" that my mother was Mexican American. I could have passed as just another white graduate of Harvard Law School, and indeed, when I joined Heller Ehrman it was as but another *Harvard Law Review* editor.

The day arrived when I was told that I would be elected partner in six months. While this news was gratifying in a way, I was never really comfortable with law firm life. Material wealth is not a principal factor in my motivational scheme of things. Living in a small apartment with few amenities was fine with me, even though friends laughed at my sparsely furnished, one-bedroom apartment in Berkeley, where I paid about $300 a month in rent. In some ways Heller Ehrman reminded me of Harvard; partners tended to be the sons and daughters of professionals, the children of privilege. As at Harvard, I tended to spend most time with colleagues from similar class backgrounds, down-to-earth guys like Sergio Garcia, Carl Johnson, Robert Hawk, and Bruce MacMillan, whether or not they were Latino.

Life at a big San Francisco law firm could be exciting, and I learned a lot. I could write persuasive briefs, take depositions without being pushed around or intimidated by opposing counsel, and I even got some trial experience, though litigation sometimes brought out the meanness of the playground fights of my youth. In practice, I learned about immigration law and spent large amounts of time on *pro bono* endeavors. But the offer of a partnership helped me put things in perspective, and to see more clearly than ever that there was something missing from my work at a private law firm. The *pro bono* work I was able to do for Heller Ehrman was intellectually engaging and morally satisfying, but the financial dynamics of law firms were changing in the early 1980s, as pressure mounted for attorneys to reduce their *pro bono* commitments. Mine were often seen as an "overload" to my regular billable assignments and I felt squeezed by work demands. I wanted to do something different, something more. I wanted a family that, unlike the one I grew up in, would remain intact.

Chapter 8

A Latino Law Professor

My lack of enthusiasm about working at a big law firm and my interest in social justice, particularly in immigration issues, had led me to contemplate a teaching career, and I began actively looking for a job in the fall of 1988. The prospect of writing on subjects of my choice was appealing. I also worried about the demands of practicing law and about the toll they would take on my family life. The example of attorneys who had been at the firm for long was not encouraging. Many were divorced. Of those who weren't, most spent little time with their children. Six months away from partnership, I left Heller Ehrman to pursue another path.

I had been interested in teaching law at least as far back as my first judicial clerkship, and I decided that the time had come to pursue that long-deferred goal. I learned that the Association of American Law Schools provides a standardized form resume that makes it easier for law schools to review large volumes of faculty candidates. Along with assorted biographical and employment history, the form asks about racial background. For as far back as I can remember I have classified myself as Chicano, but before I checked that box, I wondered aloud to my wife Virginia what I should do. "Are you ashamed of being Mexican?" she asked. I checked the Chicano box but worried that law schools in search of a bona fide Latino might view me as an imposter.

One of my first interviews for a teaching position took place in the office of a senior professor. After the initial pleasantries, the question came—a question never squarely posed to me in private practice but apparently on the minds of many faculty appointment committees: "How did you get to be Mexican?"[1] That at least is how I translated the question. Though the nature of the inquiry was not unfamiliar to me, the interrogator ordinarily asked in a more diplomatic way. The professor's bluntness placed me on notice of the intensity of racial politics in academia.

My job search, admittedly, was half-hearted. Gainfully employed and content, if not enthusiastic, about my legal career, I was not worried about unemployment. Moreover, I had no idea just how scarce law teaching jobs are, and my experience of being wined and dined by law firms made me complacent. I soon learned, however, just how different legal academia was from private practice.

As Stephen Carter, the law professor at Yale acknowledged with respect to his hiring,[2] I was in some demand in the teaching market because of my background. My self-classification as Chicano on the Association of American Law Schools (AALS) standardized form no doubt enhanced my teaching prospects.[3] Latinos are few and far between in legal education, and at various times have been in demand. (This demand may have come and gone, however. While eighteen Latinos joined legal academia in 1991, only two came on board in 1997.) Indeed, some Latinos of mixed ancestry have been told that their job prospects would improve if they identified themselves as Mexican American. A mixed Latino friend of mine was told just that by the chair of an appointments committee at a Los Angeles law school. "That's what we're looking for," she said.

Though I had consistently classified myself as Mexican American in the past and did so again when applying for teaching posts, it soon became clear that a Kevin Johnson who checked the Chicano box on the AALS form would definitely be questioned on the subject. Self-conscious as ever, I worried about being accused of attempting to reap the undeserved benefits of affirmative action.

My racial identity undoubtedly played a role in my job search. When Judge Reinhardt recommended me for a faculty position at Hastings during my clerkship with him, he wrote that because my mother was Mexican American, I might qualify as a "minority"; Hastings never contacted me. When I began work at Heller Ehrman, I applied for a teaching position at Hastings and was invited to a polite lunch with the faculty appointments committee, but Hastings never followed up after that lunch. When I went through the AALS process and checked the Chicano box, Hastings enthusiastically invited me for a full set of interviews. It was evident to me that the Mexican Kevin Johnson was hotter property than the Anglo one.

The AALS sponsors an annual faculty recruitment conference, known as the "meat market," where law school representatives and prospective job candidates get together for a marathon weekend of interviews. I attended the conference in Washington D.C. in the fall of 1988.

Many law schools invited me for an interview. For some reason, southern law schools found me especially interesting. The "meat market" was aptly named: lots of sharply-dressed job applicants scrambling for the same jobs, law professors who lacked the polish of corporate attorneys grilling applicants in mass quantities. Unlike the traditional law firm interview process, in which one or two attorneys politely interviewed each applicant, anywhere from two to ten law professors would interview a candidate in a confrontational setting. Faculty members tended to ask substantive questions about a candidate's beliefs and challenged his or her ideas, often with a minimum of tact or diplomacy.

As a candidate, like many others I am sure, I found it impossible to answer questions without irritating someone in the room. It was all too easy to get caught in the crossfire of law professors arguing with each other over whether a new hire should be, say, a corporate specialist or not. Some schools, UCLA and Michigan for example, appeared uninterested in my candidacy but felt obligated to go through the motions of an interview anyway. More than ten years later, I am still waiting for my rejection letter from Michigan.

My first interview at the AALS conference, with a law school in Texas, set the tone. As I walked in, the faculty chair of the appointments committee politely asked if I wanted a cup of coffee. "Yes," I said and moved toward the coffee pot on the other side of the room to serve myself a cup. The chair quickly told a law student, a woman with a pleasant Southern drawl, to get me a cup of coffee, which made me uncomfortable to say the least. Later in the interview, one junior faculty member encouraged me to write on immigration law, only to be challenged by a senior curmudgeon who proclaimed "Well, that immigration stuff is interesting, but we need people to teach the bread-and-butter courses, like corporations. What do you say to that?"

After this inauspicious beginning, I immediately canceled almost all my other interviews and booked a flight to San Francisco that afternoon. This rash move certainly narrowed my options, but I had no idea how scarce academic jobs were or how badly I wanted one.

Despite my half-hearted commitment to the process, a number of schools invited me for an interview with the entire faculty. It was during an on-campus interview that the senior professor asked me "how I got to be Mexican." The brashness of the inquiry revealed to me some of the differences between law firm and academic life, where issues of race often are dealt with more openly than in the "real" world.

Curiosity and confusion about my racial identity was not limited to the hiring process. Not long after I had earned tenure at U.C.

Davis, a friend on the faculty appointments committee at another law school, a "top twenty" school according to one ranking, invited me to interview for a job there. I accepted the invitation and the day went extraordinarily well, at least from my end of the table. Indeed, I gave a paper in what may have been my best presentation ever. I received many compliments and felt positive about the experience. The next day began with a breakfast at which the dean of the law school told me bluntly that although the school did not have any "regular" faculty positions open, the central administration might give the law school an additional slot for a "minority hire."[4] This all was news to me. He continued, "Before we can offer you a job, we will have to check to see if you qualify as a minority." These few words quickly brought me back to earth. Maybe the previous day had not gone so well after all. At the time, this school was among the Hispanic National Bar Association's "Dirty Dozen" law schools, a select group with no Latino faculty members. I declined the offer. Later, after the same law school succeeded in hiring a Latina, it was removed from the Dirty Dozen list.

All in all, these incidents represent the exception, not the rule, in my academic life. Davis is a collegial environment with little of the rancor that prevails on many law school faculties. I began teaching at Davis 1989 and was granted tenure in 1992. Many Latinos, other minorities, and women are not nearly so fortunate. Although the number of tenured women and minorities in legal academia is on the rise, I hear almost daily of a woman or minority locked in a tenure battle.

Despite the relative peacefulness of academic life, I do experience moments of awkwardness and racial uncertainty. While Virginia and I were shopping for a house in Davis, we ran across a local newspaper, the *Davis Enterprise,* with a front-page article about the hiring of three new "professors of color," myself, Arturo Gándara, a Chicano from southern New Mexico, and Evelyn Lewis, an African American. There had been no minorities on the faculty the year before. My worry about teaching began in earnest. The students and faculty, I feared, might not really be getting the minority professor they wanted. I was glad that there were two "real" minorities joining the faculty with me. After I began at Davis, one well-intentioned colleague, musing about the costs of college, suggested that I was fortunate that my three children would be eligible for minority scholarships. A somewhat naive secretary of South American ancestry joked that I was being classified as a "professor of color" by law students who were protesting the lack of minority law professors. These incidents, however, are the exceptions to the rule.

I heard through the grapevine that a Latino law professor at a top-ten law school had suggested to a friend of mine that I should take my mother's maiden name. Another friend told me that if I had a Spanish surname, my work would have a better chance of acceptance in the elite law reviews and I would be pursued by the "top ten" schools. I confess that I had considered a name change on my own—I had briefly but not too seriously toyed with the idea of adding my wife's surname (Salazar) to mine. I might avoid the question, "How did you get to be Mexican?" that way. But after spending more than thirty years as Kevin Johnson, I did not want to appear opportunistic.

The relevance of something so simple as a name to one's racial identity reveals just how much race is a social construction. To some people, I look white enough. But change my name to Kevin Johnson Gallardo or Kevin Johnson Salazar and my social identity would be instantly transformed. I once met a young Latino professor who had a Spanish surname and dark complexion. After I explained my background to him, he matter-of-factly mentioned that his mother was white and his father was Mexican American, a possibility that had not crossed my mind. Mixed-race people with Spanish surnames have much less explaining to do about their backgrounds.

Names do affect how one is treated. In one of my first years at Davis, I agreed to moderate a panel discussion at a student-organized conference on violence along the U.S.-Mexico border. Later, to my chagrin, I received a copy of a letter to U.C. Davis Chancellor Ted Hullar from former Commissioner of the INS Alan Nelson (who later successfully sponsored Proposition 187), complaining that the program was one-sided and that a Mexican flag had been displayed in the classroom where the conference had taken place. Oddly, Nelson had sent copies of his letter to me and Jim Smith, another conference participant and faculty colleague, but not to our colleague Arturo Gándara, who also moderated a discussion at the conference. Perhaps Nelson assumed that someone named Gándara would lack an open mind on the subject.

Class issues come up in relations with my colleagues as well. Once I was at a colleague's home with two other couples for dinner. A doctor started railing about welfare mothers who have babies in order to get more benefits. It soon became clear that he was really attacking African American welfare mothers. The host skillfully and vociferously debated him, but the doctor would not relent, offering story after story that he claimed demonstrated abuse of the system by "those welfare mothers." Hoping to end the argument and move on, I finally mentioned that I had been raised on welfare, that not all single mothers abuse welfare, and that even assuming some abuse, punitive measures will most adversely affect children, not the parent who arguably abused the system. The doctor continued his rantings. "I understand that some people get out of poverty," he said, and went on to intimate that those who don't have only themselves to blame. It was a long evening.

Affirmative Action in Academia

Once I received tenure, heavy committee assignments, the bane of the lives of many law professors, were not long in coming. I served two years on the student admissions committee, four years on faculty appointments, and one year on a dean search committee before becoming Associate Dean for Academic Affairs in July 1998. The time spent on these administrative matters takes its toll on research and scholarship.[5] More importantly, these assignments forced me to deal concretely with the issue of affirmative action.

More or less unquestioned during its heyday in the 1970s and 1980s, affirmative action came under direct attack in the 1990s. The Supreme Court's famous decision in *Regents of the University of California v. Bakke*,[6] which challenged the admissions practices of the U.C. Davis medical school, ruled that racial *quotas* were unconstitutional but left the door open to consideration of race in admissions decisions for the purpose of promoting diversity. *Bakke*'s vitality came into question over the years. The highly publicized court decision in the Cheryl Hopwood case (which found that the University of Texas law school had acted unconstitutionally in denying admission to Hopwood, a white applicant)[7] the Regents of the University of California's decision to bar the consideration of race in student admissions,[8] and the California "Civil Rights" Initiative[9] (limiting the voluntary use of affirmative action by the state of California), all represented a retreat from the affirmative action measures permitted by *Bakke*. The maze of legal prohibitions made it extremely difficult to take steps to maintain a diverse student body.

When I began my teaching career, the U.C. Davis School of Law, as directed by University of California policy, embraced affirmative action, but its policy was not clearly defined. Some members of the admissions committee considered race a factor in evaluating applications, but were often less than explicit about this. People with disadvantaged backgrounds and minorities who had overcome other disadvantages were generally favored. Given the *ad hoc* nature of the system, actual admissions outcomes rested on the shoulders of the individuals on the committee.

As a member of the admissions committee, I not infrequently had disagreements with my colleagues about particular applications. One memorable stalemate—over the application of the daughter of Mexican immigrants who worked in the fields of the Central Valley of California—lasted for weeks. There were some success stories, however: a Chinese American woman who grew up in difficult economic circumstances but achieved her dream of fighting for immigrants; a salt-of-the earth daughter of a steel worker from the Rust Belt who had taught school in South Central Los Angeles; a working-class Chicano admitted off the wait list who made the most of his law school years working in the immigration clinic.

Though generally supportive of affirmative action, I have concerns about its implementation, as do others who want to increase the number of minorities in various institutions in U.S. society.[10] A major obstacle to a diverse student body is the Law School Aptitude Test (LSAT), to which law schools pay careful attention in making admissions decisions. The much-publicized annual ranking of law schools by *U.S. News and World Report* relies on the median LSAT score as an important indicator of student selectivity. Despite lively debate over how well the LSAT serves as a predictor of minorities' law school performance,[11] it weighs heavily in admissions decisions at many law schools, including U.C. Davis, and has devastating effects on minority enrollment, especially for African Americans and Latinos. Add to this the passage of new legal prohibitions on the use of race as a factor in admissions, and the job of ensuring a diverse student body becomes extremely difficult.

In the 1997–98 academic year, Boalt Hall, Berkeley had a single African American in its entering class. Partly as a result of this, the U.S. Department of Education initiated an investigation into possible discrimination by all of the U.C. law schools.

A recurring though generally unexamined question is how to treat applicants of mixed backgrounds for affirmative action purposes. Individual determinations have to be made about these students, which requires a careful review of their files. It also requires examination of the purposes of affirmative action, including providing reparations for minorities previously injured by governmental and private discrimination and ensuring a diverse student body in order to foster a rich learning environment for all students. The consideration of such complexities, however, takes significant time and resources, which many schools, for a variety of reasons, do not devote to the admissions process.

Faculty appointments also involve difficult affirmative action issues. Under the system in place at many law schools, including U.C. Davis, the faculty votes on candidates after a long and complicated search process. All too often, the pool is narrowed by a focus on traditional credentials such as the "eliteness" of the law school attended, whether or not the applicant served on the law review and had a clerkship with a prestigious judge—all areas in which racial minorities are seriously underrepresented. Though there is much discussion of the qualities of the candidates, affirmative action is rarely raised, at least not explicitly. Despite the minimal discussion of race and gender at faculty meetings, such issues almost certainly affect the votes cast by individual faculty members.

Law faculties also participate in the selection of deans, a task with which the U.C. Davis law faculty found itself preoccupied during my first year of teaching. During the selection process, I was able to get to know former state Supreme Court Justice Cruz

Reynoso, one of the most decent persons I have ever met. A hero to California's Mexican American community, Reynoso labored in the trenches as an attorney with California Rural Legal Assistance, a group that serves rural farmworkers. I had met Reynoso when he was a California Supreme Court Justice through a law school friend who had clerked for him. A couple of years later, long after I thought he would have forgotten me, I was walking back to Heller Ehrman with a group of summer clerks after a lunch for the Legal Aid Society of San Francisco. As our group approached the old Supreme Court building in downtown San Francisco, our paths crossed and we started talking. As was customary for Cruz, as he is known by most people, he talked as if we were old friends continuing yesterday's chat. After he veered off toward the Supreme Court building, the summer clerks asked who he was. "Justice Cruz Reynoso," I replied to their astonishment. Of course, the story says more about Cruz Reynoso's graciousness than about me.

A storm of controversy surrounded Reynoso's candidacy for the deanship at U.C. Davis, and Chancellor Hullar ultimately vetoed his candidacy. Though the law school faculty was given no official reason for this, there were rumors that the agricultural business interests did not want Reynoso, a long-time thorn in their side in his fight for the rights of farmworkers, to lead the only University of California law school in California's agricultural heartland. Reynoso's appointment would unquestionably have focused media attention on the law school and might have drawn political heat from Pete Wilson, the Republican governor of the state.

Latina/o Law Professors

In pursuing a teaching job, I was soon introduced to Michael Olivas at the University of Houston, who devotes countless hours to organizing the loose band of Latino law professors in this country.

As of the fall of 1998, fewer than 130 Latinos (out of about 5,700 professors) taught in U.S. law schools. In addition to staying in touch with many of us individually, Olivas sends newsletters with recent information and the current roster of Latino law professors. He also organizes a dinner for Latino law professors at the Association of American Law Schools' annual meeting, and many of us look forward to this opportunity to let our guards down with friends and acquaintances. In contrast to the elite cliqueishness and one-upmanship of the conference generally, this dinner is generally a warm, friendly occasion.

Like Latinos in the larger society, those in legal academia reflect great diversity. Professors of Puerto Rican, Cuban, and Mexican ancestry predominate, though there are a great many other varieties. Ideologically, Latino law professors are far from homogeneous and in fact cover the political spectrum.

In recent years, a group of Latino law professors organized by law professor Frank Valdes has created a genre of legal scholarship known as critical Latino, or LatCrit, theory. Critical Race Theory, born in the 1980s of discontent with the white-dominated Critical Legal Studies movement, focused attention on race as a central organizing principle in U.S. society. Concerned that Critical Race Theory was not focusing on issues of importance to the Latino community, such as immigration, bilingual education, international human rights, and Latino identity and diversity, LatCrit scholars began analyzing issues from a uniquely Latino perspective. Though some Latino scholars, like myself, had focused in their scholarship on issues of special importance to Latinos,[12] LatCrit theory was the first organized attempt to concentrate specifically on Latino issues. Conferences held in La Jolla, California in 1996, San Antonio, Texas in 1997, and Miami, Florida in 1998[13] produced published symposia and reflected the dynamism of this movement.[14]

The "Stealth Reviewer"

Since I became a tenured professor at U.C. Davis, I have been regularly asked by other schools to review the scholarship of candidates for tenure or other promotion. So far, all but one of the reviews I have been asked to perform have been of minority candidates. A coincidence? Probably not. Though happy to perform the task, I initially wondered why so many faculties called on me, a relatively junior professor. A Latina explained, "You're a great reviewer because the other members of the faculty see a generic 'American' name on the letter, assume you're white, and do not discount your opinion." The all too common view is that a minority cannot review another minority's work without bias. I thus serve as the "stealth reviewer," an invisible Latino who can fool the uniformed and avoid the Latino discount.

This is not paranoia. One tenured Mexican American I know had twelve outside reviewers (as opposed to the usual two to four) evaluate his candidacy for tenure, conceivably so as to dilute the input of two minority reviewers. (The chair of that committee repeatedly asked if I was black!) Once I wrote a favorable review for a Latina who was nevertheless persuaded to withdraw her tenure candidacy in the face of strong opposition. The chair of the committee apparently had it in for her from the outset, believing that she was a hiring mistake. Even after he torpedoed her tenure candidacy, he wondered why my evaluation of her article had been supportive, though mine was not the only favorable letter. He asked another Latino on his faculty if Kevin Johnson was a Latino, which I found perplexing. "Come on," said the person who had told me the story, "you know why. He wanted to discount your letter as a Latino reviewing the work of another Latino."

The racial dynamics of the review process cannot be ignored. Favorable reviews of Latino scholars by other Latinos—and this is true of minority reviews generally—may be discounted by some faculty members as biased. A negative review of a Latino's work by another Latino, however, will be given great weight, in what I call the "amplification effect." If a person's work gets a poor review "even" from another Latino, it must *really* be bad. Of course, no one seems to worry about bias when a white reviewer evaluates a white candidate's scholarship.

Students

The students at U.C. Davis are bright, energetic, and generally friendly. I have enjoyed watching their transformation from nervous first-year law students to competent lawyers. U.C. Davis enjoys a high bar passage rate—usually hovering around 90 percent for first time takers of the California bar exam—so almost all of our graduates who want to can go on to practice law.

Over the years, I have spent a great deal of time each week counseling law students, particularly minority law students. Many work very hard but (like most law students everywhere) do not do as well as they had hoped. Many of them suffer from a never-ending feeling of inadequacy and uncertainty about their belonging, feelings with which I can empathize. Minority students tend to feel added pressure because some believe that they are less qualified than their non-minority classmates. White male students have directly questioned the qualifications of two of my tutors (the Davis equivalent of teaching assistants), both minority women. One of them told his tutor that she got her position because of affirmative action.

I have been struck by the diversity of Latino law students at U.C. Davis. There are many students of mixed backgrounds, including some like me with Anglo surnames. Some Chicanos' families have been in the United States for generations; others are immigrants.

One remarkable student, Miguel Valdavinos, entered the country unlawfully from Mexico as a child and grew up in urban South Central Los Angeles; he became a first-rate student, head of our Moot Court board and a successful advocate in our trial practice competition—a real U.C. Davis success story. There are other Chicano students from well-off backgrounds with all of the advantages of growing up in the upper middle class. There are light-skinned Latinos and more indigenous appearing Latinos, Central Americans, Mexican Americans, and mixed Latinos, such as the mixed Latina of German and Peruvian parentage. This diversity has sometimes caused rancor in the La Raza Law Students Association. Along with differences in background, physical appearance, and national origin, ideological differences inevitably emerge as well.

Each year, the La Raza Law Students Association organizes a banquet honoring the distinguished U.C. Davis graduate Lorenzo Patiño, a revered judge who died in his prime. A student selected by the membership receives the Patiño award, and all La Raza graduating students are honored. Every year, the number of "Latino" students surprises me. I would never have guessed that some of them—with their Anglo surnames, physical appearance, and lack of community involvement—were Latinos.

Every so often students play the "race card" with me. A student in immigration law once came to my office in the middle of the semester to ask about the final examination, a common occurrence dreaded by professors. The student's deeper concerns about the class, however, soon became apparent. He expressed frustration that in his view I was not building on the material and had failed to link the various subjects by a common thread. In addition, he said, the class was too "pro-immigrant." I listening intently, growing increasingly uneasy. He said that my class would be better if I taught more like two white male colleagues.[15] Then he told me that he was half-Mexican too! His Anglo surname and "white" physical appearance suggested to me that he was the product of a college fraternity, not anything like me.

Would I have had a similar discussion with one of my own law school professors? Absolutely not. At Harvard, the typical response to such a complaint would probably have been, "Who do you think you are? Get out of here!" I was left wondering whether, if I were older, grayer, and "whiter," I would have had such an encounter.

Another student, a self-proclaimed liberal, attempted to satisfy the law school's writing requirement under my direction. I asked him to re-draft several versions of his paper, which needed plenty of work. When he complained that my standards were too high, I concurred that my standards were indeed high and pointed out that I had warned him of this at the outset. Not satisfied, he took his complaint to the dean. I wondered whether this student would have acted the same way if I had been a distinguished white male professor.

Another white student from a wealthy family attempted to curry favor by telling me out of the blue that she "thought in Spanish." Although I can speak some Spanish, I have never "thought" in Spanish and I told her as much. Along with a group of other students, she later complained to the dean that my civil procedure assignments were excessive, though they were identical to those I had given in previous years.

Contrast these incidents with four unhappy minority women who came to my office to complain about my final exam in immigration law. They claimed that the exam was too difficult and an unfair test of their mastery of the subject. All had done well in the course, and one of them earned the highest grade in the class. All went on to do great things in law. Though I was confronted in a way that my colleagues probably would not have been, the complaint of these students was not that I should be more like my white colleagues, but that my exam did not reflect the things that I valued. And they approached me directly, rather than trying to make trouble for me by going to the dean.

I am grateful to minority law students for lobbying on my behalf for the law school's Distinguished Teaching Award, which I received in 1993. Latino students generally learn of my Mexican American background through word of mouth. Each year new students trying to pigeon-hole me in terms of my racial background. At a gathering of civil procedure students, a Korean American student once asked me point blank, "What ethnicity are you?" Taken aback, I slowly explained my mixed ancestry.[16] Over the years, a number of Asian American students have wondered aloud about my background. One student told me that her civil procedure class made bets about it. Such speculation is not limited to students. While serving on a California State Bar committee on legal services to the poor, I met a Mexican American lawyer from East Los Angeles and mentioned that my mother had lived there years before. He replied that many Japanese Americans lived in his neighborhood and asked if my mother was Japanese. "No," I said, and he quickly changed the subject.

In academia, I generally have not suffered the disadvantages, including but not limited to racial slurs and slights, which many minority law professors have. Many fine men and women of color in the legal academy regularly experience a great many more indignities than I ever will. For example, a few years ago, dead fishes were left in the law school's faculty mailboxes of a Mexican American professor, an African American professor, one who devoted his life to death penalty cases, and another who defended the rights of immigrants.[17] I was spared. The culprits, presumably disgruntled students, were never caught.

My experiences at U.C. Davis illustrate the complexities of race and class in modern-day America, both inside and outside academia. Racial politics within the academy, while in some ways more "civilized" than outside, can be treacherous. Issues of affirmative action and racial identity lurk around every corner. Students with mixed backgrounds attend my law school, but not all mixed students are created equal. Some are committed to working with the Latino community, others are not. Some might "pass" as Anglo, others cannot. Some come from families that recently immigrated to the United States, others have been here for generations. Some have Spanish surnames, others are named Holman, Eichler—or Johnson.

Chapter 9

My Family/Mi Familia

On a balmy day in May of 1992, an all-white jury in Simi Valley had just acquitted the white officers of the Los Angeles Police Department in the savage beating of African American Rodney King, a beating that had been captured on videotape and broadcast repeatedly on television for the nation to see. Outrage and violence followed the verdict, and by evening, South Central Los Angeles was in flames. Watching the live television coverage, I worried that my wife and I had brought our one-year-old daughter Teresa into a violent, racially divided world. I wondered how I would explain the violence to Teresa some day. Sadly, each generation in the United States has had to explain racial outbursts like this. My father told me of the Watts uprising in 1965. I worried about what catastrophic event Teresa would have to explain to her children.

In October 1987, I married Virginia Salazar, a Mexican American woman from La Puente in the San Gabriel Valley, not all that far from where I lived as a youngster in Azusa. Decisions of the heart cannot be rationalized, but I felt an almost immediate affinity for Virginia. We both grew up knowing good times and bad. We were both raised in assimilationist households, and Virginia's parents did not teach her to speak Spanish for the same reason my mother did not teach me. We both felt comfortable with Mexican American culture, and we were both among the few in our families who had attended college. Perhaps at some unconscious level Virginia reminded me of the Mexican American girls I had crushes on in elementary and junior high school in Azusa.

Virginia and I are both private people, perhaps a remnant of the more traditional Mexican culture described by Octavio Paz and Richard Rodriguez.[1] She introduces herself as Virginia to new acquaintances, but her family calls her Ginger, a nickname given her by her older sister, Michelle, who could not pronounce "Virginia" as a toddler. "Ginger," she thinks, creates too many negative images—the immediate association for our generation is the caricature of a buxom movie star on the popular 1960s sitcom "Gilligan's Island"—to be part of anyone's first impression.

Virginia earned her undergraduate degree from Loyola Marymount, a small Catholic university in southern California near Los Angeles International Airport. Working her way through college as a waitress and at several other jobs, Virginia also took out student loans to pay private school tuition. She was working two jobs to repay these loans when we met in June 1986, teaching science and math at St. Bernard's High School, a Catholic school in Playa del Rey, and waiting tables on weekends. She lived with two close friends from college, a Japanese American from Hawaii and an African American from Los Angeles. Even with her down-to-earth nature, I worried about introducing Virginia to my mother and was careful to explain that, despite the Harvard education, I came from a humble background.

Virginia has five sisters, all quite different from each other. One thing they have in common, however, is their view of *cholos* and *cholas*—Mexican youth gang members—as deviant and disrespectful of family.[2] Being Mexican American in La Puente was the norm, not something that made anyone feel "different." Her sisters do not dwell on their Mexican ancestry, though they are aware of their heritage. For example, Velia, who married a Texan with a drawl, flew back to Lubbock, Texas to attend his mother's funeral. At the funeral, Velia overheard some mourners whispering, "Who's the Mexican?" She was the only one there.

The most bookish person in her family, Virginia is also the most socially conscious. Her racial sensibilities coincide with my own, though she is far more comfortable with who she is than I am with my own racial identity. Being a Mexican American woman, she is not oblivious to racism. She once called me at work to object to a *New York Times* article about the Unabomber's longstanding correspondence with Juan Sanchez Arreola, a farm worker from Mexico. Virginia was outraged that after referring to Sanchez by name, the article went on to say,

> "We only knew each other by letters," *the Mexican* said. . . . In a gradual role reversal, *the Mexican* began the correspondence as a supplicant but ended it years later as an advisor.[3]

Why use the term "Mexican" when "Sanchez" would have done just as well? If the Unabomber's pen-pal had been from England, would he have been referred to in this way as "the Englishman"? Maybe, but I doubt it. The characterization stripped Sanchez of his individuality and relegated him to the "Mexican" category. In this way the *Times* article added another element of evil to the mad Unabomber: he associated with a "Mexican!"

We know some people from Sonoma County, in northern California's famed wine country. Whenever we see them, they inevitably raise the subject of the great "Bracero program" of the 1950s,[4] which allowed Mexican laborers to come to this country on a temporary basis. "We need a new Bracero program. It was good for everyone," is the standard refrain. Virginia and I always wonder—do they always bring this up because of our ancestry? Or because of my interest in immigration law? The Bracero program had been largely dismantled by the time we were in kindergarten. Though one might wonder whether this is racial paranoia, our feelings are real.

Virginia and I live in a predominantly white college town. Because our children Teresa and Tomás are so fair, she sometimes feels that parents at parks think that she is a nanny; she has in fact been overtly mistaken for one. This is not an uncommon problem. One of Virginia's cousins in Phoenix, Arizona, who has a dark complexion and fair children, has also been mistaken for her children's nanny. This offensive presumption speaks volumes about white society's view of Mexican American women and reinforces stereotypes of them as outsiders fit only to care for the children of whites.[5]

Virginia's tight-knit family reflects the diversity of the Mexican American community. Her father, Joe Salazar, is from Arizona. Most of his family have darker complexions. Her mother Mary Helen is fair and comes from a large family in downtown Los Angeles, where for years her parents ran a small store on the outskirts of South Central Los Angeles. Virginia went to college and majored in biology; Michelle was graduated from Long Beach State with a degree in home economics; Christy, Velia, and Jolene did not go to college, though all are hard-working folks devoted to their jobs. The sisters run the gamut of physical appearances.

Virginia's extended family is close. Not long after I met her, we went to the wedding of her Uncle Willie's daughter. I ran into Uncle Willie, who I later learned makes a great *menudo,* at the wedding reception, which was held in a bowling alley in Azusa, and I congratulated him on his daughter's marriage. Willie, a butcher, is built like one—strong and stocky. He warned me jokingly but seriously that I should treat Virginia well. "Mexican families are like the Mafia, you know what I mean," he cautioned, apparently assuming I was white. I got the message. After a shot of tequila, we parted friends.

Virginia's father, an affable fellow and hard-working sheet metal worker, is always ready and willing to help friends and family. A long-time resident of southern California, Joe is well aware of the anti-Mexican motive behind the call for immigration reform. He believes, in fact, that public concern with immigration focuses exclusively on Mexicans,[6] and he complained about the 1996 police beating of an undocumented man and woman after a high speed chase in Riverside, which was captured on videotape but, unlike the Rodney King incident, was basically ignored by the media.[7] At the same time, as a Mexican American from Arizona whose family came to the United States generations ago, Joe understands that he is different from recent Mexican immigrants. After Virginia and I moved to Sacramento and bought a house, I began working in the yard. When I complained about the time-consuming nature of yardwork, Virginia reminded me that her father keeps a beautiful, immaculate yard. The next time we visited, I asked Joe how he did it. He replied, "I just pay the Mexicans to do it."

Virginia's grandfather, Joe Salazar Senior, was a character. Fending for himself from early in life, he was truly a self-made man. Joe worshipped his family and worked many different jobs to support them, driving trucks, paving roads, and selling plastic buckets. He also understood racism against Mexicans much better than I ever could, having experienced it firsthand throughout his life in Arizona. We once discussed the death penalty, which he supported and I opposed. "But if we have the death penalty, they will be killing the Mexicans," I cautioned. Joe Sr. thought a minute and conceded that I had a good point. Quite a storyteller, he had many tales of discrimination against Mexican Americans. He loved to talk about his days in the artillery during World War II, and often said, "We would have won the war sooner if they would have let Mexicans do more."

After Joe Sr. died in 1996, Virginia's grandmother Velia ran across a copy of a letter to the editor he had written that was published by the *Arizona Republic* and signed "Private Joe Salazar." During World War II, the paper had run a story accompanied by pictures of children, including Joe Jr., with a caption stating that the children were from foreign countries. Joe Sr.'s nationality was given as "Mexican." Angered by this presumptuous error of fact, especially when he was fighting for his country in the Philippines, Joe's letter emphasized that he was born in Arizona, as were his parents and grandparents, and that they were all U.S. citizens.

The birth name of my mother-in-law, Mary Helen, is Maria Elena (just like my younger daughter's). As with most of her brothers and sisters, a nun in parochial school Anglicized her name. Arturo became Arthur, Roberto became Bobby, Teresa was pronounced the English way. Maria Louisa was transformed into Mary Louise, and Luis was known as Louie. Still, Mary Helen recognizes her racial identity. A few years ago, my mother, Mary Helen, and Joe were on their way to visit us in Sacramento for Thanksgiving, heading north on Interstate Highway 5, which cuts through the heart of rural California with its Anglo-Mexican tensions. A monotonous, less than scenic route, I-5's saving grace is that it is the fastest way to travel the length of the state. My in-laws and mother stopped to eat at a restaurant along the highway, where they sat and sat at the table but were never served. Feeling snubbed and certain that they had been discriminated against, they eventually left without eating.

My wife's family embraced me and my Mexican background wholeheartedly. I heard secondhand that it was a topic of conversation among them and that some relatives were even pleased when they learned of it. In some ways, I could fit into a picture of Mexican Americans as well as into a picture of Anglos. I have occasionally been told—usually by Mexican Americans trying to be inclusive—that I "look" Mexican.

Because both Virginia and I have dark brown hair and brown eyes, we expected our babies to have the same. We were surprised when our daughter Teresa was born with blue eyes and light-colored fuzz on her head, but we adjusted to the unexpected. Though my father had blond hair and blue eyes, we had no idea that Virginia also carried a recessive gene for blue eyes. Her mother's sister, *Tia* (Aunt) Teresa, was the only one of ten children with blue eyes. Friends, acquaintances, and even strangers quipped endlessly that Virginia must have been "sleeping with the mailman," jokes that were old before Teresa even got home from the hospital. My standard response was to inform people that our mail carrier was a woman. Over the years, Teresa's appearance has continued to be a topic of conversation. When we told our Japanese American doctor that our firstborn had blond hair and blue eyes, he remarked that this was "good," implicitly suggesting that the alternatives were "not so good" or even "bad."

We were even more startled when our next child, Tomás, had the same light fuzz and blue eyes and even fairer skin. Our third child, Maria Elena, whom we call Elena, has the brown eyes and hair that we originally expected from all of our children. A family friend once remarked that Elena was the only one of our children who "looks like a Chicano." Another friend admired Elena's "tan." The differences in their physical appearance do not escape Teresa and Tomás. Both have taken classes in Ballet Folklorico, Mexican folkdancing, at a housing project in nearby Woodland. At age five Teresa remarked that Elena would be a good Ballet Folklorico dancer. "Why to you say that?" her mother asked. "Because Elena looks like all the other dancers," Teresa responded.

In analyzing the social construction of whiteness, Ruth Frankenberg found it "startling" to learn that a parent of a light-skinned Anglo/Mexican child cut off from the Mexican American community feared that the child might develop anti-Mexican sentiment.[8] But I have precisely those fears, and they are supported by my family history. Color often serves as a proxy for race in U.S. society. Adults classify people by skin color. Recall President George Bush's reference to his grandchildren as "little brown ones." I worry that my children will make distinctions based on skin color and that society will do the same with respect to them. As my mother's and grandmother's mythical Spanish heritage suggests, it is not unheard of, even today, for Latinos to deny their heritage.

Virginia and I took great care in choosing names for our children. We gave each child their mother's surname, Salazar, as a middle name. We also tried to pick names that were neither too "ethnic" nor too "white-bread." This was fairly easy for Teresa and Elena, but we had a more difficult time agreeing on a boy's name. She rejected my suggestions, which included names like Emilio and Esteban. Our ultimate choice, Tomás, which we thought fit into the not-too-ethnic category, sparked discussion among the extended family. Some, particularly from my side of the family, asked and others undoubtedly wondered why we had chosen "Tomás." They evidently found it "too Spanish." Why not a good American name like "Thomas"? they might have thought. I learned that my mother, who saw our choice of the name as "anti-assimilationist" on some level, and others in my family questioned our decision.

Some people openly wonder about the name Tomás Johnson in ways to which I have become increasingly sensitive. Once a doctor called a pharmacy to order some medicine for Tomás's ear infection. I overheard him repeat the name. "Yeah, Tomás Johnson. I don't know why they picked that one." Intimidated by the simple Spanish, some people will often call my son Thomas. I started to worry early on that our son would accumulate baggage simply because of his name. I once asked him whether he wanted to be called Tomás, Thomas, or Tommy. "Just plain old Tomás," he said simply. "I'm just plain old Tomás."

We came to an important crossroads after the birth of Teresa and Tomás. We lived at the time in an old, comfortable bungalow in a racially and socioeconomically mixed neighborhood in downtown Sacramento. We decided to move to more homogeneous, suburban Davis, which we thought would be better and safer for our children. The Davis schools have what is known as a Spanish immersion program, in which children begin kindergarten and are taught all of their subjects exclusively in Spanish. (By passing Proposition 227 in 1998, a measure that effectively forbids bilingual education, California voters put the future of this innovative voluntary program in jeopardy.) As they progress through the grades, students are exposed to more English. We certainly understood the advantages of bilingual education in California, feeling disadvantaged ourselves on that score. Because the immersion program included a more diverse group of children than the other schools and included some native Spanish speakers, we valued the exposure to different cultures that the program provided. At the same time, we worried about experimenting with Teresa's future. Would the program make it harder for her to learn to read and write in English? In the end, we decided to enroll her, in part because she was so enthusiastic about the prospect of speaking with her grandparents in Spanish.

There were a number of Spanish-speaking children of migrant farm laborers, most of them from Mexico, in Teresa's kindergarten class. The migrant children left the school in the late fall and returned in the spring, when their parents came back to California for the harvests. Helping out in the classroom, I observed that these children seemed just as bright as, and were quieter and better-behaved than, many of the other students in the class, though as a rule they seemed shy. This was understandable given the foreign environment.

Catholicism

My wife and I were married in a Catholic Church in Los Angeles in August 1987. Virginia is more religious than I am and wanted to marry in the church, which was also important to her family and to my mother. (Years later, when we were having trouble selling our house in Sacramento, I was digging in a flower bed in the backyard and found a small statue of the Virgin Mary, which she had placed there because it was supposed to help us sell the house. Not long after I found the statue, which I left in place, the house sold.)

To marry in the church, we had to attend a full-day class on finances, birth control, and rudimentary Catholic theology. The presentation on "finances" taught such things as how to balance your checkbook and cautioned against over-extending yourself on credit cards. Similarly, we were taught that the rhythm method constituted the church's officially sanctioned method of birth control. I was also required to meet with the priest, who asked me pointed questions about my relationship with Virginia that I found a little ridiculous. "Have you seen her naked?" he asked from his side of a beautiful wooden desk. I readily provided the answer he wanted, hoping to get out of there as quickly as possible and move on to the rehearsal dinner.

Catholicism is a complex aspect of many Mexican Americans' identity. My own views of the Catholic Church have changed considerably over the years. In college I blamed the church for exacerbating my mother's problems, especially her inability to deal with divorce, and I disagreed (and still do) with the Vatican's stand on birth control and abortion. I have, however, come to appreciate the social justice aspect of Catholic theology. I was inspired by the liberation theology behind the church's good work in war-torn El Salvador, which helped me see that the church can be an active agent for positive change. The work of Catholic organizations like Cristo Rey in Lansing, Michigan, which provides food, health care, and other services to the Mexican American community, can only be commended. The Catholic Church also has been at the forefront on immigration issues.[9] When California experienced a nativist, anti-Mexican revival in the 1990s, one of the institutions to take a vocal stand in opposition was the Catholic Church.

I am not, however, an apologist for the church—far from it. Like many modern American Catholics, I cannot defend its positions on sexuality, sexual orientation, abortion, birth control, or the refusal to ordain women priests. Catholicism is important to me, and I suspect to many Latinos, for cultural as well as religious reasons. Many Latinos grow up in a culture permeated by the Catholic Church, with pictures of the Virgin Mary, the Virgin of Guadalupe (a symbol of the Chicano movement of the 1960s), and Jesus Christ on the walls of their homes. César Chávez prayed with farmworkers. As they are for many "secular Christians," holidays like Christmas and Easter are less religious occasions for me than traditional opportunities for the family to come together. At the same time, my childhood exposure to the church has left its mark. At Harvard, Catholic mass was one of the few settings in which I felt comfortable and "normal," not that I attended mass regularly then. Even if they wanted to, many Latinos—just like many Irish and Italians—could not break free from the influence of Catholicism on their lives. Whatever one's religious views, the Catholic Church is an important part of Mexican American culture in the Southwest.

The Catholic faith does, of course, have deep religious meaning in the lives of many Latinos. A few days after our daughter Teresa was born, my mother began asking when she was going to be baptized. While Virginia and I took some time to make the arrangements, largely because of the church's many bureaucratic requirements, my mother began to worry that if Teresa died she would be condemned to eternity in purgatory. I could have dismissed her fear as ignorance, but my mother literally worried herself sick about it.

Baptism is a cultural marker for many Mexican Americans, a chance for families to come together to celebrate a birth and reinforce the family. We ultimately had Teresa and Tomás baptized at what is popularly known as *La Placita*, a Catholic Church on Olvera Street in downtown Los Angeles.[10] *La Placita* is the church of many new immigrants to Los Angeles, especially Mexicans and Central Americans. It imposes few requirements for baptism and serves the community of unwed mothers. At Teresa's baptism, the ceremony was conducted in Spanish, and the priest chastised others in the group that day for having children out of wedlock, which seemed wrong to me. After the lecture, he asked all of the mothers to stand for his blessing. About half the people in the church stood up. Then he asked the fathers to stand. I stood with one or two others.

My family's background is far from remarkable. A great many Latinos intermarry and have children. The racial background of Latinos is a mixture and promises to become even more mixed with increasing rates of intermarriage. More intermarriage also means more diversity in physical appearance. I wonder how that will play out in my own family. Will Elena's fortunes be different from those of her fairer-skinned, blue-eyed brother and sister? If she turns out to be less well off in some way, will it be because of her complexion—or because she is the youngest of three children or because she hung out with the wrong crowd?

Given my own experience, I wonder whether my children will accept, deny, downplay, or ignore their Mexican backgrounds. It might be easy enough for Teresa to call herself Terry, drop her middle name of Salazar, and join a sorority in college. Tomás could follow a similar path. Elena could call herself Helen. Only time will tell.

Chapter 10

Lessons for Latino Assimilation

The conventional wisdom in the United States has long been that immigrants should assimilate into the American mainstream.[1] The "melting pot" metaphor says that it is both possible and desirable for immigrants to blend into the dominant Anglo culture, and that immigrants have a positive obligation to assimilate—to learn English, shed their "foreign" culture, and become "American."[2]

At the same time, many whites refuse to accept minorities, whether they try to assimilate or not, because of physical and other differences. In response, minority scholars in recent years have forcefully challenged the assimilationist ideal for racial minorities on philosophical,[3] historical, sociological, and psychological grounds.[4] They have responded to the limits and ironies of the assimilationist ideal with a constructive multicultural ethic, in which people of color are respected and valued. Multiculturalism—the view that minorities should proudly assert their difference from the majority—can be thought of as the mirror image of assimilationism.[5]

In reality, assimilation occurs to some extent among all immigrant groups,[6] but the process has not always been smooth. Virtually every wave of immigrants to the United States encountered difficulty adjusting at first.[7] But most European immigrants eventually became an established and accepted part of Anglo-American society, virtually indistinguishable—in terms of skin color, language, and cultural heritage, broadly speaking—from those who came before them.[8]

The assimilation process has been much more problematic for people of color than for European immigrants.[9] In the late nineteenth century, for example, Chinese immigrants helped build this country and got their thanks when Congress passed a series of laws designed to exclude them on the grounds (among others) that they were unwilling and unable to assimilate.[10] As the U.S. Supreme Court emphasized in rejecting a challenge to one of the infamous exclusion laws, which effectively prohibited immigration from China, "It seemed impossible for [the Chinese] to assimilate with our people or to make any change in their habits or modes of living."[11] Similarly, the Court justified internment of Japanese Americans during World War II on the grounds that "social, economic, and political conditions . . . have intensified [Japanese] solidarity and in large measure prevented their assimilation as an integral part of the white population."[12]

Like other people of color, Latinos in the United States have found it difficult to assimilate into the mainstream, whether they immigrated to this country or were born here.[13] Whereas a German or Irish American finds relatively easy acceptance into the culture, Latinos are often treated as unwelcome outsiders looking to cash in on America's bounty.[14] As a group, even those with deep roots and a long history in the United States have not fully assimilated,[15] despite the government's efforts at various times to "Americanize" them.[16] One need look no further than the many separate and unequal Latino communities in U.S. cities for evidence that assimilation, at least as reflected in the conception of America as a melting pot, is far from complete. Although some argue that intermarriage will facilitate Latino assimilation over time,[17] intermarriage and racial mixture have occurred for centuries, yet Latinos and other minorities remain outside the political and economic mainstream.

Anti-immigration advocates accuse today's immigrants, particularly those from Latin America, of refusing to assimilate by maintaining their language and culture and by living in separate enclaves.[18] Latino intellectuals like Linda Chávez and Richard Rodriguez have added fuel to the fire by strongly encouraging "Hispanics" to assimilate and by criticizing Latino leaders who encourage ethnic separation.[19]

The attacks of pro-assimilationists notwithstanding, Latin American immigrants have in fact assimilated and adapted, in varying degrees, to life in the United States, often against the odds. Persons of Mexican ancestry, including native Spanish speakers, tend to learn English by necessity.[20] In California, Latino men have a higher rate of participation in the labor market than *any* racial group, including Anglos.[21] As many studies have concluded, "Latinos appear to have behaviors and values very similar to those held by middle-class Anglos in the areas of family life, work ethic, health outcomes and education."[22]

Like African Americans, however, Latinos have not achieved full political or economic integration. On the contrary, as the twentieth century draws to a close, the perceived assimilation problem has grown with the changing demographics of immigration.[23] Physical, cultural, and linguistic differences present major obstacles to the acceptance of today's immigrants by the dominant culture. In fact, the latest cohort of Asian and Latin American immigrants must surmount many of the same hurdles faced by Chinese and Japanese immigrants in the past. Even as the new immigrants acculturate, Anglo society continues to view Latinos, with their Spanish language and surnames, their non-Anglo Saxon culture, and their different physical appearance, as foreign, different, "other."[24]

The experience of even the most fully assimilated Latinos illustrates the limits of the assimilationist ideal. Gung-ho assimilationist Linda Chávez resigned as President of U.S. English, an organization devoted to ending bilingual education and establishing English as the official language, after a crude anti-Latino memorandum written by the organization's founder came to light. The memorandum questioned whether "Hispanics" could be educated, spoke of the "Latin American onslaught," and expressed concern over the fertility rates of Latinos, stating, "Perhaps this is the first instance in which those with their pants up are going to get caught by those with their pants down!"[25]

Professor Margaret Montoya has eloquently described how Chicanas wear "masks" in interactions with whites, as she herself did while a student at Harvard Law School.[26] The much-publicized story of Joe Razo, a Chicano at Harvard College who fashioned himself as a "homeboy" and was later convicted of committing armed robberies during summer vacation, demonstrates the precarious nature of Latino assimilation even among those who may appear to have achieved success.[27]

Complete assimilation may not be possible even for Latinos, like myself, of mixed backgrounds who do not necessarily "look" Latino. As Greg Williams and Judy Scales-Trent have shown in writing about their experiences as fair-skinned African Americans, it is not easy to wash your hands of your background. For me, being raised by a Chicana and growing up with Latinos made blending into the Anglo mainstream a stressful experience.[28] There is always the danger that comments made in my presence will irritate, hurt, or simply make me uncomfortable.[29] As some of the stories with which I began this book suggest, some Anglos may see me as part of their club and assume that I will to join them in baiting those inferior Mexican "foreigners."

Latinos of unmixed background can have similar experiences.

My wife was once paid the "compliment" in college that she did not "look" Mexican. What exactly did this remark mean? That Virginia was light-skinned and Mexicans were supposed to be dark? That she was attractive and Mexicans were not? That Mexicans look "different" but Virginia looked "normal"? Whatever the intentions of the speaker, the comment was offensive and she never forgot it.

Diversity within the Latino community helps explain why some Latinos may find it easier than others to assimilate. Phenotype is an important assimilation variable, and assimilation is usually easier for fairer-skinned Latinos than for others. They shed their "foreignness" and blend into the crowd more easily than the more indigenous-looking. Fair-skinned Cuban Americans, for example, have found it easier than other Latino national origin groups to assimilate economically, politically, and socially.[30] Puerto Ricans, in contrast, some of whom are black, are the least likely Latino group to be assimilated in these ways.[31] In many Mexican Americans, "the Indian racial types predominate. Most are dark of complexion with black hair, traits inherited in large part from their Indian ancestors. But many are blond, blue-eyed, and white, while others have red hair and hazel eyes."[32]

Until racial and cultural background becomes as "transparent" as whiteness, it seems that full assimilation will be impossible.[33] But is such "transparency" really desirable? To assimilate fully, people of Latino ancestry would have to ignore or eliminate any consciousness of their cultural background and heritage and strive to be "white." Some Latinos are more willing to attempt this than others. One can only wonder about the damage to an individual's psyche that results from living a hidden life, suppressing a Latino identity while fearing that some day someone may discover that you are an imposter.

Mexican immigrants have a unique experience among Latinos

in that the United States and Mexico share a border more than 1,000 miles long. This geographical proximity has enabled a large population of unnaturalized Mexican immigrants to live in the United States.[34] Although some of them have assimilated to some degree culturally and otherwise, they have not become integrated into the political process.[35] Though recent revisions to Mexican law permitting dual nationality may change this, significant numbers of Mexican immigrants view naturalization and U.S. citizenship as a betrayal of one's Mexican nationality and heritage. They live by the code "born a Mexican, die a Mexican." Consider Richard Rodriguez's description of his father's naturalization:

> When he decided to apply for American citizenship, my father told no one, none of his friends, those men with whom he had come to this country looking for work. American citizenship would have seemed a betrayal of Mexico, a sin against memory. One afternoon, like a man with something to hide, my father slipped away. He went downtown to the Federal Building in Sacramento and disappeared into America.[36]

Many Mexican citizens resist naturalization for other reasons than allegiance to Mexico; becoming a naturalized citizen is a long, complicated, and, to many people, daunting process.[37] Others resist full assimilation into the American mainstream because they do not want to relinquish their Mexican identity and are slow to acknowledge a new transnational identity spanning two nations.[38] But until the political and economic integration of Latino noncitizens occurs, assimilation will remain far from complete.[39]

A considerable body of academic commentary has addressed the voluntary adoption of a racial or ethnic identity. The title of Mary C. Water's book—*Ethnic Options: Choosing Identities in America*[40]—nicely captures the essence of the concept. As Ken Karst has observed,

> identity itself *is* a myth—a myth of origin, or destiny, or both. We "make up people," inventing categories, giving each category not only a label but an imagined history and an imagined behavioral script—and then deciding, Yes or No, whether particular individuals should be assigned to the category.[41]

Inventing an identity, however, is not always an option; there are limits to the identities one can choose. "In every circumstance choices are exercised not by free agents or autonomous actors, but by people who are compromised and constrained by the social context."[42] Indeed, minorities of certain phenotypes have a racial identity thrust upon them. A dark-skinned African American and a fair-complexioned Latino simply do not have the same identity choices available to them. Society treats those with dark skin as "black" regardless of how they see themselves,[43] but may treat the fair Latino as white.[44]

Discrimination based on physical appearance certainly presents an obstacle to Latinos who want to adopt a racial identity different from that which society assigns them. In essence, dark-skinned or indigenous-looking Latinos have a socially constructed "race" imposed on them. Fairer Latinos have different experiences and face different choices, just as Latinos with Anglo surnames generally have more choice than people with Spanish surnames.

Constraints on choice are reflected in the surveys showing that African Americans and Mexican Americans, even those of mixed ancestry, are more consistent in ethnic affiliation than white ethnics over time.[45] It is noteworthy, however, that significant differences exist in this regard among Latinos. Puerto Ricans offer more consistent responses than Mexicans, who again are more consistent in their identification than Cubans.[46] Not coincidentally, Puerto Ricans, the most economically deprived of all Latino national origin groups, include a significant black population, while many Cuban Americans, the most economically well off of all Latinos, tend to be fair-skinned.

Even when identity choice does exist, it is not without limits. Finding and becoming comfortable with one's racial identity is probably one of the most difficult things a member of a racial minority will ever face. Denial of one's background exacts a psychological toll that may outweigh the benefits of the higher status and prestige accorded to whiteness. But it is not difficult to understand why many mixed and fair-skinned Latinos choose a white identity. Those who embrace their Latino identity face many costs and few concrete benefits.

Besides the emotional turmoil involved in coming to grips with one's background,[47] identity selection exposes a person to the judgment of others. Latinos risk rejection for refusing to assimilate, challenges to their Latino authenticity, and accusations of trying to cash in on affirmative action benefits. The constant questioning by others of my own identity takes an emotional toll. Rarely a day goes by that my identity is not called into question. Many people assume that I am white because of my surname and appearance and openly wonder how it is possible that a Latino could be named Johnson, how I could have children named Teresa, Tomás, and Elena, or why I am so interested in "Latino issues."

I have also been accused by whites of refusing to assimilate when I embrace my Latino identity. And I have been charged—by both Latinos and whites—with identifying myself as Latino only in order to take advantage of affirmative action benefits. The myth remains that there are many affirmative action benefits to be gained by identifying as Latino. I do know some persons of mixed Anglo/Latino background who identified only for purposes of affirmative action in college and law school admission and may have benefitted because of that identification. But the number of Latinos in higher education and the professions is so small as to suggest that we would do well to focus on more significant social justice issues.[48]

As this book attests, I exercised a good deal of choice in embracing a Mexican American identity. Born with light skin and an Anglo surname, I have been able to "pass" as white in many settings. There have been times when I could have hidden my background or simply pretended that I was white without raising an eyebrow. At times in my life, such as at the law firm, I have been more or less oblivious to my Mexican ancestry and have simply done my work. Still, to say that I had free choice would be an overstatement. I grew up with a Mexican American mother and grandmother and until the seventh grade lived in a mixed working-class white and Mexican American community. To deny that part of my background and life history would have been painful, if not impossible. The support of my wife has helped me to become more comfortable and confident in my identity as a Mexican American and, at the same time, has helped me deflect challenges to that identity.[49]

My blond-haired, blue-eyed brother Michael made a different choice. He recognizes our family history and treats it as just that—as historical fact with little relevance to his daily life. My half-brother Robby, who looks a bit like me, followed Michael's example in fashioning his racial identity. They neither deny their Mexican American heritage, as our mother did, nor openly embrace it as I have done.

Latino Diversity

The stories in this book illustrate an important characteristic of the Latino community. In spite of overwhelming evidence to the contrary, many people consider Latinos to be a monolithic group.[50] In fact, Latinos in the United States are extremely heterogeneous and include persons of Mexican, Cuban, Puerto Rican, Central American, and other Latin American ancestry.[51] Diversity of national origin, which varies by region in this country,[52] is simply the beginning. Latinos differ widely in terms of race (as that term is conventionally used), immigration status, duration in this country, circumstances under which they came, social class, linguistic abilities, and cultural background.[53] Latinos even speak different kinds of Spanish.[54] My nuclear family exemplifies this diversity: a half-Mexican American, half-Anglo man who looks more white than Mexican and speaks some Spanish, a Mexican American woman who speaks some Spanish, three children who are three-fourths Mexican American, two with blond hair, blue eyes, and light skin and one with dark brown hair, brown eyes, and an olive complexion.

Discrimination based on physical appearance varies greatly among Latinos. While a relatively minor problem for some, it looms larger in the lives of Latinos with more indigenous appearances.[55] Mexican Americans who fit the stereotype—dark-skinned with indigenous features—are more likely than other Mexican Americans to be stopped, questioned, or worse, by immigration authorities in border communities. Having the physical appearance of a stereotypical Mexican can lead to distinctly "special" treatment.[56] In one highly publicized incident, the Border Patrol stopped Eddie Cortez, a third-generation Mexican American who happened to be the conservative Republican mayor of a small southern California city, because he fit the "profile" of an "illegal alien."[57]

Though light-skinned Mexican Americans are usually not subjected to the same level of harassment, they may suffer "microaggressions," such as having racial insults made in their presence. They may also be disparaged by fellow Mexican Americans as "gabachos," slang for Anglos.[58] Rejection by Latinos does not necessarily mean acceptance by Anglos, or vice versa, and light-skinned Mexican Americans often feel trapped in a no-man's land, belonging to neither world.

Black-skinned Latinos face an entirely different set of assimilation obstacles. They cannot "pass" as white and are often seen not as Latino but as African American, with the harsh stigma U.S. society attaches to being black. Black Latinos, as some Puerto Ricans and Cubans have learned, find it difficult to assimilate and are, on the average, less well off socioeconomically than other persons of Latin American ancestry in the United States. The negative reaction to the Cuban refugees who came to this country in the Mariel boatlift of 1980, including the reaction of some Cuban Americans, stemmed in part from the fact that many were black.[59]

Because of Latino heterogeneity, physical appearance alone is an unreliable indicator of racial authenticity. My friend Elvia Arriola, for example, described me in an article as a "'white-looking' Latino,"[60] a description that made me uneasy. To describe a Latino this way is to reinforce the stereotype that all Latinos are dark-skinned.[61] In fact, I know many full-blooded Latinos, including Jorge Castañeda, the famous Mexican intellectual, who look as "white" as I do. My physical appearance has generated a variety of responses from Anglos. Besides the occasional suspicions that I am Asian, some people have told me that I look something like Jimmy Smits, the Latino actor. Indeed, a law school friend called me Sifuentes after Smits's character on the popular 1980s television show "L.A. Law." Another white acquaintance once told me with delight that I looked like Richard Ramirez, the infamous "Night Stalker" who was convicted of a series of heinous murders in Los Angeles in the 1980s.[62] I am never sure how to respond to these statements about my physical appearance, which cut to the core of my being.

Latinos in the United States trace their ancestors to every corner of Latin America, yet political efforts in recent years have tended to homogenize them. This is ironic because political tensions often run high between Latinos of different national origin, and pan-Latino coalition building often breaks down over national differences that overshadow any collective "Latino" identity. Cuban Americans, for example, historically have been more politically conservative than other Latinos.[63] Some tensions are more class-oriented, but national origin often plays a part there, too. Because the average income of persons of Mexican, Puerto Rican, and Cuban ancestry in the United States varies substantially,[64] it is not surprising that there are also political differences between these groups, including cleavages on such hot-button issues as civil rights, affirmative action, welfare, and electoral representation.[65]

Huge differences in language also differentiate the Latino community. While many speak Spanish, some do not.[66] Spanish is still classified by Anglo society as a foreign language, even though it has long been part of Southwestern culture and was spoken in some regions long before they became part of the English-speaking United States.

Though many Latinos speak Spanish, this obviously does not determine their ethnicity. Vociferous assimilationists would have Latinos forsake Spanish for English, but many Latinos have maintained Spanish as a part of their culture in the face of constant attacks. In California, more than 60 percent of Latino voters voted against the initiative known as Proposition 227, which would end bilingual education in the public schools; many presumably saw it as an attack on Latinos. (The measure passed overwhelmingly.)[67]

At the opposite end of the spectrum, there are Latinos striving to assimilate into the American mainstream who have deliberately eliminated the Spanish language from their homes. I learned what Spanish I know in school rather than at home. I still feel somewhat ill at ease at gatherings where Spanish is the primary language and am reminded on those occasions of this unfortunate aspect of my family history.

Though a Spanish surname may affect one's life experiences, it too is an imperfect indicator of Latino heritage. Intermarriage and racial mixture have produced many Latinos of mixed background with Anglo surnames.[68] "Even if one could identify with precision which surnames connote Hispanic ethnicity, the question remains whether the name was obtained through marriage or adoption rather than birth."[69] United Nations ambassador Bill Richardson, a former congressman from New Mexico who served as chair of the Congressional Hispanic Caucus, is a prominent Latino leader with a Latina mother and Anglo father.[70] (Political columnist Robert Novak once questioned Richardson's Latino credentials by emphasizing that he is "half Hispanic. Everybody calls him Hispanic. He's half Anglo too.")[71] Former football star Jim Plunkett, son of William Plunkett and Carmen Blea, is Latino.[72] Born in Mexico, the actor Anthony Quinn is of mixed Irish-Mexican parentage.[73] Baseball legend Ted Williams, the last player to bat .400 in a season, was half Mexican American, though he is rarely seen as Latino (nor does he identify himself as such).[74] The father of the famous sociologist Julian Samora, author of many works on Latinos, was named Fred Harris.[75] One wonders whether Samora's work would have focused on Latinos if his last name had been Harris.

To complicate matters further, some well-known Latinos, such as actor Martin Sheen, born Ramon Estevez,[76] and singer Vikki Carr, born Florencia Bisenta de Casillas Martínez Cardona,[77] changed their names to enhance their careers. The pressure to change rich Spanish names to rather bland Anglo-Saxon ones subtly affects the community by robbing Latinos of opportunities to see Latino public figures clearly. The changing of Spanish surnames only contributes to Latino invisibility and reinforces the belief that Latinos do not belong in polite society. Even if other Latinos knew the racial history of stars like Sheen and Carr, the fact that these public figures felt compelled to change their names—to "whiten" themselves—in order to succeed, underlines the negative connotations of Latino identity. Though times may be changing, we still see relatively few figures with Spanish surnames in mainstream popular culture.

Trying to sort people out by their surnames becomes even more complicated when the names are changed by marriage. Some mixed Anglo/Latino women born with Anglo surnames take their Latino husband's Spanish surname when they marry. Even if they identified themselves as Latinas before marriage, they are probably asked fewer questions about their backgrounds afterwards. In contrast, some mixed Anglo/Latino women with Spanish surnames may keep their surnames, and Latino identity, upon marrying.[78] To complicate matters further, some schools have counted Anglo women married to Latinos as "Latinas" in order to inflate the number of Latino faculty members.[79]

Additional complications arise with the children of mixed Anglo/Latino marriages. Children are most commonly given the surname of their father; in the case of children with an Anglo father and Latina mother, the child's Latino heritage can be hidden.[80] Clearly surname alone cannot always reveal whether a person is "Latino."

As this discussion demonstrates, the Latino community is extremely heterogeneous, and this diversity will only increase with increasing intermarriage between racial groups. The political and economic consequences of this diversity must be addressed in searching for strategies to achieve political and economic participation. Differences within the Latino community often hinder consensus building and complicate efforts at social change. For example, although the Latino leadership has resisted restrictive immigration "reforms," some Latino citizens support such measures.[81] Activists who attempt to gloss over these differences face charges that the leadership is out of touch with the rank and file.[82] Any attempt to create a consensus within the Latino community must recognize the diversity within the community as a critical first step.

Four important components of Latino identity that may serve as the basis for Latino coalition building are family, ethnicity, religion, and the Spanish language.[83] These factors form the basis for the common Anglo belief that Latinos are "foreign" and may serve as rallying points around which unity can be built.[84] By focusing on the core of Latino identity, Latinos may seek and perhaps demand a political voice.[85] To achieve change within the political process,[86] coalitions need to be built both within the Latino community and with other subordinated groups.[87]

Latino diversity, however, causes practical problems that must be addressed with respect to affirmative action and related programs. As Supreme Court Justice Anthony Kennedy has pointed out, one federal agency was required "to trace an applicant's family history to 1492 to conclude that the applicant was 'Hispanic' for purposes of a minority tax certificate policy."[88] Assuming that race will be a factor in future governmental programs,[89] other questions arise. Should differences within the Latino community affect eligibility for affirmative action programs? Specifically, should immigrants from Latin America—as opposed to Latino citizens—be eligible for affirmative action? These and related questions raise potentially divisive issues for the Latino community. For example, Mexican Americans whose families have lived in this country for generations may have a stronger claim to remedial affirmative action than do recent immigrants from Latin America.[90] At the same time, inequities may result when Latino immigrants are eligible for affirmative action programs designed to remedy pervasive systemic discrimination against African Americans.[91] Making new immigrants eligible for benefits may not provide adequate recompense for past discrimination against U.S. citizens; immigrants have not descended from persons subject to centuries of racial subordination in this country.[92] The issue becomes even muddier, however, when immigrants of color become the victims of discrimination once they arrive in the United States, or when they come to this country because of U.S. foreign policy in their native countries.[93]

Some opponents of affirmative action, notably Peter Brimelow in the anti-immigrant polemic *Alien Nation,*[94] claim that Latino activists have constructed a false identity for purposes of securing affirmative action and other benefits. True, Latinos are an exceedingly diverse lot, and care must be taken not to essentialize or oversimplify the Latino experience.[95] But accusations like Brimelow's obscure the fact that Latinos share common interests, political and otherwise, because society classifies and treats them as a homogeneous group.

The racial demographics of the United States in the last third of the twentieth century have seen a dramatic increase in Latinos and Asian Americans as a proportion of the population.[96] Race relations in the United States today are therefore far more complex than they were a century ago, and, over time, the Latino community is likely to become more diverse. As Deborah Ramirez puts it, "it's not just black and white anymore."[97] Largely because of intermarriage,[98] more multi-racial people live in the United States than ever before.[99] This means that any sound analysis of race relations must focus broadly on all racial minorities.[100]

The choices and limits confronting persons of Anglo/Latino background in a highly charged era of identity politics are both similar to and different from the identity issues facing persons of mixed black/white origin. In analyzing the identity choice of white/brown people, one must consider their prospects for full integration into the mainstream.

Mutiracialism: The Final Piece of the Puzzle

The increasing number of multi-racial people in the United States has generated legal difficulties because "the American legal system today lacks intermediate or 'mixed race' classifications."[101] This country has a long tradition of simply ignoring the existence of mixed-race people. The so-called "one drop" rule, for example, classified as "African American" all persons who possessed "one drop" of "black" blood.[102] Though it made racial classifications administratively convenient for discriminatory purposes, this rule classified as "black" an entire array of persons who varied greatly in terms of parentage and physical appearance.

When naturalization laws required that a noncitizen be either "white" or of African descent to naturalize, the courts had to grapple with how to classify persons of mixed heritage. Faced with the question whether a noncitizen with an English father and a mother who was half-Chinese and half-Japanese was "white," one court emphasized that "a person, one-half white and one-half of some other race, belongs to neither of those races, but is literally a *half-breed.*"[103] Following this reasoning and the one-drop rule, the courts consistently found that mixed-race persons were not "white" and were therefore ineligible for naturalization.[104]

As these examples show, mixed-race people have been marginalized when not ignored altogether. The court's derogatory characterization of them as "half-breeds" exemplifies this marginalization.[105] Historically, academic theories have supported this treatment of mixed-race people. At the end of the nineteenth century, for example, scientists believed that a child of black and white parents was inferior,[106] a racist notion that still survives today in some quarters.[107] The mixed heritage of Mexicans led to similar conclusions. As T.J. Farnham wrote in 1840,

> No one acquainted with the indolent, mixed race of California, will ever believe that they will populate, much less, for any length of time, govern the country. The law of Nature which curses the mulatto here with a constitution less robust than that of either race from which he sprang, lays a similar penalty upon the mingling of the Indian and white races in California and Mexico. They must fade away. . . .[108]

Though animosity toward mixed-race people may be on the wane, "the rich diversity literally embodied by Multiracial people [has been] hidden from view, hidden from discourse, hidden from recognition and thus, invisible."[109] Lacking intermediate classifications, the law constructs a neat, dichotomous, unreal world.[110]

In the 1990s the Bureau of the Census stirred up controversy by considering the addition of a multi-racial category to its racial classification scheme.[111] Some African American leaders objected that mixed-race people who had always identified as black might begin to identify themselves as "multiracial," thereby diluting the strength of blacks in electoral representation, affirmative action, and federal contracting programs.[112]

The multiracial issue was again brought to national attention in 1997 by professional golfing sensation Tiger Woods, who claimed not to be African American, as many assumed, but "Cablinasian," a mixture of Caucasian, African, Indian, and Asian.[113] Some African Americans were offended that Woods, in their view, was denying that he was black. Whatever his declared racial background, however, Woods was the subject of slurs and hate mail from people who assumed that he was African American.[114]

The number of multiracial people in the United States will undoubtedly increase in the future, but how this may affect political and racial subordination in this country is far from clear. By blurring the lines between racial categories, multiracial people may destabilize the racial status quo. One might hope that the increasing number of multiracial people will build sympathy among members of dominant society as they become more familiar with, even related to, racial minorities.[115] Increasing numbers of multiracial children of mixed marriages may also be cause for hope.[116] Interracial marriages, however, have occurred for centuries without a radical racial transformation. Given this nation's racial history, one must guard against too optimistic an outlook.

Racial mixture is nothing new to Latinos. As the product of a long history of intermixture of Spanish, Indian, African, and other peoples, Mexican Americans, and Latinos more generally, represent a diverse mixture of races. In sharp contrast to the clear, unequivocal racial categorization schemes constructed by U.S. law and society, "Latinos, and especially Mexican Americans, have been conditioned by their history . . . to accept racial ambiguity and mixture as 'normal.'"[117] In contrast to the dim view of racial mixture taken by Anglo colonizers, Mexican philosophers saw it as a positive contribution to a *raza cosmica* or "cosmic race."[118] Like the boundaries between the races, Americans consider the U.S.-Mexico border a physically fixed location, while Mexicans refer to it as *la frontera* in much the same way that nineteenth-century Americans envisioned the American frontier.[119] Though Latinos may accept racial ambiguity more readily than whites, U.S. society has traditionally imposed rigid racial classifications that raise difficult identity issues for persons of mixed Latino heritage.

Animus toward mixed Anglo/Latinos is generally less virulent than hostility toward other mixed-race persons,[120] perhaps because of the long history of intermarriage between Anglos and persons of Mexican ancestry in the Southwest. For example, when my Uncle Brown-eyes married his Mexican American wife Rosie in the 1940s, few Anglos raised an eyebrow. Things would have been much different, I suspect, had he married a black woman.

Some mixed-background Latinos may be treated as "white" by the rest of society,[121] but as with light-skinned blacks, the decision to "pass" has its costs. Professor Cheryl Harris offers the sad example of the great pain her grandmother suffered in living two lives, working by day as "white" and returning home each night as black.[122]

In the Southwest, to be stigmatized by Anglos as "Mexican" places one at a distinct disadvantage in certain circumstances. Like my mother and grandmother, some Latinos therefore attempt to pass as Spanish,[123] but this brings other kinds of pain. My mother's assimilation ordeals are an example of the psychological and other costs. My own experience as a mixed Anglo/Latino, though far less severe, has had its own share of pain.

Adrian Piper has captured the double-edged quality of the phenomenon of "passing" in her eloquent description of the experiences of an African American woman who could have passed as white but chose not to.[124] Some blacks demanded proof that she was black; other subjected her to racial slurs. Then there were those who accused her of calling herself black only in order to reap affirmative action benefits. In addition, Piper resented fair-skinned family members who sealed themselves off from the rest of the family in their attempt to pass as white. Though they achieved higher status that way, they left their black family behind, with all the emotional turmoil and sadness that this entailed.

Attempts to "pass," moreover, are not always successful, as my mother and grandmother learned at great cost. I well understand the Catch-22 in which Piper was caught. Being true to yourself subjects you to public scrutiny. Life under a microscope can be disorienting, uncomfortable, and burdensome. And like her, I vacillate between understanding and resentment of the efforts of others to pass as white, with all the privileges and burdens that "passing" brings.[125]

Whatever the assimilation route taken by Latinos who appear "white," it is clear that their life experiences and identities are shaped by the knowledge that to be white is to be at the pinnacle of the social hierarchy in the United States. Those who embrace their minority identity suffer a different set of costs from those who reject it. The point is that both choices come with costs—costs from which whites are generally immune.

There is no clear or easy answer to the question of how a person should classify herself when given an either/or choice rather than one that better reflects the complexities of race in modern America. Since there are no agreed-upon rules, identity choice by definition is arbitrary. As Linda Chávez, the daughter of a Latino father and a British-Irish mother, explained, she had "very little identification with my mother's background. I always thought of myself as Latina despite the fact that I didn't speak Spanish."[126] Or take the case of the prominent federal judge, Harold Medina, whose father was a Mexican immigrant and mother an Anglo.[127] Though Medina is listed among Latinos in the *Hispanic Almanac,*[128] another book claims that Reynaldo Garza, though he was appointed to the bench more than a decade after Medina, was the first Mexican American federal judge because "political figures . . . were unaware of [Medina's] Mexican roots" at the time of his confirmation.[129]

Some mixed Latinos classify themselves as white, others as Latino. Some identify as Latino at one time in their lives, perhaps in response to affirmative action considerations, but not at another. Without a clear classification rule, there is no clearly acceptable course of conduct.[130] Although one can understand that circumstances may lead to a change of identity (one may begin to identify with a particular group because of education, for example), strategic box checking should not be condoned. Minority identification for the purpose of gaining affirmative action and other benefits should in fact be discouraged and condemned as not serving any legitimate function, particularly when it is done exclusively to manipulate affirmative action programs for personal gain.

The ambiguity of racial classifications for mixed Latinos can be seen in the controversy involving Maria Hylton, a law professor with one white Australian and one black Cuban parent, who identified herself as black rather than Latina when she was being considered for a faculty position at Northwestern University School of Law in Chicago.[131] But was Hylton black? An African American professor at Northwestern claimed that because her background differed from that of most African Americans in the United States, she was not.[132]

Conundrums like these have led to increased academic attention to the experiences of multiracial peoples[133] in the form of a new field of Critical "Mixed Race" Theory.[134] Although African American legal scholars of white and African American parents have written books documenting their experience,[135] there has been surprisingly little analysis of mixed Anglo/Latinos. But consider the diverse backgrounds of a few Latina and Latino law professors: a Latina with a "Cuban black" father and a mother who was the daughter of Italian immigrants;[136] a "Mexican, Irish, Jewish, Woman, Heterosexual, Aunt, Law Professor, Californian, Bostonian, Tusconian, middle child, professional" grappling with multiple identities;[137] a Latino who is the son of a fourth-generation Irish father and a Salvadoran immigrant mother;[138] a Latina with a Mexican immigrant mother and a Canadian father;[139] one whose father was Irish and mother Mexican;[140] a Latino from New Mexico whose mother was "Mexican American, his father Anglo-American";[141] and a Latina "born in Cuba [who] grew up in Puerto Rico."[142]

The identity complexities in my own life suggest some of the issues that society must grapple with in the future. For the most part, I have been accepted by both the Mexican American and

Anglo communities. At the same time, I am self-conscious about where I fit in, fully aware that racial politics are a treacherous minefield. I am occasionally reminded in no uncertain terms that I might not be employed, or at least not by as good a law school, were it not for my Mexican American ancestry. Tenure has not cleared up the uncertainty or stopped the questions and reminders. Though I have only one Mexican American parent, my own Latino identity illustrates the volitional nature of racial identity. Assimilation, racial choice, and Latino diversity all come into play when I pose the question of where mixed Anglo-Latino persons—half brown, half white—fit into the heated identity politics of the modern United States.

As increasing numbers of multiracial people in the United States mature, they will grapple with some of the issues with which I have struggled. Mixed Latinos do not fit neatly into the dominant Anglo culture. At the same time, they may be viewed with suspicion by some Latinos. My experience has been that others await an explanation when I claim to be Mexican American, especially in the academic world, with its unique brand of racial politics.

Ultimately, persons of mixed background are left little space in the modern debate over race relations. With the increasing number of mixed-race Latinos and mixed-race people generally in the United States, one might expect more blurring of the physical differences traditionally used to demarcate the so-called races. Telling who is white and who is not on the basis of physical appearance will become increasingly difficult. How society will address these racial complexities remains far from clear.

Chapter 11

What Does It All Mean for Race Relations in the United States?

The lessons to be learned from the history of race relations in this country obviously are not limited to Latinos alone. Issues of race in the modern United States have become increasingly complex. If there ever was a black-and-white world demarcated by slavery and freedom, we no longer live there. Asians, Latinos, Native Americans and other racially subordinated peoples all press for redress of civil rights violations, sometimes even vying with each other for relief. Society often pits their demands against each other, sometimes with violent results, as when complex African American, Korean, and Latino tensions—which the media analyzed in terms of African American and Korean conflict—boiled over in South Central Los Angeles in May 1992. If society continues to ignore the cries of the oppressed in the United States, we will, in all likelihood, see this violent episode repeated.

As immigration and intermarriage increase, so will the complexity of racial issues in a multiracial society. The United States is a much more racially mixed nation today than it was in 1950, as a glance at any major American city will attest. For better or worse, my hometown of Los Angeles may allow us a glimpse of the future of race relations in America. But Los Angeles is not the only place undergoing racial change. Hmong and Mexican immigrants have settled in the Midwest, Sikhs in the Central Valley of California, Vietnamese refugees on the Gulf Coast. Demographic transformations are taking place across the nation and they increase the complexities of race and class in modern-day America. The pressing question, to paraphrase Rodney King's elegant simplicity, is whether Latinos, Asian Americans, African Americans, Native Americans, whites, and others can just get along. We can only hope.

Because of the institution of slavery and its legacy, African Americans have suffered unparalleled disadvantages in U.S. society.[1] Other racial minorities have been subordinated by the majority as well. The people of California terrorized the Chinese population in the mid-and-late nineteenth century. In addition to direct physical violence against Chinese immigrants, the United States Congress passed laws prohibiting Chinese immigrants from coming to our shores. About a century later, another nativist outburst resulted in new laws that more subtly affected immigrant populations largely from Asia and Latin America.[2] People of Mexican ancestry in the Southwest continue to suffer from the vestiges of U.S. conquest more than 150 years ago.[3]

Many people view race relations as a static hierarchy, with blacks at the bottom, whites at the top, and other groups in between. However, race relations in the multiracial, multicultural United States constantly shift and change, ebb and flow depending on the social, political, and economic circumstances of the day.[4] Those who are serious about social change must seek to understand how the complexities operate as a whole in maintaining racial subordination.

The interrelationship between the subordination of various minority groups can be seen throughout history. In the American Southwest, the United States provoked a war with Mexico as a part of the political struggle to maintain slavery of blacks, a war that ended in 1848 with the Treaty of Guadalupe Hidalgo, an instrument that helped ensure the subordination of persons of Mexican ancestry in this country. In the 1880s, whites and blacks, enjoying new political rights under the Fourteenth Amendment, joined forces to pass the laws preventing Chinese immigration to the United States. A hundred years later, Asian Americans became the "model minority" in this country, which many whites took as proof that the poverty of African Americans and Latinos is their own fault.

Despite the complexities, the media, social commentators, and academics have traditionally focused attention on civil rights issues as conflict between African Americans and whites. In light of the legacy of chattel slavery in the United States, the subsequent reign of Jim Crow, and modern, more subtle forms of discrimination against African Americans, the traditional focus is understandable. To achieve racial justice in the United States, however, the subordination of other peoples of color—Latinos, Asian Americans, Native Americans, and other minorities—must be accounted for in the national civil rights debate. As the controversy surrounding President Clinton's race relations commission revealed, this project may at times cause tension among minority communities. However, continued treatment of civil rights issues as black and white will exacerbate, not reduce, tensions.

Inter-ethnic conflict, whether Asian against African American, Latino against Asian, or some other variation, has proven time and again to be counterproductive. Such hostilities divert important energy that should be focused on the true source of the problem. Latinos should know that African Americans and Asian Americans are not responsible for their place in the social hierarchy. Similarly, African Americans and Asian Americans must know that Latinos cannot be blamed for their social and political status. Minority coalitions must be built that will move beyond racial divisiveness and work to change the racial status quo.

In analyzing issues of race in the modern United States, we also must keep in mind that racial questions go beyond skin color. As many have argued persuasively, race is a social, not a biological, construction.[5] The United States has seen the construction, deconstruction, and reconstruction of races at various times in its history. At various points in this nation's history, U.S. society has classified Irish and Jewish immigrants as distinctly different and inferior "races."[6] Similarly, society has vacillated in its treatment of Latinos, specifically Mexican Americans, sometimes classifying them as non-white and other times as white without the privileges that typically accrue to whiteness.[7]

Latino identity, like any racial or ethnic identity, is complex. The simple question "Who is Latino in the United States?" is just the beginning. We must also ask where people of mixed Anglo-Latino heritage fit into the racial dynamics of the United States. These difficult questions must be considered by society as well as by Latinos individually. Little attention has been given to defining who is Latino or where mixed-race persons fit into the overall scheme of things. Latinos come in all forms. We are light, dark, Spanish-speaking, English-fluent, bilingual, immigrants (legal and undocumented), refugees, citizens, Mexican, Cuban, Puerto Rican, Central and South American. But to varying degrees, we are all treated as foreign, different, "the Other." For some, Latino identity is more voluntary than membership in other minority groups. Because "Latino" is a fluid category, we should expect great movement in and out of the community. Similarly, because physical appearance and cultural markers make Latino identity voluntary for some, we can expect an increase in the number of Latinos who "come out" in the future.

Matters have improved. The voluntariness of Latino identity in the United States has changed over time. We no longer live in an era when Mexican Americans in the Southwest routinely deny their rich heritage in an attempt to pass as white. Sensibilities have changed with the growth of Chicano activism in the 1960s and of multiculturalism in the 1980s and 1990s. More Latinos now take pride in their culture, rejecting the Spanish masks worn by so many for so long. Latinos today enjoy greater freedom than in the past to embrace their history and take pride in their indigenous Latin American roots.

U.S. society continues to grapple with some of the problems of racial classification. Mixed Latino/Anglos have been largely ignored in this debate. The Census Bureau flap over whether to include a "multiracial" category on its form was resolved by allowing persons to check multiple boxes, though this still fails to deal with Latinos who by definition are mixed-race or *mestizaje*. Some racial minorities view Latinos as white, which is how the census classifies them ("Hispanic" is an ethnic, not a racial, category), though they do not enjoy all the benefits of whiteness and are still the victims of segregation and discrimination in the United States.

Linda Chávez and other assimilationists trust that intermarriage and racial mixture will result in racial harmony in the twenty-first century. Increasing numbers of multiracial people undoubtedly will blur racial lines. But history (in the United States and throughout the world) suggests that racism will not die a quick or easy death. This nation has a long history of racial classification and discrimination, even when, as in the case of nineteenth-century Irish and Eastern European immigrants, "racial" differences are subtle or non-existent. Rather than the demise of racism, the increase of multiracial people may result in new forms of racial subordination. Society will construct new races, perhaps based on lightness or darkness of skin color, language, culture, or religion. The bloody war in Bosnia in the 1990s, to name just one of the ethnic and racial conflicts going on around the world, offers a chilling possibility.

Some claim that racial minorities, especially immigrants of color, refuse to assimilate. They point to the more or less successful assimilation of European immigrants as a model for other minorities,[8] but ignore the limits that the majority imposes on the assimilation of racial minorities. Unlike European immigrants, many racial minorities cannot blend into society after a generation or two. With their differences in skin color and physical appearance, racial minorities are invariably discriminated against in one way or another. This explains why the descendants of Chinese immigrants in the late 1800s may still be subjected to racial slurs today, while the ancestors of Irish immigrants of roughly the same period generally are not. It explains why the ancestors of Japanese immigrants are not as fully assimilated as German immigrants of the same era. It explains why many Mexican Americans, including those who can trace their ancestors in this land to the days before the U.S. conquest of the Southwest, live in separate and unequal communities in cities across the nation.

Ultimately, assimilation is much more complicated than the optimistic pro-assimilationists would have it. Even minorities who appear white, and therefore face many fewer obstacles to acceptance and assimilation than their darker-skinned brothers and sisters, cannot always forget their pasts—nor should they be required to as a condition of social acceptance. Even many of those who wish to do so must resign themselves to living in a quasi-white status, with some of the benefits of whiteness and many of the costs of their racial and cultural ancestry. I have experienced this ambiguity in my life on the border between two worlds, belonging partly to each but fully to neither.

For many racial minorities, full assimilation into dominant Anglo-Saxon society is impossible, and so they have opted to establish a peaceful place of their own, adopting a multicultural outlook as a positive response to the limits of assimilation. Despite centuries of coexistence of African American and white people in the United States, blacks remain largely outside the political and economic mainstream. Asian Americans and Latinos have faced similar though different experiences. While it is in many ways tantalizing, full-fledged assimilation is not likely, much less inevitable, for many racial minorities. Of course, some blacks, Asian Americans, Latinos, and Native Americans have joined the middle and upper classes and assimilated through intermarriage. Many, however, have not. To blame them for remaining unassimilated is to ignore the racism that permeates U.S. history and society.

One area greatly in need of further exploration is the role of class in racial subordination in the United States. Class issues are particularly important to Latinos, in part because their physical difference from whites is not as pronounced as the difference between blacks and whites. Economic assimilation, obviously, is one prerequisite to political and social integration.

Large portions of the Latino community have been plagued by poverty. As of 1997, Latinos represented the poorest minority group in the United States. In the Southwest, racial discrimination, part and parcel of securing a labor force for Southwestern agricultural interests, has been inextricably linked to economic domination. Generations of Mexican American and Mexican immigrant farm workers have been marginalized through the intersection of class and race. The squalor endured by persons of Mexican ancestry in impoverished *colonias*—semi-rural, unincorporated subdivisions along the borders—gives the lie to the claims of the of the assimilationist Pollyannas.[9] Puerto Ricans, formally longtime citizens of the United States but still denied full membership rights, have suffered economic subordination as well.[10]

This book, I hope, is one of the first installments in the study of the complexity of the Latino community in the United States. This study is long overdue, given the dramatic changes that have taken place over the course of the twentieth century. The Latino community for all too long has remained invisible and forgotten in society's attempt to address civil rights. Ultimately, to ensure racial justice and to avoid civil unrest and mass discontent, we must address the grievances of the Latino community. The alternatives, including the outburst of violence seen in the wake of the Rodney King verdict in 1992, should be sobering for us all. Only time will tell whether this nation will live up to its reputation as the bellwether of freedom, equality, and justice for all.

Notes

Preface

1. Jerome McCristal Culp, Jr., "Autobiography and Legal Scholarship and Teaching: Finding the Me in the Legal Academy," *Virginia Law Review* 77 (1991): 539, 540.

2. For example, Professor Stephen Carter found it necessarily to correct his understanding of an event central to his book's analysis of affirmative action. Stephen L. Carter, *Reflections of an Affirmative Action Baby* (New York: Basic Books, 1991), pp. 47–69. See also Stephen L. Carter, "'Best Black' Syndrome: My Bitter Memory; Somehow, for 20 Years, I Was Haunted by a Slight that Never Happened," *Washington Post,* Oct. 13, 1991, p. C5.

Chapter 1 Introduction

1. The irony did not escape me that he recently had visited Texas, "long considered [Chicanos'] Mississippi" (Michael A. Olivas, "Torching Zozobra: The Problem with Linda Chávez," *Reconstruction* 2 [1993]: 48, 50).

2. I say "inevitable" because jokes like these often are made in informal settings. See Richard Delgado, "Alternative Dispute Resolution Conflict as Pathology: An Essay for Trina Grillo," *Minnesota Law Review* 81 (1997): 1391, 1398.

3. This type of experience is not uncommon for racial minorities who "look" white. Judy Scales-Trent, for example, tells of an incident in which a cab driver made a racist comment in her presence. She observes that she is alert to such comments that call her identity into question (*Notes of a White*

Black Woman [University Park, Pa.: Pennsylvania State University Press, 1995], p. 13). In a similar vein, Mary Coombs notes that "I find myself in the position to hear anti-Semitic remarks and jokes more easily because my name allows me to pass unless and until I consciously and explicitly 'come out'" ("Interrogating Identity," *Berkeley Women's Law Journal* 11 [1996]: 222, 240 n.97; *African-American Law & Policy Report* 2 [1996]: 222, 240 n.97).

4. Barbara J. Flagg analyzes the "transparency" of whiteness in "'Was Blind, But Now I See': White Race Consciousness and the Requirement of Discriminatory Intent," *Michigan Law Review* 91 (1993): 953, 957–58.

5. See generally Mari J. Matsuda et al., *Words That Wound: Critical Race Theory, Assaultive Speech, and the First Amendment* (Boulder: Westview, 1993).

6. I prefer the term Latino to "Hispanic," a term coined by the U.S. government for census purposes. See Angel R. Oquendo, "Re-Imagining the Latino/a Race," *Harvard BlackLetter Law Journal* 12 (1995): 93, 96–99. Suzanne Oboler analyzes various difficulties in the construction of Latino identities in *Ethnic Labels, Latino Lives: Identity and the Politics of (Re)Presentation in the United States* (Minneapolis: University of Minnesota Press, 1995). I use Latin*o* throughout this book for sake of simplicity, without meaning to marginalize Latin*as*.

7. For a critical view of autobiography in legal scholarship, see Anne M. Coughlin, "Regulating the Self: Autobiographical Performances in Outsider Scholarship," *Virginia Law Review* 81 (1995): 1229. For responses, see Richard Delgado, "Coughlin's Complaint: How to Disparage Outsider Writing, One Year Later," *Virginia Law Review* 82 (1996): 95; Jerome McCristal Culp, Jr., "Telling a Black Legal Story: Privilege, Authenticity, 'Blunders,' and Transformation in Outsider Narratives," *Virginia Law Review* 82 (1996): 69; and Robert L. Hayman, Jr. and Nancy Levit, "The Tales of White Folk: Doctrine, Narrative, and the Reconstruction of Racial Reality," *California Law Review* 84 (1996): 377, 400 n.83, 429 n.158.

Despite the claims that autobiography is used by outside scholars for fame and fortune (see Coughlin, "Regulating the Self," pp. 1232, 1283–84), my instincts told me that this work would not enhance my career. Nonetheless, I believed it important to publish this book because it raises issues of general importance to the Latino community that have not been discussed in traditional legal scholarship. See also Susan Rubin Suleiman, *Risking Who One Is* (Cambridge, Mass.: Harvard University Press, 1994), p. 214: "The only kind of autobiography I find truly essential, to read *or* write . . . is the kind that tries to recover, through writing, an irrecoverable absence." Cf. Randall L. Kennedy, "Racial Critiques of Legal Academia," *Harvard Law Review* 102 (1989): 1745, 1810–19, where Kennedy explains why he rejected advice not to publish an article because of his belief in the need for full academic discussion of issues of race.

8. In "Some Thoughts on the Future of Latino Legal Scholarship," *Harvard Latino Law Review* 2 (1997): 101, I contend that Latino legal scholarship promises to change the fact that Latinos are forgotten in the constructive dialogue to improve race relations in the United States. Daniel A. Farber and Suzanna Sherry note that storytelling may be particularly useful as a way of filling informational gaps about lesbians and gays who are "closeted" and about whose lives information may be unavailable ("Telling Stories Out of School: An Essay on Legal Narratives," *Stanford Law Review* 45 [1993]: 807, 829n.119).

9. Mary Helen Ponce, *Hoyt Street* (Albuquerque: University of New Mexico Press, 1993), p. x.

10. See Linda Chávez, *Out of the Barrio* (New York: Basic Books, 1991) and Richard Rodriguez, *Hunger of Memory* (Boston: Godine, 1981).

11. Bureau of Census data show that the poverty rate among Hispanics in the United States has surpassed that of blacks and that Hispanics constitute almost one-fourth of all the poor in the nation (Carey Goldberg, "Hispanic Households Struggle Amid Broad Decline in Income," *New York Times*, Jan. 30, 1997, p. A1).

12. In "An Essay on Immigration Politics, Popular Democracy, and California's Proposition 187: The Political Relevance and Legal Irrelevance of Race," *Washington Law Review* 70 (1995): 629, I analyze the anti-Mexican, not just anti-"illegal alien," element of the Proposition 187 campaign in California.

13. See, e.g., David A. Hollinger, *Postethnic America* (New York: Basic Books, 1995) and Mary C. Waters, *Ethnic Options: Choosing Identities in America* (Berkeley: University of California Press, 1990).

14. See Philip Tajitsu Nash, "Multicultural Identity and the Death of Stereotypes," in *Racially Mixed People in America*, ed. Maria P. P. Root (Newbury Park, Calif.: Sage, 1992), p. 330: "Those of us with parents of two distinct 'racial' backgrounds are a visible reminder that *everyone* is multicultural and deserves to be treated as a multifaceted individual."

15. For the experiences of a mixed Anglo/Mexican American who is a self-proclaimed "güera," see Cherríe Moraga, *Loving in the War Years* (Boston: South End, 1983), pp. 50–59.

16. As this suggests, many persons categorize others by skin color. Bill Piatt recounts the story of President George Bush's referring to his grandchildren, who have a Mexican American mother, as "little Brown ones" (*Black and Brown in America* [New York: New York University Press, 1997], p. 158).

17. For a general discussion of the increasing number of mixed-race people in the United States, see Gabrielle Sándor, "The 'Other' Americans," *American Demographics,* June 1994, p. 36.

18. See James McBride, *The Color of Water* (New York: Riverhead, 1996), Scales-Trent, *Notes of a White Black Woman,* and Gregory Howard Williams, *Life on the Color Line* (New York: Dutton, 1995).

19. The Census Bureau projects that because of immigration and high fertility rates, Latinos will surpass African Americans as the largest minority group in the United States by 2005, and will constitute about one-fourth of the total U.S. population (Katharine Q. Seelye, "The New U.S.: Grayer and More Hispanic," *New York Times,* March 27, 1997, p. B16).

20. For data on the increasing rate of interracial marriages and children, see 62 Fed. Reg. 36,874, 36,901 (July 9, 1997).

21. Peggy C. Davis, in "Law As Microaggression," *Yale Law Journal* 98 (1989): 1559, 1561–62, analyzes the human need to categorize people in terms of race. Charles R. Lawrence III, in "The Id, the Ego, and Equal Protection: Reckoning With Unconscious Racism," *Stanford Law Review* 39 (1987): 317, 336–39, discusses the psychological phenomenon of "categorization" in the development of racial stereotypes. Linda Hamilton Kreiger contends that much modern discrimination can be explained by cognitive theory and unintentional categorization errors ("The Content of Our Categories: A Cognitive Bias Approach to Discrimination and Equal Employment Opportunity," *Stanford Law Review* 47 [1995]: 1161). Cf. John D. Ayer, "Isn't There Enough Reality to Go Around? An Essay on the Unspoken Promises of Our Law," *New York University Law Review* 53 (1978): 475, which analyzes generally the law's failure to consider the realities of human existence. For an analysis of the costs and benefits that categories may have on self-identity, see Ruth Colker, *Hybrid: Bisexuals, Multiracials, and Other Misfits under American Law* (New York: New York University Press, 1996), pp. 15–38.

22. In recognizing Latino diversity, I do not mean to question the intention

or results of affirmative action programs. Though far from perfect, these programs serve important functions. For an articulation of the affirmative action rationales for various minority groups, see Charles R. Lawrence III and Mari J. Matsuda, *We Won't Go Back* (Boston: Houghton Mifflin, 1997) and Paul Brest and Miranda Oshige in "Affirmative Action for Whom?" *Stanford Law Review* 47 (1995): 855. In "Understanding Affirmative Action," *Hastings Constitutional Law Quarterly* 23 (1996): 921, David Benjamin Oppenheimer argues for retaining affirmative action programs.

23. See Johnson, "Some Thoughts on the Future of Latino Legal Scholarship," pp. 127-29.The growing critical Latina/o, or LatCrit, theory movement in legal academia has focused attention on the treatment of Latina/os as foreigners. For important foundational readings on this and related subjects, see *The Latino/a Condition: A Critical Reader,* Richard Delgado and Jean Stefancic, eds. (New York: New York University Press, 1998), and Jean Stefancic, ""Latino and Latina Critical Theory: An Annotated Bibliography," *California Law Review* 85 (1997): 1509; *La Raza Law Journal* 10 (1998): 423.

24. Leslie Espinoza aptly captures the self-doubt experienced by a Mexican American who is successful by traditional standards: "My life is so surprising to me, so unexpected. It makes two things easier to believe: there are very few others like me, and because there are so few, my success must be a mistake, an aberration" ("Masks and Other Disguises: Exposing Legal Academia," *Harvard Law Review* 103 [1990]: 1878, 1884).

Chapter 2 A "Latino" Law Student? Law 4 Sale at Harvard Law School

1. Joel Seligman, *The High Citadel* (Boston: Houghton Mifflin, 1978), p. 5.

2. In comparison, a student entering law school in 1997 at U.C. Davis, a public school with relatively low fees, paid more than this.

3. See, e.g., Scott Turow, *One L: An Inside Account in the Life in the First Year at Harvard Law School* (New York: Putnam, 1977) and Richard D. Kahlenberg, *Broken Contract: A Memoir of Harvard Law School* (New York: Hill and Wang, 1992). In addition, a fictitious movie later made into a television series, "The Paper Chase," dramatized the life of a first-year law student at Harvard.

4. 97 F. Supp. 5 (D.P.R. 1951).

5. See, e.g., Margaret E. Montoya, "Mascaras, Trenzas, y Greñas: Un/Masking the Self While Un/Braiding Latina Stories and Legal Discourse," *Harvard Women's Law Journal* 17 (1994): 185, 201–9, and *Chicano-Latino Law Review* 15 (1994): 1, 18–26.

6. I define a Latino professor here as a professor on Michael Olivas's list of Latino law professors.

7. See Seligman, *High Citadel,* p. 7.

8. See *Regents of the University of California v. Bakke,* 438 U.S. 265, 313–20 (1978) (Powell, J.).

9. See Montoya, "Mascaras," pp. 191–92.

10. For the importance of community ties of minorities in the related area of faculty hiring, see Ian Haney López, "Community Ties, Race, and Faculty Hiring: The Case for Professors Who Don't Think White," *Reconstruction,* Winter 1991, p. 46.

11. For a discussion of why educational institutions benefit from over-inclusion in the definition of racial minorities for purposes of affirmative action, see John Martinez, "Trivializing Diversity: The Problem of Overinclusion in Affirmative Action Programs," *Harvard BlackLetter Law Journal* 12 (1995): 49.

12. J. Anthony Lukas documents this history through the lives of three families in *Common Ground: A Turbulent Decade in the Lives of Three American Families* (New York: Knopf, 1985).

13. See Ruth Marcus, "Black Law Group Supports Boycott of Harvard Course," *Washington Post,* Aug. 18, 1982, p. A3 and "Minority Groups Assail Course at Harvard Law," *Washington Post,* July 26, 1982, p. A5. There was only one tenured woman on the faculty at the time. One protester carried a sign proclaiming "One Tenured Black, One Tenured Woman—One Sorry Situation" (Ruth Marcus, "Law Students Divided: Course on Race Bias Stirs Row at Harvard," *Washington Post,* Jan. 13, 1983, p. A2).

14. Bell discusses this episode in *Confronting Authority: Reflections of an Ardent Protester* (Boston: Beacon, 1994).

15. "Notes from the Dean," *Harvard Law School Bulletin,* Spring 1983, p. 4.

16. See Marcus, "Law Students Divided," p. A2.

17. "Harvard Students Call for Affirmative Action," *New York Times,* Nov. 26, 1982, p. A17.

18. See Kimberlé Crenshaw, Neil Gotanda, Gary Peller, and Kendall Thomas, eds., *Critical Race Theory: The Key Writings That Formed the Movement*

(New York: New Press, 1995), p. xxi for a description of the class and its genesis.

19. For a summary of important works in the field, see Crenshaw et al., *Critical Race Theory* and Richard Delgado, ed., *Critical Race Theory: The Cutting Edge* (Philadelphia: Temple University Press, 1995). For sustained criticism, see Daniel A. Farber and Suzanna Sherry, *Beyond All Reason* (New York: Oxford University Press, 1997).

20. Cherríe Moraga, *The Last Generation* (Boston: South End, 1993), p. 145.

21. See Duncan Kennedy, "Legal Education as Training for Hierarchy," in *The Politics of Law*, ed. David Kairys (rev. ed.; New York: Pantheon, 1990), p. 38.

22. See Note, "In Defense of Tribal Sovereign Immunity," *Harvard Law Review* 95 (1982): 1058. Student notes in the *Harvard Law Review* are published without attribution of the student author.

23. *Connecticut v. Teal*, 457 U.S. 440 (1982) and *American Tobacco Co. v. Patterson*, 456 U.S. 63 (1982) are analyzed in Case Comment, "The Supreme Court, 1981 Term," *Harvard Law Review* 96 (1982): 278.

24. See ibid., p. 106, analyzing *Rogers v. Lodge*, 458 U.S. 613 (1982).

25. See Barack Obama, *Dreams from My Father: A Story of Race and Inheritance* (New York: Random House, 1995), p. 10. When Obama was elected president of the review, the media reported that he was black, despite his mixed-race background. See Anthony Flint, "First Black Chosen Head of Harvard Law Journal," *Boston Globe*, Feb. 6, 1990, p. 17.

26. See generally Eleanor Kerlow, *Poisoned Ivy: How Egos, Ideology, and Power Politics Almost Ruined Harvard Law School* (New York: St. Martin's, 1994).

27. See "Harvard Law Review Selects Minority Editors," *New York Times*, Oct. 10, 1982, p. 30.

28. Christopher D. Cameron, comments, *Harvard Law Review, Centennial Album* (1987): 47.

29. John O. McGinnis, comments, *Harvard Law Review, Centennial Album* (1987): 48.

30. Kathryn Hoff-Patrinos, comments, *Harvard Law Review, Centennial Album* (1987): 47-48.

31. "Notes from the Dean," *Harvard Law School Bulletin*, Spring 1982, p. 4.

32. See David E. Sanger, "A Vote But No Early Verdict at Harvard's Law Review," *New York Times*, May 10, 1981, sec. 4, p. 20.

33. Ibid.

34. Margot Slade and Eva Hoffman, "Ideas and Trends in Summary, Law Review's New Criteria," *New York Times,* Jan. 17, 1982, sec. 4, p. 6.

35. See ibid.

36. See "Harvard Law Review Selects Minority Editors," p. 30.

37. See Kerlow, *Poisoned Ivy,* p. 183.

38. *Harvard Law Revue,* April 16, 1983, p. 3 n.6, cites a fictitious publication entitled "Johnson, 'That Sobering Interview Process,' *Jack Dan. L. Rev.*"

39. Ibid., p. 13 n.6 (bold in original). To further belittle me, the parenthetical states that the book was written "under influence of cocaine."

40. Ibid., p. 13. In addition, I am listed on the back cover of the *Revue* as the author of an article entitled, "Why I'd Prefer a Course in Machine Shop to One in Federal Courts."

41. For a discussion of this event at Harvard Law School and the controversy it provoked, see Kerlow, *Poisoned Ivy,* pp. 169–98.

Chapter 3 My Mother: One Assimilation Story

1. For a literary account of losing touch with family and the blurring of family lines among Mexican farmworkers, see Helena María Viramontes, *Under the Feet of Jesus* (New York: Dutton, 1995).

2. Since I moved away in the 1970s, the racial mix of the San Gabriel Valley has changed significantly due to the settlement of Asian immigrants there. See National Board of Changing Relations Project, *Changing Relations: Newcomers and Established Residents in U.S. Communities* (New York: Ford Foundation, 1993) pp. 15–16, which observed demographic changes in Monterey Park, a city in San Gabriel Valley, as part of a study of conflict between minority groups. See also Robert S. Chang and Keith Aoki, "Centering the Immigrant in the Inter/National Imagination," *California Law Review* 85 (1997): 1395, 1417–46; *La Raza Law Journal* 10 (1998): 309, 331–360, for an analysis of the multiracial political dynamics of Monterey Park.

3. For an analysis of the images of mothers in Latin culture, see Elizabeth M. Iglesias, "Rape, Race, and Representation: The Power of Discourse, Discourses of Power, and the Reconstruction of Heterosexuality," *Vanderbilt Law Review* 49 (1996): 869, 915–29.

4. Stories play an important role in Mexican American culture. For stories told by Mexican American grandparents, see Yxta Maya Murray, "Merit-

Teaching," *Hastings Constitutional Law Quarterly* 23 (1996): 1073; Michael A. Olivas, "The Chronicles, My Grandfather's Stories, and Immigration Law: The Slave Traders Chronicle as Racial History," *St. Louis University Law Journal* 34 (1990): 425; and Christopher D. Cameron, "Border Views: Immigration Reform Bashes Mexican Americans," *El Paso Times*, April 24, 1994, p. 26.

5. Attempts by Mexican Americans to "pass" as white are not uncommon. "Some Mexicans, despite their strong indigenous faces, will confide that they have a French grandmother" (Rodolfo F. Acuña, *Anything But Mexican* [London, New York: Verson, 1996], p. 8). Mexican Americans in the Southwest often claim a "fantasy [Spanish] heritage" (Carey McWilliams, *North From Mexico* [rev. ed.; New York: Greenwood, 1990], pp. 43–53).

6. The efforts to "pass" as Spanish, in combination with a dislike for Mexican immigrants (see below), may reflect the self-hatred that sometimes motivates minority identification with the dominant group. See Gordon W. Allport, *The Nature of Prejudice* (Cambridge, Mass.: Addison-Wesley, 1979 ed.), pp. 150–53.

7. This is not to suggest that anti-Mexican sentiment is something of the distant past. For example, immigration restrictionists in the 1990s were motivated by a desire to reduce Mexican immigration. See below, chapter 10.

8. In Julia Alvarez's novel, *How the García Girls Lost Their Accents* (Chapel Hill, N.C.: Algonquin, 1991), pp. 98–99, a young Anglo tells his parents that his Latina friend is "Spanish." Rodolfo Acuña mentions efforts to characterize Mexican food and culture in Los Angeles as "Spanish" (*Anything But Mexican*, pp. 1–2).

9. Assimilationism of this kind unfortunately fits into a larger pattern among Mexican Americans in the Southwest: "Latina/o history is replete with stories about those who changed their names, lost the Spanish language . . . or deliberately married out of the culture. In short, some did whatever was necessary to be seen as not-different by the majority." Montoya, "Mascaras," p. 193. Oscar Martínez describes Mexican American assimilationists in *Border People* (Tucson: University of Arizona Press, 1994), pp. 93–95.

10. This experience is common. See, e.g., Steven W. Bender, "Consumer Protection for Latinos: Overcoming Language Fraud and English-Only in the Workplace," *American University Law Review* 45 (1996): 1027, 1032 n.17, and Christopher David Ruiz Cameron, "How the García Cousins Lost Their Accents: Understanding the Language of Title VII Decisions Approving English-Only Rules as the Product of Racial Dualism, Latino Invisibility, and Legal

Indeterminacy," *California Law Review* 85 (1997): 1347, 1364n.73; *La Raza Law Journal* 10 (1998): 261, 278n.73.

11. See Montoya, "Mascaras," pp. 189–90.

12. As this suggests, one way to assimilate is by adopting the dominant society's views about race. For example, Professor Gerald Torres's father, although he was personally discriminated against in buying a house, nevertheless voted for an initiative to repeal fair housing laws. Torres's story is recounted in Charles R. Lawrence III, "Foreword: Race, Multiculturalism, and the Jurisprudence of Transformation," *Stanford Law Review* 47 (1995): 819, 834–35.

13. In *The Politics of Experience* (New York: Pantheon, 1967), pp. 77–81, R. D. Laing explains the "double bind theory" of schizophrenia, which posits that being treated inconsistently, often by one's parents as a child, predisposes a person toward mental illness. In "Toward a Theory of Schizophrenia," *Behavioral Science* 1 (1956): 251, Gregory Bateson, Dan D. Jackson, Jay Haley and John Weakland define the "double bind" as "a situation in which no matter what a person does, he 'can't win.'"

14. Laing, *Politics of Experience,* pp. 78–79 (emphasis in original).

15. For an analysis of the role of gender and poverty in the psychological status of women, see Patricia Perri Rieker and M. Kay Jankowski, "Sexism and Women's Psychological Status" in *Mental Health, Racism, and Sexism,* ed. Charles V. Willie et al. (Pittsburgh: University of Pittsburgh Press, 1995).

16. For analysis of intersectionality, see Kimberlé Crenshaw, "Mapping the Margins: Intersectionality, Identity Politics, and Violence Against Women of Color," *Stanford Law Review* 43 (1991): 1241, and Angela P. Harris, "Race and Essentialism in Feminist Legal Theory," *Stanford Law Review* 42 (1990): 581.

Chapter 4 My Father: Planting the Seeds of a Racial Consciousness

1. For an analysis of the political evolution of Watson, who ran as the Populist candidate for President in 1904, see C. Vann Woodward, *The Strange Career of Jim Crow,* (2d rev. ed.; New York: Oxford University Press, 1966), pp. 89–99.

2. Years later at U.C. Berkeley, I took a course from Harry Edwards, a prominent sociologist who had been involved in organizing this historic

event. See generally Harry Edwards, *The Revolt of the Black Athlete* (New York: Free Press, 1969).

Chapter 5 Growing Up White?

1. For an introduction to Serrano, see Kevin R. Johnson, "Los Olvidados: Images of the Immigrant, Political Power of Noncitizens, and Immigration Law and Enforcement," *Brigham Young University Law Review* 1993 (1993): 1139, 1233–34.

2. See Bill Ong Hing, *To Be An American* (New York: New York University Press, 1997), pp. 37–43, for discussion of Padilla.

Chapter 6 College: Beginning to Recognize Racial Complexities

1. Richard Rodriguez describes a similar experience in self-identification, even after publicly voicing opposition to affirmative action. See Richard Rodriguez, *Hunger of Memory,* pp. 152–53.

2. In "'A People Distinct from Others': Race and Identity in Federal Indian Law and the Hispanic Classification in OMB Directive No. 15," *Texas Tech Law Review* 26 (1995): 1219, 1252-53, Luis Angel Toro discusses the phenomenon of "box checking" by persons falsely identifying themselves as belonging to a racial minority in order to obtain employment and educational benefits.

3. Murieta, a legendary figure (either a hero or a villain depending on the version of history one believes), was a gold miner killed by Anglos in Calaveras County, California. See Julian Samora and Patricia Vandel Simon, *A History of the Mexican-American People* (Notre Dame, Ind.: Notre Dame University Press, 1993), pp. 114–15 and Richard Rodriguez, *Days of Obligation* (New York: Viking, 1992), pp. 137–48.

4. Ruben Navarette, *A Darker Shade of Crimson* (New York: Bantam, 1993), p. 105.

5. Montejano later published an important book analyzing Mexican subordination in Texas. See David Montejano, *Anglos and Americans in the Making of Texas, 1836–1986* (Austin: University of Texas Press, 1987).

6. Mario Barrera, *Race and Class in the Southwest* (Notre Dame, Ind.: Notre Dame University Press, 1979).

7. See Mary C. Waters, *Ethnic Options,* p. 44.

Chapter 7 A Corporate Lawyer: Happily Avoiding the Issue

1. See David G. Savage, "Crusading Liberal Judge Keeps High Court Busy," *Los Angeles Times,* March 3, 1996, p. A3.

2. See Ana Puga, "Civil Rights Post Delights, Frustrates Deval Patrick," *Boston Globe,* Nov. 26, 1994, p. 1. As assistant attorney general, Deval was criticized for the highly publicized decision of the Justice Department to reverse its position in a "reverse discrimination" suit brought by a white teacher.

3. See Carole Hicke, *Heller Ehrman White & McAuliffe: A Century of Service to Clients and Community* (San Francisco: Heller Ehrman White & McAuliffe, 1991) pp. 3, 16–17.

4. See, for example, Gerald P. López, *Rebellious Lawyering* (Boulder: Westview, 1992); Michael A. Olivas, "'Breaking the Law' on Principle: An Essay on Lawyers' Dilemmas, Unpopular Causes, and Legal Regimes," *University of Pittsburgh Law Review* 52 (1991): 815.

5. Brief for Plaintiffs-Appellants, *Committee of Central American Refugees v. Immigration and Naturalization Service,* Case Nos. 85–2329, 85–2752, pp. 40–41 (Jan. 6, 1986).

6. For a discussion of the importance of terminology in the treatment of immigrants, see Kevin R. Johnson, "'Aliens' and the U.S. Immigration Laws: The Social and Legal Construction of Nonpersons," *University of Miami Inter-American Law Review* 28 (1996–97): 263.

7. See *Committee of Central American Refugees v. INS,* 795 F.2d 1434 (9th Cir. 1986), *as amended,* 807 F.2d 769 (9th Cir. 1987). In a case raising similar issues, a court permanently enjoined the Immigration and Naturalization Service from engaging in practices that discouraged Salvadorans in detention from applying for asylum, interfered with their right to counsel, and encouraged them to agree to "voluntarily" depart the country. See *Orantes-Hernandez v. Thornburgh,* 919 F.2d 549 (9th Cir. 1990).

8. Similarly, Bill Ong Hing, who grew up in a mixed community with many Mexican Americans in a small town in Arizona, describes affinities for Mexican immigrant clients. See Hing, *To Be An American,* p. 36.

9. See Marjorie Miller, "Right-Wing Salvadoran Politician Killed in Ambush," *Los Angeles Times,* Nov. 29, 1989, p. A5.

10. See Douglas Farah, "Left Killed Activist, Says Duarte," *Washington Post,* Jan. 6, 1988, p. A15.

11. See Arthur Golden, "Salvadoran Theologian Won't Be Frightened Into Leaving," *San Diego Union-Tribune,* Nov. 24, 1990, p. A2.

12. See Raymond C. Marshall, "Minority Hiring Made High Priority," *National Law Journal,* Oct. 23, 1989, p. S3.

13. See Jana Eisinger, "Firms Step Up Hiring Gay and Lesbian Lawyers," *New York Times,* Feb. 7, 1992, p. B6.

Chapter 8 A Latino Law Professor

1. Derrick Bell and Richard Delgado describe a similar incident in which a light-skinned Hispanic with a Spanish surname was asked at an interview "why she had indicated on her form that she was a Hispanic" ("Minority Law Professors' Lives: The Bell-Delgado Survey," *Harvard Civil Rights-Civil Liberties Law Review* 24 [1989] 349, 362). Berta Esperanza Hernandez Truyol relates a story about a Latina being interviewed for a teaching position who was questioned about her parents' professions and was told that Chicano students would be unable to relate to her ("Building Bridges—Latinas and Latinos at the Crossroads: Realities, Rhetoric, and Replacement," *Columbia Human Rights Law Review* 25 [1994]: 369, 408–10).

2. See Carter, *Reflections of An Affirmative Action Baby,* pp. 4–5.

3. A significant percentage of faculty members, particularly at the elite law schools, are hired more informally through word of mouth. See Martha S. West, "Gender Bias in Academic Robes: The Law's Failure to Protect Women Faculty," *Temple Law Review* 67 (1994): 67, 166–67.

4. In "Rodrigo's Tenth Chronicle: Merit and Affirmative Action," *Georgetown Law Journal* 83 (1995): 1711, 1713–14, Richard Delgado's fictional professor, Rodrigo, learns that he has been hired under a "special opportunity appointment" for minorities.

5. For survey results on the time pressures minority professors face because of committee responsibilities, see Bell and Delgado, "Minority Law Professors' Lives," pp. 349, 355–56, 363–64.

6. 438 U.S. 265 (1978).

7. See *Hopwood v. Texas,* 78 F.3d 932 (5th Cir.), *cert. denied, sub nom.,* 518 U.S. 1033 (1996).

8. For a description of the genesis and impact of the Regent's resolution, see Jeffrey B. Wolff, "Affirmative Action in College and Graduate Admissions," *SMU Law Review* 50 (1997): 627.

9. See *Coalition for Economic Equality v. Wilson,* 110 F.3d 1431 (9th Cir.), upholding the initiative in the face of equal protection challenge, *cert. denied,* 118 S. Ct. 397 (1997).

10. Susan Sturm and Lani Guinier make the case for an in-depth study of admissions criteria in "The Future of Affirmative Action: Reclaiming the Innovative Ideal," *California Law Review* 84 (1996): 953.

11. See Leslie G. Espinoza, "The LSAT: Narratives and Bias," *American University Journal of Gender & the Law* 1 (1993): 121, Daria Roithmayr, "Deconstructing the Distinction Between Bias and Merit," *California Law Review* 85 (1997): 1449; *La Raza Law Journal* 10 (1998): 363, and Sturm and Guinier, "The Future of Affirmative Action," pp. 968–97.

12. See, for example, Richard Delgado and Victoria Palacios, "Mexican Americans as a Legally Cognizable Class Under Rule 23 and the Equal Protection Clause," *Notre Dame Law Review* 50 (1975): 393; Johnson, "*Los Olvidados*"; George A. Martínez, "Legal Indeterminacy, Judicial Discretion and the Mexican-American Litigation Experience," *U.C. Davis Law Review* 27 (1994): 555; Montoya, "Mascaras,"; and Olivas, "The Chronicles, My Grandfather's Stories, and Immigration Law."

13. Symposium, "Difference, Solidarity, and Law: Building Latina/o Communities Through LatCrit Theory," *UCLA Chicano-Latino Law Review* 19 (forthcoming 1998); Symposium, "LatCrit: Latinas/os and the Law," *California Law Review* 85 (1997): 1087 and *La Raza Law Journal* 10 (1998):1; Symposium, "LatCrit Theory: Naming and Launching a New Discourse of Critical Legal Scholarship," *Harvard Latino Law Review* 2 (1997): 1; Colloquium, "International Law, Human Rights, and LatCrit Theory," *University of Miami Inter-American Law Review* 28 (1996–97): 177; Colloquium, "Representing Latina/o Communities: Critical Race Theory and Practice," *La Raza Law Journal* 9 (1996): 1.

14. For important foundational readings in the LatCrit movement, see Richard Delgado and Jean Stefancic, eds., *The Latino/a Condition.*

15. For a similar incident, see Bell and Delgado, "Minority Law Professors' Lives," pp. 349, 359. Derrick Bell has described an incident in which, during his visit at Stanford, students complained about his teaching and the law school responded by having other professors give lectures in his place. See Derrick Bell, *Confronting Authority,* pp. 115–16.

16. Other mixed Latinos no doubt have had similar experiences. Rachel F. Moran, for example, reports an incident in which a student told a Latina law

professor about a "rumor" that she was Latina and her explanation of her ancestry ("Full Circle," in *Critical Race Feminism: A Reader*, ed. Adrien Katherine Wing [New York: New York University Press, 1997], pp. 113–16).

17. For a similar incident, see Jennifer M. Russell, "On Being a Gorilla in Your Midst, or, The Life of One Blackwoman in the Legal Academy," *Harvard Civil Rights-Civil Liberties Law Review* 28 (1993): 259. Russell recounts the emotions of an African American law professor upon being confronted with a picture of a gorilla left anonymously in her faculty mailbox.

Chapter 9 My Family/Mi Familia

1. See Octavio Paz, *The Labyrinth of Solitude* (New York: Grove, 1961), p. 29: "The Mexican . . . seems to me to be a person who shuts himself away to protect himself: his face is a mask and so is his smile. . . . He is jealous of his own privacy and that of others. . . . The Mexican is always remote, from the world and from other people. And also from himself." See Richard Rodriguez, *Hunger of Memory*, pp. 176–82, for a similar description.

2. Margaret E. Montoya explains how, in a middle-class Mexican American family, a "pachuco" or "cholo" is a sign of deviance, delinquency, betrayal to family and community, and low class ("Lines of Demarcation in a Town Called Frontera: A Review of John Sayles' Movie 'Lone Star,'" *New Mexico Law Review* 27 [1997]: 223, 231).

3. James Brooke with David Barboza, "In Letters, Window on Life of the Unabom Suspect," *New York Times*, April 10, 1996, p. A1 (emphasis added).

4. See generally Kitty Calavita, *Inside the State: The Bracero Program, Immigration, and the I.N.S.* (New York: Routledge, 1992) for analysis of the "guest worker" program.

5. For a study of Mexican American women in the domestic service industry, Mary A. Romero, *Maid in the U.S.A.* (New York: Routledge, 1992).

6. See Kevin R. Johnson, "Free Trade and Closed Borders: NAFTA and Mexican Immigration to the United States," *University of California at Davis Law Review* 27 (1994): 937, 969 n.114.

7. I analyze the significance of this horrible incident in Kevin R. Johnson, "Some Thoughts on the Future of Latino Legal Scholarship," *Harvard Latino Law Review* 2 (1997): 123–125.

8. Ruth Frankenberg, *White Women, Race Matters* (Minneapolis: University of Minnesota Press, 1993), p. 130.

9. See Michael Scaperlanda, "Who is My Neighbor? An Essay on Immigrants, Welfare Reform, and the Constitution," *Connecticut Law Review* 29 (1997): 1587, for a discussion of the relationship between immigration reforms and Catholic theology.

10. For a negative description of *La Placita* as a haven for "illegal" immigrants, see Peter Skerry, *Mexican Americans: The Ambivalent Minority* (New York: Free Press, 1993), pp. 61–62.

Chapter 10 Lessons for Latino Assimilation

1. See Kevin R. Johnson, "Civil Rights and Immigration: Challenges for the Latino Community in the Twenty-First Century," *La Raza Law Journal* 8 (1995): 42, 67–72. See generally Milton M. Gordon, *Assimilation in American Life* (New York: Oxford University Press, 1964), for a historical analysis of assimilation in the United States.

2. See Kenneth L. Karst, *Belonging to America* (New Haven, Conn.: Yale University Press, 1989), pp. 83–84; William M. Newman, *American Pluralism* (New York: Harper and Row, 1973), p. 59. See also Sylvia R. Lazos Vargas, "Deconstructing Homo[geneous] Americanus: The White Ethnic Immigrant and Its Exclusionary Effect," *Tulane Law Review* 71 (1998): 1493, which analyzes the assimilation mandate that U.S. society imposes on racial minorities as part of the cultural myth of homogeneity.

For a highly romanticized view of immigrant assimilation, see Peter D. Salins, *Assimilation, American Style* (New York: Basic Books, 1997). On the issue of speaking English, see Arthur M. Schlesinger, Jr.'s *The Disuniting of America* (New York: Norton, 1992), pp. 107–10. Schlesinger criticizes bilingual education as the result of a "flood of immigration from Spanish-speaking countries" and emphasizes that "a common language is a necessary bond of national cohesion." Bill Ong Hing analyzes the tension between pro-assimilationists and cultural pluralists in "Beyond the Rhetoric of Assimilation and Cultural Pluralism: Separatism and Conflict in an Immigration-Driven Society," *California Law Review* 81 (1993): 863.

3. See, e.g., George A. Martínez, "Latinos, Assimilation, and the Law: A Philosophical Perspective," (unpublished manuscript on file with the author). See also John O. Calmore, "Random Notes of an Integration Warrior," *Minnesota Law Review* 81 (1997): 1441, 1474–76, which characterizes multiculturalism as the rejection of assimilation.

4. See Lazos, "Deconstructing Homo[geneous] Americanus," for a discussion of critiques of assimilation in social science literature.

5. Martínez, "Latinos, Assimilation, and the Law."

6. See Nathan Glazer and Daniel P. Moynihan, *Beyond the Melting Pot* (2d ed.; Cambridge, Mass.: MIT Press, 1970) p. xxxiii. Glazer and Moynihan note that each immigrant ethnic group brought a distinctive culture that was shaped by U.S. culture to forge a new identity.

7. See generally Oscar Handlin, *The Uprooted* (2d ed.; Boston: Little, Brown, 1973), which documents these difficulties.

8. See Karst, *Belonging to America*, pp. 81–104.

9. Cf. Nathan Glazer, *We Are All Multiculturalists Now* (Cambridge, Mass.: Harvard University Press, 1997), pp. 114–15, which recognizes that racial difference has made African American assimilation close to impossible. For further exploration of this theme, see Kevin R. Johnson, "The New Nativism: Something Old, Something New, Something Borrowed, Something Blue," in *Immigrants Out! The New Nativism and the Anti-Immigrant Impulse in the United States*, ed. Juan F. Perea (New York: New York University Press, 1997), p. 165.

10. See generally Ronald Takaki, *Strangers From a Different Shore* (Boston: Little, Brown, 1989), pp. 79–131, which recounts the history of Chinese immigration to the United States.

11. The Chinese Exclusion Case (*Chae Chan Ping v. United States*), 130 U.S. 581, 595 (1889).

12. *Hirabayashi v. United States*, 320 U.S. 81, 96 (1943). For a discussion of how some of these stereotypes survive to this day, see Robert S. Chang, "Toward an Asian American Legal Scholarship: Critical Race Theory, Post-Structuralism, and Narrative Space," *California Law Review* 81 (1993): 1241, 1252–58; *Asian Law Journal* 1 (1993): 1, 12–19.

13. See Carlos Villarreal, "Culture in Lawmaking: A Chicano Perspective," *U.C. Davis Law Review* 24 (1991): 1193, 1196–1215 for an analysis of the psychological and other costs on Chicanos exacted by assimilation pressures. See also Rachel F. Moran, "Foreword—Demography and Distrust: The Latino Challenge to Civil Rights and Immigration Policy in the 1990s and Beyond," *La Raza Law Journal* 8 (1995): 1, 13–24, which contrasts the immigration experience of Latinos with that of other groups and notes the emergence of a transnational identity among some Latin American immigrants, particularly those from Mexico.

14. See, e.g., Kevin R. Johnson, "Some Thoughts on the Future of Latino Legal Scholarship," pp. 118–19, which describes an incident in which Latino member of Congress Luis Gutierrez was told by a law enforcement officer at the Capitol to go back to where he came from and discusses generally the treatment of Latinos as foreigners; Kevin R. Johnson, "Free Trade and Closed Borders," pp. 949–50, which recounts an incident at a conference where a fifth-generation Chicano speaking on human rights abuses along the U.S.-Mexico border was asked by a person in the audience why, if things were so bad in this country, he did not go "back" to Mexico.

15. See generally George J. Sánchez, *Becoming Mexican American* (New York: Oxford University Press, 1993), which analyzes Mexican cultural adaptation in Los Angeles in the face of a lack of economic mobility. See also Toro, "'A People Distinct from Others,'" pp. 1250–51, which reviews the evidence of a lack of Latino assimilation.

16. See Hing, *To Be an American,* pp. 19–20, which describes Americanization campaigns of the early twentieth century. The United States Commission on Immigration Reform recently recommended that the Immigration and Naturalization Service pursue "Americanization" efforts by promoting naturalization. See U.S. Commission on Immigration Reform, *Legal Immigration: Setting Priorities* (Washington, D.C.: U.S. Government Printing Office, 1995), pp. 175–200.

17. See, e.g., Chávez, *Out of the Barrio,* pp. 139–40.

18. See, e.g., Peter Brimelow, *Alien Nation* (New York: Random House, 1995), which advocates a drastic reduction in immigration levels because of the alleged failure of non-Anglo Saxon immigrants to assimilate, and Richard D. Lamm and Gary Imhoff, *The Immigration Time Bomb* (New York: Truman Talley, 1985) pp. 76–98, which contends that Latin American and other immigrants do not assimilate, thus causing a "splintered society."

19. See Chávez, *Out of the Barrio* and Rodriguez, *Hunger of Memory.*

20. See Rodolfo O. de la Garza et al., *Latino Voices* (Boulder: Westview, 1992), p. 42, which reports survey results showing that over 60 percent of U.S.-born Mexican Americans speak only English or more English than Spanish in the home.

21. See David E. Hayes-Bautista et al., *No Longer a Minority* (Los Angeles: UCLA Chicano Studies Research Center, 1992), p. 11, fig. 2, which presents labor market participation data from 1940–1990.

22. Ibid., p. 33. See also Hing, "Beyond the Rhetoric," p. 877: "Study after

study demonstrates . . . that the vast majority of immigrants take on cultural traits of the host community."

23. Until 1965, the national origins quota system in the U.S. immigration laws limited immigration from many developing, non-white nations and favored immigration from northwestern Europe. See Stephen H. Legomsky, "Immigration, Equality and Diversity," *Columbia Journal of Transnational Law* 31 (1993): 319, 326–30. Lifting the quotas in 1965 allowed a more diverse group of immigrants to come to the United States. See Jeffrey S. Passel and Barry Edmonston, "Immigration and Race: Recent Trends in Immigration to the United States," *Immigration and Ethnicity,* ed. Barry Edmonston and Jeffrey S. Passel, 1994, p. 31.

24. Asian Americans also are frequently categorized as "foreign." See Pat K. Chew, "Asian Americans: The 'Reticent' Minority and Their Paradoxes," *William & Mary Law Review* 36 (1994): 1, 33–38; Cynthia Kwei Yung Lee, "Race and Self-Defense: Toward a Normative Conception of Reasonableness," *Minnesota Law Review* 81 (1996): 367, 429–38, 441–52.

25. Chávez describes this incident in *Out of the Barrio,* pp. 91–92.

26. See Margaret E. Montoya, "Mascaras," pp. 185, 192–201, 206–09. See also Leslie G. Espinoza, "Masks and Other Disguises," p. 1885: "Minority legal scholars, in order to get where they are, have spent a lifetime disguising their difference, hoping that the difference will not disqualify them from achievement."

27. Ruben Navarrette, Jr., in *A Darker Shade of Crimson,* pp. 117–38, describes the incident and discusses the heavy pressures on Chicanos at Harvard.

28. Hing, "Beyond the Rhetoric," pp. 891–92, notes that some African Americans, to avoid stress, prefer living in predominantly black communities over integrated ones.

29. Chester M. Pierce, in "Stress Analogs of Racism and Sexism: Terrorism, Torture, and Disaster in Mental Health," in *Mental Health, Racism, and Sexism,* ed. Charles V. Willie et al. (Pittsburgh: University of Pittsburgh Press, 1995), pp. 277, 281, states that "probably the most grievous of offensive mechanisms spewed at victims [of] racism and sexism are microaggressions . . . subtle, innocuous, preconscious, or unconscious degradations, and putdowns." Peggy C. Davis, in "Law as Microaggression," analyzes "microaggressions," subtle slights and putdowns of African Americans, and the perception of law as a series of microaggressions.

30. See María Cristina García, *Havana USA* (Berkeley: University of California Press, 1996), pp. 108–19. This may be in part because government assistance has been provided to political refugees from Cuba but has not been provided, for example, to Mexican immigrants. See Silvia Pedraza-Bailey, "Cuban Political Immigrants and Mexican Economic Immigrants: The Role of Government Policy in Their Assimilation," in *Hispanic Migration and the United States,* ed. Gastón Fernández et al. (Bristol, Ind.: Wyndham Hall, 1987), p. 68. Distinctions, however, should be made between different waves of Cuban immigrants. The Cubans who came before 1980, mostly upper class and white, experienced greater acceptance in the United States than Cuban immigrants who came over in the Mariel boatlift, which included a significant number of black Cubans.

31. Glazer and Moynihan, in *Beyond the Melting Pot,* pp. 86–136, analyze the assimilation difficulties Puerto Ricans have experienced in New York City. See also Chávez, *Out of the Barrio,* pp. 139–59, which discusses the "Puerto Rican exception" to Latino assimilation.

32. Samora and Simon, *History of the Mexican-American People,* p. 8.

33. Barbara J. Flagg, "'Was Blind, But Now I See,'" p. 957, analyzes the transparency concept. For a study of the construction of whiteness, see Ruth Frankenberg, *White Women, Race Matters;* Ian Fidencio Haney López, *White By Law* (New York: New York University Press, 1996); David Roediger, *Towards the Abolition of Whiteness* (London, New York: Verso, 1994).

34. Johnson, "Civil Rights," pp. 51–55, discusses the implications of low naturalization rates of Mexican immigrants on Latino electoral participation and suggests possible solutions. See also U.S. Department of Justice, *1994 Statistical Yearbook of the Immigration and Naturalization Service* (Washington, D.C.: U.S. Government Printing Office, 1996), p. 132, table K, which shows that, for immigrants admitted in fiscal year 1977, the naturalization rate was only 17.6 percent for Mexican immigrants compared to over 60 percent for immigrants from the Soviet Union, the Philippines, and China.

35. Rodolfo O. de la Garza and Louis DeSipio, in "Save the Baby, Change the Bathwater, and Scrub the Tub: Latino Electoral Participation After Seventeen Years of Voting Rights Act Coverage," *Texas Law Review* 71 (1993): 1479, 1511–13, analyze the negative impact of a large noncitizen population and high immigration levels on Latino electoral participation.

36. Richard Rodriguez, *Days of Obligation,* p. 50.

37. See generally David S. North, *The Long Gray Welcome* (Washington,

D.C.: NALEO Education Fund, 1985), which analyzes deficiencies in the naturalization process, and U.S. Commission on Immigration Reform, *Legal Immigration,* pp. 184–200, which recommends that the Immigration and Naturalization Service reduce delays in naturalization.

38. See Moran, "Foreword," pp. 13–24, for an analysis of this identity.

39. See Karst, *Belonging to America,* pp. 92–94.

40. Waters, *Ethnic Options: Choosing Identities in America.*

41. Kenneth L. Karst, "Myths of Identity: Individual and Group Portraits of Race and Sexual Orientation," *UCLA Law Review* 43 (1995): 263, 283–84.

42. Ian F. Haney López, "The Social Construction of Race: Some Observations on Illusion, Fabrication, and Choice," *Harvard Civil Rights-Civil Liberties Law Review* 29 (1994): 1, 47.

43. See ibid., p. 9; Karst, "Myths of Identity," p. 307. Although physical appearances may be changed to some extent, (see Haney López, *White By Law,* pp. 191–92), there are limits. Efforts to straighten one's hair, for example, will not change the fact for many African Americans that society treats them as blacks.

44. Berta Esperanza Hernández Truyol, in "Building Bridges—Latinas and Latinos at the Crossroads," p. 427, notes that some Latinos "appear 'white' in the 'Anglo' sense."

45. See Waters, *Ethnic Options,* pp. 37–38. Blacks and Mexican Americans gave a consistent response 94.2 percent and 88.3 percent of the time, respectively, while Irish gave a consistent response 57.1 percent of the time, and English, Scottish, and Welsh persons lagged behind that at 55.1 percent.

46. Ibid., p. 38, reports that over 96 percent of Puerto Ricans, over 88 percent of Mexicans, and over 83 percent of Cubans responded consistently to questions about ethnic identity.

47. See, e.g., Williams, in *Life on the Color Line,* who describes his experiences in this regard.

48. See, e.g., Michael A. Olivas, "The Education of Latino Lawyers: An Essay on Crop Cultivation," *Chicano-Latino Law Review* 14 (1994): 117, which presents data showing that despite affirmative action, there are relatively few Latinos teaching and studying law.

49. Haney Lopez, in *White By Law,* p. 192, acknowledges that one's choice of marriage partner may affect one's racial identity.

50. Johnson, "Civil Rights," pp. 67–72, analyzes Latino diversity.

51. Alejandro Portes, in "From South of the Border: Hispanic Minorities

in the United States," in *Immigration Reconsidered: History, Sociology, and Politics,* ed. Virginia Yans-McLaughlin (New York: Oxford University Press, 1990), p. 160, analyzes the diverse experiences of Mexican Americans, Puerto Ricans, and Cuban Americans in the United States. See also Alex M. Saragoza et al., "History and Public Policy: Title VII and the Use of the Hispanic Classification," *La Raza Law Journal* 5 (1992): 1, 3–4, 25–27, which notes the diversity among persons who fall within the category of "Hispanics" and the implications of this diversity.

There is heterogeneity in other minority communities as well. See generally William E. Cross, Jr., *Shades of Black* (Philadelphia: Temple University Press, 1991), which studies the diversity in the African American community, and Bill Ong Hing, *Making and Remaking Asian America Through Immigration Policy, 1850–1990* (Stanford, Calif.: Stanford University Press, 1993), which considers how immigration policies have affected development of various Asian American communities in United States.

52. For example, in California in 1990, 80 percent of the Latino population was Mexican American, compared to 2 percent Puerto Rican and 1 percent Cuban. See Fredric C. Gey et al., *California Latina/Latino Demographic Data Book* (Berkeley: California Policy Seminar, 1993), p. 9, table 1–3. Latino population demographics in Miami and New York City, for example, differ dramatically.

53. See Portes, "From South of the Border," pp. 160–61. See also Samora and Simon, p. 8, which observes "great diversity of physical, social, and cultural traits" among the Mexican American community, and Saragoza et al., "History and Public Policy," p. 4, which remarks that "there are no indelible physical characteristics, language, or cultural forms that are shared by all of the people south of the U.S.-Mexico border that would invariably unify them under one ethnic or racial term."

54. Alexander Rainof, in "How to Best Use an Interpreter in Court," *California State Bar Journal* 55 (1980): 196, mentions the existence of nineteen major Spanish dialects and offers examples of variations among them.

55. Several studies document the impact of phenotype on Latinos. Carlos H. Arce, Edward Murguia, and W. Parker Frisbie, in "Phenotype and Life Chances Among Chicanos," *Hispanic Journal of Behavioral Science* 9 (1987): 19, conclude that Mexican Americans with European physical appearance have better "life chances" than do Mexican Americans with indigenous features. Martha Menchaca, in "Chicano Indianism: A Historical Account of Ra-

cial Repression in the United States," *American Ethnologist* 20 (1993): 583, 599, scrutinizes the history of laws applied to Mexicans and concludes "that the skin color of Mexican-origin people strongly influenced whether they were to be treated by the legal system as white or as non-white." Edward E. Telles and Edward Murguia, in "Phenotypic Discrimination and Income Differences Among Mexican Americans," *Social Science Quarterly* 71 (1990): 682, find that although Mexican American incomes in all phenotypic groups lag far behind those of non-Hispanic whites, earnings of Mexican American males with dark and native American phenotype earn significantly less income than do lighter Mexican American males with a more European phenotype.

56. See J. Jorge Klor de Alva, "Telling Hispanics Apart: Latino Sociocultural Diversity," in *The Hispanic Experience in the United States,* ed. Edna Acosta-Belén and Barbara R. Sjostrom (New York: Praeger, 1988), pp. 106, 114. See, for example, *Gonzalez-Rivera v. INS,* 22 F.3d 1441, 1447 (9th Cir. 1994), the case in which the Border Patrol stopped an undocumented Mexican because of his "Hispanic appearance." In a related vein, Richard Rodriguez, in *Hunger of Memory* pp. 115–16, describes the harsh treatment given his darker-skinned sister in grade school and college, and her relief when her children were born with fair skin.

57. This incident is described in Lee Romney, "Over the Line?" *Los Angeles Times* (San Gabriel Valley ed.), Sept. 2, 1993, p. J1.

58. In Rick P. Rivera's *A Fabricated Mexican* (Houston: Arte Publico, 1995), pp. 79–81, a Mexican American accuses another man of being a *gabacho,* slang for Anglo. Richard Delgado, in "Rodrigo's Fourteenth Chronicle: American Apocalypse," *Harvard Civil Rights-Civil Liberties Law Review* 32 (1997): 275, 299, and n.115, mentions that *pocho* is Spanish slang for a person of Mexican ancestry "who does not speak Spanish and has lost touch with his or her roots."

59. Maria Cristina Garcia, in *Havana USA,* p. 68, notes that 15 to 40 percent of Marielitos were black, compared to 3 percent of 1959–73 immigrant population from Cuba. Earl Shorris, in *Latinos* (New York: Norton, 1992), p. 64, notes that the first wave of Cubans were mostly white and educated while many in the later group were black with limited education.

60. Elvia R. Arriola, "LatCrit Theory, International Human Rights, Popular Culture, and the Faces of Despair in INS Raids," *University of Miami Inter-American Law Review* 28 (1996–97): 245, 247 n.10.

61. For an analysis of Latino stereotypes in popular culture, see Clara E. Rodríguez, ed., *Latin Looks: Images of Latinos and Latinas in the U.S. Media* (Boulder: Westview, 1997).

62. See "Night Stalker Gets Death; 'You Don't Understand' Killer Says," *Los Angeles Times,* Nov. 7, 1989, p. P1.

63. For an optimistic appraisal of the potential for Cubans to join a broader coalition, see Max J. Castro, "Making Pan Latino: Latino Pan-Ethnicity and the Controversial Case of the Cubans," *Harvard Latino Law Review* 2 (1997): 179.

64. De la Garza et al., *Latino Voices,* p. 84, shows that at the time of the survey, 25.5 percent of Mexicans, 45 percent of Puerto Ricans, and 19.7 percent of Cubans surveyed earned less than $13,000 while 11 percent of Mexicans, 4.6 percent of Puerto Ricans, and 25.6 percent of Cubans earned in excess of $50,000.

Internal divisions exist within national origin groups as well, such as that between Mexican Americans and recent Mexican immigrants. See generally David G. Gutíerrez, *Walls and Mirrors: Mexican Americans, Mexican Immigrants, and the Politics of Ethnicity* (Berkeley: University of California Press, 1995), which analyzes the impact of Mexican immigration on the Mexican American community in the United States and discusses the existence of restrictionist sentiment among established Mexican Americans.

65. See de la Garza et al. *Latino Voices,* p. 84, which shows that 34.2 percent of Cubans surveyed, as compared to 15.4 percent of Mexicans and 22.7 percent of Puerto Ricans, identified themselves as "conservatives."

66. See Shorris, *Latinos,* pp. 181–82: "Third or fourth generation Latinos who live in suburbs of Minneapolis or Atlanta have no more reason to know Spanish than Polish-Americans need to know Polish or German-Americans to know German." See also Frank Valdes, "Foreword: Under Construction—LatCrit Consciousness, Community and Theory," *California Law Review* 85 (1997): 1087, 1127–32; *La Raza Law Journal* 10 (1998): 1, 41–46, for analysis of issues of essentialism raised by Spanish language usage among Latinos.

67. For an analysis of exit poll data, see Amy Pyle, Patrick J. McDonnell, and Hector Tobar, "Latino Voter Participation Doubled Since '94 Primary," *Los Angeles Times,* June 4, 1998, p. A1.

68. See Samora and Simon, *History of the Mexican-American People,* p. 8. For an analysis of some of the complexities Latinas face when they keep their own surnames, see Yvonne M. Cherena Pacheco, "Latino Surnames: Formal and Informal Forces in the United States Affecting the Retention and Use of the Maternal Surname," *Thurgood Marshall Law Review* 18 (1992): 1.

69. *United States v. Changco*, 1 F.3d 837, 841 n.1 (9th Cir.) (Kozinski, J.) (citation omitted), cert. denied, 510 U.S. 1019 (1993).

70. Nicolás Kanellos, *The Hispanic Almanac* (Detroit: Visible Ink, 1994), p. 201.

71. "Syndicated columnist Robert Novak Discusses President Clinton's Cabinet Choices," *Show: Equal Time* (CNBC News Transcripts), Dec. 16, 1996.

72. Jim Plunkett and Dave Newhouse, *The Jim Plunkett Story* (New York: Arbor House, 1981), pp. 19–20.

73. See Kanellos, *Hispanic Almanac*, p. 555.

74. See Toro, "A People Distinct," p. 1259, footnote citing "The Best and Worst of 1993," *Hispanic*, Dec. 1993, p. 22.

75. See Julian Samora, *Mestizaje: The Formation of Chicanos* (Stanford, Calif.: Stanford Center for Chicano Research, 1996), p. 9.

76. See Johnson, "Civil Rights," p. 82 n.200. Ironically, Sheen appeared sufficiently "white" to portray the famous Confederate General Robert E. Lee in the movie "Gettysburg," (Turner Home Entertainment 1993).

77. See Kanellos, *Hispanic Almanac*, p. 595.

78. According to Amy L. Unterburger et al., *Who's Who Among Hispanic Americans* (2d ed.; Detroit: Gale Research, 1992), p. 71, Linda Chávez, whose mother is Anglo, is married to Christopher Gersten.

79. See Olivas, "Education of Latino Lawyers," p. 129.

80. See Piatt, *Black and Brown in America*, p. 43.

81. See generally Gutierrez, *Walls and Mirrors*.

82. See Skerry, *Mexican Americans: The Ambivalent Minority*, pp. 217–49.

83. See Hayes-Bautista et al., *No Longer a Minority*, p. 34, for a summary of the quantitative data supporting this statement.

84. See Johnson, "Some Thoughts on the Future of Latino Legal Scholarship," pp. 117–29.

85. Cf. Kimberlé Williams Crenshaw, "Race, Reform, and Retrenchment: Transformation and Legitimation in Antidiscrimination Law," *Harvard Law Review* 101 (1988): 1331, 1336, which contends that "the Black community must develop and maintain a distinct political consciousness. . . . History has shown that the most valuable political asset of the Black community has been its ability to assert a collective identity and to name its collective political reality."

86. George A. Martínez, in "Legal Indeterminacy, Judicial Discretion and the Mexican American Litigation Experience," documents the failure of law and litigation to change the status of Mexican Americans in the United States.

See generally Richard Delgado and Jean Stefancic, *Failed Revolutions: Social Reform and the Limits of Legal Imagination* (Boulder: Westview, 1994), for a general analysis of the limits on achieving social change through law.

87. Charles R. Lawrence III, in "Foreword: Race, Multiculturalism, and the Jurisprudence of Transformation," pp. 828–47, analyzes the need for, as well as obstacles to, building multiracial coalitions.

88. *Metro Broadcasting, Inc. v. Federal Communications Commission,* 497 U.S. 547, 633 n.1 (1990) (Kennedy, J., dissenting) (citation omitted).

89. Questions about implementing affirmative action may become moot if the Supreme Court, as at least one court has, finds affirmative action to be unconstitutional. See *Hopwood v. Texas,* 84 F.3d 720 (5th Cir.), *cert. denied sub nom.*, 508 U.S. 1033 (1996). In any event, political forces may limit, if not abolish, affirmative action. See *Coalition for Economic Equity v. Wilson,* 110 F.3d 1431 (9th Cir.), *cert. denied,* 118 S. Ct. 397 (1997) (upholding California initiative prohibiting state's use of racial preferences); William H. Honan, "Admissions Change Will Alter Elite Campuses, Experts Say," *New York Times,* July 22, 1995, sec. 1, p. 7, which reports that the Board of Regents of University of California passed a resolution prohibiting the use of race in student admissions.

90. Brest and Oshige, in "Affirmative Action for Whom?" p. 890, suggest that different Latino national origin groups deserve different treatment in affirmative action programs for education.

91. See, e.g., Brimelow, *Alien Nation,* pp. 218–19; Richard D. Kahlenberg, *The Remedy* (New York: Basic Books, 1996), pp. 74–80, 114.

92. Kahlenberg, "The Remedy," raises issues surrounding immigrant eligibility for affirmative action. See also Peter H. Schuck, "Alien Rumination," *Yale Law Journal* 105 (1996): 1963, 2000–04. Michael Lind, in *The Next American Nation* (New York: Free Press, 1995), pp. 116, 131, suggests that "Hispanics" and immigrants should not be eligible for affirmative action. Frank H. Wu, in "The Limits of Borders: A Moderate Proposal for Immigration Reform," *Stanford Law & Policy Review* 7 (1996): 35, 51–54, analyzes the complex relationship between immigration and affirmative action debates in the modern United States. See Christopher Edley, Jr., *Not All Black and White* (New York: Hill and Wang, 1996), p. 174, for the argument that because of racism against blacks in United States, black immigrants should be eligible for affirmative action.

93. See Lawrence and Matsuda, *We Won't Go Back,* pp. 262–64.

94. Brimelow, *Alien Nation.* Skerry, in *Mexican-Americans,* pp. 308–09, criticizes the imprecision of the term "Hispanic." For a criticism of Brimelow's much-publicized book as an attack not only on immigrants but on all Latinos, see Kevin R. Johnson, "Fear of an 'Alien Nation': Race, Immigration, and Immigrants," *Stanford Law & Policy Review* 7 (1996): 111.

95. Cf. Harris, "Race and Essentialism in Feminist Legal Theory," which criticizes the gender essentialism in feminist legal theory that erases experiences of women of color.

96. Deborah Ramirez, in "Multicultural Empowerment: It's Not Just Black and White Anymore," *Stanford Law Review* 47 (1995): 957, 960–62, reviews demographic data showing that people of color increased from 10 to 25 percent of the U.S. population between 1960 to 1990.

97. Ibid.

98. Schuck, in *Alien Nation,* p. 1999, summarizes statistical data showing that intermarriage rates are increasing dramatically among various racial groups. It is important to keep in mind that intermarriage rates for Mexican Americans and Anglos vary regionally, with the border region having much lower rates than the interior. See Oscar Martínez, *Border People,* pp. 64, 325n.5.

99. See Ramirez, "Multicultural Empowerment," pp. 964–69, for a discussion of the practical issues raised by increasing numbers of multiracial persons. Alex M. Johnson, in "Destabilizing Racial Classifications Based on Insights Gleaned from Trademark Law," *California Law Review* 84 (1996): 887, analyzes the significance of the multiracial status of African Americans and contends that multiracial identity may destabilize the system of racial categorization. For a summary of the issues implicated by the growth in the multiracial population, see Bijan Gilanshah, "Multiracial Minorities: Erasing the Color Line," *Law & Inequality Journal* 12 (1993): 183.

100. See Richard Delgado, "Rodrigo's Fifteenth Chronicle: Racial Mixture, Latino-Critical Scholarship, and the Black-White Binary," *Texas Law Review* 75 (1997): 1181.

101. Neil Gotanda, "A Critique of 'Our Constitution is Color-Blind,'" *Stanford Law Review* 44 (1991): 1, 25; see Karst, "Myths of Identity," pp. 299–305.

102. See Everett V. Stonequist, *The Marginal Man* (New York, Chicago: C. Scribner's Sons, 1937), p. 24; Lawrence Wright, "One Drop of Blood," *New Yorker,* July 25, 1994, p. 46. See, for example, *Plessy v. Ferguson,* 163 U.S. 537,

541 (1896), the landmark case that rejected the equal protection claim of a person of seven-eighths white and one-eighth black blood. For the argument that the "one drop" rule helped build African American solidarity in the fight against racial injustice, see Christine B. Hickman, "The Devil and the One Drop Rule: Racial Categories, African Americans, and the U.S. Census," *Michigan Law Review* 95 (1997): 1161.

103. *In re* Knight, 171 F. 299, 301 (E.D.N.Y. 1909) (emphasis added). See Haney López, *White By Law,* p. 61, which analyzes *In re* Knight. See also George W. Gold, "The Racial Prerequisite in the Naturalization Law," *Boston University Law Review* 15 (1935): 462, 494–96, which summarizes case law analyzing whether "half-breeds" were white for purposes of naturalization.

104. Kevin R. Johnson, "Racial Restrictions on Naturalization: The Recurring Intersection of Race and Gender in Immigration and Citizenship Law," *Berkeley Women's Law Journal* 11 (1996): 142, 151, reviews the cases. There is one important exception to this rule. Due to obligations under treaties with Mexico, the one reported decision that addressed the question concluded that Mexican nationals (by definition of mixed race) were "white" and therefore eligible for naturalization. See *In re* Rodriguez, 81 F. 337 (W.D. Tex. 1897). See also George A. Martínez, "The Legal Construction of Race: Mexican Americans and Whiteness," *Harvard Latino Law Review* 2 (1997): 321, 326–27, which analyzes the importance of *Rodriguez* in analyzing race as a social and political construct.

105. See Herbert Hovenkamp, "Social Science and Segregation Before *Brown*," *Duke Law Journal* 1985 (1985): 624, 670: "The mulatto's plight was exacerbated because he was disowned by both races and regarded as a rootless, useless half-breed."

106. See ibid., pp. 655, 657: "In the scientific view of the day a racially mixed couple . . . [was] likely to produce inferior offspring that would be a lifetime burden on society and were guaranteed to weaken and contaminate both the white and the black races."

107. Cf. Richard J. Herrnstein and Charles Murray, *The Bell Curve* (New York: Free Press, 1994), which contends that race and intelligence are linked. In *Life on the Color Line,* p. 91, Greg Williams describes his reaction to watching a television broadcast of a Ku Klux Klan leader decrying the Supreme Court's decision in *Brown v. Board of Education,* 347 U.S. 483 (1954): "He claimed that the Supreme Court was encouraging 'race-mixing' and the only result would be the 'bestial mongrel mulatto, the dreg of human society.' His nasal repetition of 'mongrel mulatto' finally hit me like a thunderbolt. He was

talking about me. I was the Klan's worst nightmare. I was what the violence directed against integration was all about. I was what they hated and wanted to destroy."

108. T. J. Farnham, *Life, Adventures, and Travels in California* (New York: Cornish, Lamport, and Co. 1840), p. 413. For an analysis of Farnham's racialization of Mexicans, see Haney López, "Social Construction of Race," pp. 29–37. Guadalupe T. Luna, in "'Agricultural Underdogs' and International Agreements: The Legal Context of Agricultural Workers within the Rural Economy," *New Mexico Law Review* 26 (1996): 9, quotes Lothrop Stoddard's description of Mexican American workers: "The Mexican 'peon' (Indian or mixed-breed) is a poverty-stricken, ignorant, primitive creature, with strong muscles and with just enough brains to obey orders and produce profits under competent direction."

109. Julie C. Lythcott-Haims, "Where Do Mixed Babies Belong? Racial Classifications in America and Its Implications for Transracial Adoption," *Harvard Civil Rights-Civil Liberties Law Review* 29 (1994): 531, 540. See Ruth Colker, "Bi: Race, Sexual Orientation, Gender, and Disability," *Ohio State Law Journal* 56 (1995): 1, 12.

110. Colker ("Bi," pp. 64–67) analyzes the failure to account for mixed-race persons and the use of two categories for gender (man or woman), sexual orientation (homosexual or heterosexual), and disability (disabled or not). Kenneth E. Payson, in "Check the Box: Reconsidering Directive No. 15 and the Classification of Mixed-Race People," *California Law Review* 84 (1996): 1233, discusses the classification problems for mixed-race persons.

111. See Colker, "Bi," pp. 14–15; Ramirez, "'Multicultural, Empowerment," pp. 968–69 n. 154. See also 62 Fed. Reg. 36,874 (July 9, 1997), which requested comments on a report considering multiracial and related categorization issues for census purposes. For an analysis of the Bureau of the Census controversy and of multiracialism generally, see Tanya Katerí Hernandez, "'Multiracial' Discourse: Racial Classifications in an Era of Color-Blind Jurisprudence," *Maryland Law Review* 57 (1998): 97.

112. See Ramirez, "Multicultural Empowerment," p. 968. For a description of the political battle over creating a multiracial category, see Linda Mathews, "Beyond 'Other': More Than Identity Rides on a New Racial Category," *New York Times,* July 6, 1996, p. 1.

113. See Michael A. Fletcher, "Woods Puts Personal Focus on Mixed-Race Identity," *Washington Post,* April 23, 1997, p. A1.

114. See Mike Aitken, "Woods Savours Troon Test," *Scotsman,* May 2,

1997, p. 35 which mentions the racism directed at Woods as a child; Larry Dorman, "The 61st Masters," *New York Times,* April 14, 1997, p. C7, which describes racist hate mail directed at Woods as a professional golfer.

115. Cf. James W. Gordon, "Did the First Justice Harlan Have a Black Brother?" *Western New England Law Review* 15 (1993): 159, which contends that Justice Harlan, author of a dissenting opinion in *Plessy v. Ferguson* that decried the separate but equal doctrine endorsed by the majority, had a half-brother who was half-black. Gordon suggests that this relationship may have influenced Justice Harlan's more enlightened thinking on issues of race.

116. Nathan Glazer, in *We Are All Multiculturalists,* pp. 129–30, expresses hope for the assimilation of Asian Americans and Latinos due to the relatively high rates of intermarriage. Compare Jim Chen, "Unloving," *Iowa Law Review* 80 (1994): 145, which embraces an image of the United States as a "Creole Republic" in which increased intermarriage and multiracial children will promote racial harmony, with Peter Kwan, "Unconvincing," *Iowa Law Review* 81 (1996): 1557, which disputes that there is a basis for such hopes.

117. Carlos A. Fernández, "La Raza and the Melting Pot: A Comparative Look at Multiethnicity," in *Racially Mixed People in America,* ed. Maria P. P. Root (Newbury Park, Calif.: Sage, 1992), pp. 126, 139. Racial mixture is referred to in Spanish as *mestizaje.* See generally Julian Samora, *Mestizaje.* African American author Adrienne D. Davis, in "Identity Notes Part One: Playing in the Light," *American University Law Review* 45 (1996): 695, 697–99, describes her experience with racial fluidity in Nicaragua.

118. Martínez, in "Mexican-Americans and Whiteness," p. 343n.128, discusses Mexican philosopher José Vasconcelos' prediction of the emergence of a *raza cosmica.* Of course, racial stratification is linked to skin color and indigenous appearance in Latin America. See generally Magnus Mörner, *Race Mixture in the History of Latin America* (Boston: Little Brown, 1967).

119. See Rodriguez, *Days Of Obligation,* pp. 84–85.

120. This implies the existence of a loose racial hierarchy. See Johnson, "Racial Restrictions," pp. 150–51, 165–66. Natsu Taylor Saito, "Alien and Non-Alien Alike: Citizenship, 'Foreignness' and Racial Hierarchy in American Law," *Oregon Law Review* 71 (1997): 261, analyzes the importance of racial hierarchy in maintaining subordination of minority groups. But cf. Chew ("Asian Americans," pp. 87–89), who argues that a "race to the bottom" by different minority groups claiming greater disadvantage was "divisive" and "not constructive."

121. In *Notes of a White Black Woman,* pp. 95–98, Judy Scales-Trent notes that her great uncle left the family to pass as white. Patricia J. Williams, in *The Alchemy of Race and Rights* (Cambridge, Mass.: Harvard University Press, 1991), p. 223, relates the story of the light-skinned African American mother of one of her relatives who left the family to pass and marry a white man.

122. See Cheryl I. Harris, "Whiteness as Property," *Harvard Law Review* 106 (1993): 1707, 1710–12. Everett Stonequist, in *Marginal Man,* pp. 189–90, 193–99, mentions the psychological problems and mental conflicts resulting from "passing" and being mistaken for another race.

123. See Guillermo Lux and Maurilio E. Vigil, "Return to Aztlán: The Chicano Rediscovers His Indian Past," in *Aztlán,* ed. Rudolfo A. Anaya & Francisco A. Lomelí (Albuquerque, N.M.: Academia/El Norte, 1989), pp. 93, 97–98, which notes that some Chicano leaders are critical of Chicanos who claim to be Spanish. Bill Piatt, in *Black and Brown in America,* p. 157, offers his experiences about Mexican Americans attempting to pass as Spanish in New Mexico. Of course, matters are complicated in some places, such as northern New Mexico, where centuries ago Spaniards in fact settled. See George I. Sanchez, in *Forgotten People* (rev. ed.; Albuquerque, N.M.: C. Horn, 1967) p. 264. But cf. Oboler, *Ethnic Labels, Latino Lives,* pp. 25–26, which contends that "Spanish Americans" in New Mexico have a "fantasy heritage" of racial purity that is used to justify retention of power and status.

124. See Adrian Piper, "Passing for White, Passing for Black," *Transition* 58 (1992): 4.

125. Stephanie Wildman, in *Privilege Revealed* (New York: New York University Press, 1996), analyzes the hidden privilege attached to whiteness.

126. Lee May, "U.S. English Chief: Controversy Spoken Here," *Los Angeles Times,* Aug. 6, 1987, part 5, p.1 (quoting Chávez). Don Kowet, "She Would Bring Back Melting Pot," *Washington Times,* Jan. 9, 1992, p. E1 notes that Chávez said that her father descended from Spanish settlers of New Mexico.

127. See Hawthorne Daniel, *Judge Medina* (New York: W. Funk, 1952), pp. 11–12.

128. See Kanellos, *Hispanic Almanac,* pp. 242–43.

129. Louise Ann Fisch, *All Rise, Reynaldo G. Garza, The First Mexican American Federal Judge* (College Station, Texas: Texas A&M University Press, 1996) p. 177n.1.

130. For an analysis of the classification conundrums facing a family of mixed Indian, African, and European descendants as described in Piri Tho-

mas, *Down These Mean Streets* (New York: Knopf, 1967), see Haney López, "Social Construction," pp. 40–44.

131. Irene Sege, "Not Black Enough?" *Boston Globe,* Feb. 9, 1995, p. 63 discusses the controversy over the appointment of Professor Maria Hylton. See also Clint Bolick, *The Affirmative Action Fraud* (Washington, D.C.: Cato Institute, 1996), p. 18, which describes the incident in the context of a general attack on affirmative action. Gloria Sandrino-Glasser, in "Los Confundidos: De-Conflating Latinos/as' Race and Ethnicity," an unpublished manuscript on file with the author, pp. 24–33, discusses the history of Cuban migration to the United States and analyzes the conflation of race and national origin with respect to Cuban identity.

132. For responses to the charge that Maria Hylton was not a bona fide black, see Leonard M. Baynes, "Who is Black Enough for You? The Stories of One Black Man and His Family's Pursuit of the American Dream," *Georgetown Immigration Law Journal* 11 (1991): 97 and Leonard M. Baynes, "Who is Black Enough for You? An Analysis of Northwestern Law School's Struggle Over Minority Faculty Hiring," *Michigan Journal of Race and Law* 2 (1997): 205.

133. See generally Paul Spickard, *Mixed Blood* (Madison: University of Wisconsin Press, 1989), which studies intermarriage between white persons and Japanese Americans, Jewish Americans, and African Americans; Root, ed., *Racially Mixed People in America,* which compiles chapters on mixed-race persons generally, including some focusing on mixed-race Latinos; Naomi Zack, *Race and Mixed Race* (Philadephia: Temple University Press, 1993), which analyzes the experience of mixed black-white persons.

134. See, e.g., Lewis R. Gordon, "Critical 'Mixed Race,'" *Social Identities* 1 (1995): 381. For analysis of the burgeoning literature in Critical Multiracial Studies, see Jean Stefancic, "Multiracialism: A Bibliographic Essay and Critique in Memory of Trina Grillo," *Minnesota Law Review* 81 (1997): 1521.

135. See Williams, *Life on the Color Line;* Scales-Trent, *Notes of a White Black Woman.*

136. Trina Grillo, "Anti-Essentialism and Intersectionality: Tools to Dismantle the Master's House," *Berkeley Women's Law Journal* 10 (1995): 16, 22–23.

137. Leslie G. Espinoza, "Multi-Identity: Community and Culture," *Virginia Journal of Social Policy Law* 2 (1994): 23, 26.

138. Haney López, "Social Construction," p. 10.

139. See Yxta Maya Murray, "The Latino-American Crisis of Citizenship," *U.C. Davis Law Review* 31 (1998): 503.

140. Moran, "Full Circle," p. 113.

141. Terry Farish, "CHOICE Interviews: Bill Piatt," *CHOICE*, Feb. 1994, pp. 898–99.

142. Hernández-Truyol, *Building Bridges*, pp. 69–70. To complicate matters further, Latinos with parents of different national origin groups may have an additional set of issues with which to grapple. See Enid Trucios-Haynes, "The Legacy of Racially Restrictive Immigration Laws and Policies and the Construction of the American National Identity," *Oregon Law Review* 76 (1997): 369, 414–15 which describes the background of a Latina with a Puerto Rican mother and a father of Panamanian-Peruvian descent.

Chapter 11 What Does It All Mean for Race Relations in the United States?

1. For the argument that the treatment of African Americans is exceptional among minority groups in the United States, see Leslie Espinoza and Angela P. Harris, "Afterword: Embracing the Tar-Baby—LatCrit Theory and the Sticky Mess of Race," *California Law Review* 85 (1997): 1585, 1596–1605; *La Raza Law Journal* 10 (1998): 499, 510–519.

2. See generally Kevin R. Johnson, "Race, the Immigration Laws, and Domestic Race Relations: A "Magic Mirror" into the Heart of Darkness," *Indiana Law Journal* 73 (1998): 1111 analyzing the significance of racism to the history of U.S. immigration law and policy.

3. See generally Rodolfo Acuña, *Occupied America: A History of Chicanos* (New York: Harper and Row, 3d ed., 1988).

4. This argument is articulated more fully in Kevin R. Johnson, "Racial Hierarchy, Asian Americans, and Latinos as 'Foreigners,' and Social Change: Is Law the Way to Go?" *Oregon Law Review* 76 (1997): 347. For a philosophical analysis, see George A. Martinez, "African-Americans, Latinos, and the Construction of Race: Toward as Epistemic Coalition," *Chicano Latino Law Review* 19 (forthcoming 1998).

5. See generally Michael Omi & Howard Winant, *Racial Formation in the United States*. 2d ed. (New York: Routledge and Kegan Paul, 1944).

6. See generally Noel Ignatiev, *How the Irish Became White* (New York:

Routledge, 1995), which discusses the transformation of Irish immigrants from a separate "race" to part of the white "race," and John Higham, *Strangers in the Land: Patterns of American Nativism, 1860–1925.* 2d ed. (New Brunswick, N.J.: 1988), which summarizes how Jews were treated as a separate race during the wave of immigration restrictionism in the 1920s.

7. See George A. Martínez, "Mexican Americans and Whiteness."

8. See generally Lazos, "Deconstructing Homo[geneous] Americanus."

9. See Jane E. Larson, "Free Markets in the Heart of Texas," *Georgetown Law Journal* 84 (1995): 179, and Guadalupe T. Luna, "'Agricultural Underdogs,'" p. 9, both of which study the squalor of the *colonias* along the U.S.-Mexico border.

10. See generally José Cabranes, "Citizenship and the American Empire," *University of Pennsylvania Law Review* 127 (1978): 391, which details the U.S. government's resistance to affording full citizenship rights to Puerto Ricans.

Bibliography

Acosta-Belén, Edna, and Barbara R. Sjostrom, eds. *The Hispanic Experience in the United States*. New York: Praeger, 1988.

Acuña, Rodolfo. *Occupied America: A History of Chicanos*. 3d ed. New York: Harper & Row, 1988.

———. *Anything but Mexican*. London, New York: Verso, 1996.

Allport, Gordon W. *The Nature of Prejudice*. Cambridge: Addison-Wesley, 1979.

Almaguer, Tomás. *Racial Fault Lines: The Historical Origins of White Supremacy in California*. Berkeley: University of California Press, 1994.

Alvarez, Julia. *How the García Girls Lost Their Accents*. Chapel Hill, N.C.: Algonquin, 1991.

Anaya, Rudolfo A., and Francisco A. Lomelí, eds. *Aztlán*. Albuquerque, N.M.: Academia/El Norte, 1989.

Arce, Carlos H., Edward Murguia, and W. Parker Frisbie. "Phenotype and Life Chances Among Chicanos." *Hispanic Journal of Behavioral Science* 9 (1987): 19.

Arriola, Elvia R. "LatCrit Theory, International Human Rights, Popular Culture, and the Faces of Despair." *University of Miami Inter-American Law Review* 28 (1996–97): 245.

Ayer, John D. "Isn't There Enough Reality to Go Around? An Essay on the Unspoken Promises of Our Law." *New York University Law Review* 53 (1978): 475.

Barrera, Mario. *Race and Class in the Southwest: A Theory of Racial Inequality*. Notre Dame: Notre Dame University Press, 1979.

Bateson, Gregory et al. "Toward a Theory of Schizophrenia." *Behavioral Science* 1 (1956): 251.

Baynes, Leonard M. "Who Is Black Enough for You? The Stories of One Black Man and His Family's Pursuit of the American Dream." *Georgetown Immigration Law Journal* 11 (1991): 97.

———. "Who Is Black Enough for You? An Analysis of Northwestern Law School's Struggle Over Minority Faculty Hiring." *Michigan Journal of Race and Law* 2 (1997): 205.

———. "If It's Not Just Black and White Anymore, Why Does Darkness Cast a Longer Discriminatory Shadow than Lightness? An Investigation and Analysis of the Color Hierarchy." *Denver Law Review* 75 (1997): 131.

Bell, Derrick A., Jr. *Race, Racism and American Law.* 3d ed. Boston: Little, Brown, 1992.

———. *Confronting Authority: Reflections of an Ardent Protester.* Boston: Beacon, 1994.

Bell, Derrick A., Jr., and Richard Delgado. "Minority Law Professors' Lives: The Bell-Delgado Survey." *Harvard Civil Rights-Civil Liberties Law Review* 24 (1989): 349.

Bender, Steven W. "Consumer Protection for Latinos: Overcoming Language Fraud and English-Only in the Workplace." *American University Law Review* 45 (1996): 1027.

———. "Direct Democracy and Distrust: The Relationship Between Language Law Rhetoric and the Language Vigilantism Experience." *Harvard Latino Law Review* 2 (1997): 145.

Bolick, Clint. *The Affirmative Action Fraud.* Washington, D.C.: Cato Institute, 1996.

Brest, Paul, and Miranda Oshige. "Affirmative Action for Whom?" *Stanford Law Review* 47 (1995): 855.

Brimelow, Peter. *Alien Nation.* New York: Random House, 1995.

Brown, Kevin. "Do African-Americans Need Immersion Schools? The Paradoxes Created by Legal Conceptualization of Race and Public Education." *Iowa Law Review* 78 (1993): 813.

Brown v. Board of Education, 347 U.S. 483 (1954).

Cabranes, José. "Citizenship and the American Empire." *University of Pennsylvania Law Review* 127 (1998): 391.

Calavita, Kitty. *Inside the State: The Bracero Program, Immigration, and the I.N.S.* New York: Routledge, 1992.

Calmore, John O. "Random Notes of an Integration Warrior." *Minnesota Law Review* 81 (1997): 1441.

Cameron, Christopher David Ruiz. "How the García Cousins Lost Their Accents: Understanding the Language of Title VII Decisions Approving English-Only Rules as the Product of Racial Dualism, Latino Invisibility, and Legal Indeterminacy." *California Law Review* 85 (1997): 1347; *La Raza Law Review* 10 (1998): 261.

Carter, Stephen L. *Reflections of An Affirmative Action Baby.* New York: Basic Books, 1991.

Castro, Max J. "Making *Pan Latino:* Latino Pan-Ethnicity and the Controversial Case of the Cubans." *Harvard Latino Law Review* 2(1997): 179.

Chang, Robert S. "Toward an Asian American Legal Scholarship: Critical Race Theory, Post-Structuralism, and Narrative Space." *California Law Review* 81 (1993): 1241; *Asian Law Journal* 1 (1993): 1.

Chang, Robert S., and Keith Aoki. "Centering the Immigrant in the Inter/National Imagination." *California Law Review* 85 (1997): 1347; *La Raza Law Review* 10 (1998): 261.

Chávez, Linda. *Out of the Barrio.* New York: Basic Books, 1991.

Chen, Jim. "Unloving." *Iowa Law Review* 80 (1994): 145.

Cherena Pacheco, Yvonne M. "Latino Surnames: Formal and Informal Forces in the United States Affecting the Retention and Use of the Maternal Surname." *Thurgood Marshall Law Review* 18 (1992): 1.

Chew, Pat K. "Asian Americans: The 'Reticent' Minority and Their Paradoxes." *William and Mary Law Review* 36 (1994): 1.

The Chinese Exclusion Case (*Chae Chan Ping v. United States*), 130 U.S. 581, 595 (1889).

Cho, Sumi K. "Korean Americans vs. African Americans: Conflict and Construction." In *Reading Rodney King/Reading Urban Uprising,* edited by Robert Gooding-Williams. New York: Routledge, 1993.

Coalition for Economic Equality v. Wilson, 110 F.3d 1431 (9th Cir.), *cert. denied,* 118 S. Ct. 397 (1997).

Colker, Ruth. "Bi: Race, Sexual Orientation, Gender, and Disability." *Ohio State Law Journal* 56 (1995): 1.

———. *Hybrid: Bisexuals, Multiracials, and Other Misfits Under American Law.* New York: New York University Press, 1996.

Colloquium, "International Law, Human Rights, and LatCrit Theory." *University of Miami Inter-American Law Review* 28 (1996–97): 177.

Colloquium, "Representing Latina/o Communities: Critical Race Theory and Practice." *La Raza Law Journal* 9 (1996): 1.

Committee of Central American Refugees v. INS, 795 F.2d 1434 (9th Cir. 1986), *as amended,* 807 F.2d 769 (9th Cir. 1987).

Coombs, Mary. "Interrogating Identity." *Berkeley Women's Law Journal* 11 (1996): 222; *African-American Law & Policy Report* 2 (1996): 222.

Coughlin, Anne M. "Regulating the Self: Autobiographical Performances in Outsider Scholarship." *Virginia Law Review* 81 (1995): 1229.

Crenshaw, Kimberlé Williams. "Mapping the Margins: Intersectionality, Identity Politics, and Violence Against Women of Color." *Stanford Law Review* 43 (1991): 1241.

———. "Race, Reform, and Retrenchment: Transformation and Legitimation in Antidiscrimination Law." *Harvard Law Review* 101 (1988): 1331.

Crenshaw, Kimberlé et al., eds. *Critical Race Theory: The Key Writings That Formed the Movement.* New York: New Press, 1995.

Cross, William E., Jr. *Shades of Black.* Philadelphia: Temple University Press, 1991.

Culp, Jerome McCristal, Jr. "Autobiography and Legal Scholarship and Teaching: Finding the Me in the Legal Academy." *Virginia Law Review* 77 (1991): 539.

———. "Telling a Black Legal Story: Privilege, Authenticity, 'Blunders,' and Transformation in Outsider Narratives." *Virginia Law Review* 82 (1996): 69.

Daniel, Hawthorne. *Judge Medina.* New York: W. Funk, 1952.

Davis, Adrienne D. "Identity Notes Part One: Playing in the Light." *American University Law Review* 45 (1996): 695.

Davis, Peggy C. "Law as Microaggression." *Yale Law Journal* 98 (1989): 1559.

De la Garza, Rodolfo O. et al. *Latino Voices.* Boulder: Westview, 1992.

De la Garza, Rodolfo O., and Louis DeSipio. "Save the Baby, Change the Bathwater, and Scrub the Tub: Latino Electoral Participation After Seventeen Years of Voting Rights Act Coverage." *Texas Law Review* 71 (1993): 1479.

Delgado, Richard. "Words That Wound: A Tort Action for Racial Insults, Epithets, and Name-Calling." *Harvard Civil Rights-Civil Liberties Law Review* 17 (1982): 133.

———. "The Imperial Scholar: Reflections on a Review of Civil Rights Literature." *University of Pennsylvania Law Review* 132 (1984): 561.

———. "'The Imperial Scholar' Revisited: How to Marginalize Outsider Writing, Ten Years Later." *University of Pennsylvania Law Review* 140 (1992): 1349.

———. "Rodrigo's Tenth Chronicle: Merit and Affirmative Action." *Georgetown Law Journal* 83 (1995): 1711.

———. "Coughlin's Complaint: How to Disparage Outsider Writing, One Year Later." *Virginia Law Review* 82 (1996): 95.

———. "Rodrigo's Fourteenth Chronicle: American Apocalypse." *Harvard Civil Rights-Civil Liberties Law Review* 32 (1997): 275.

———. "Rodrigo's Fifteenth Chronicle: Racial Mixture, Latino-Critical Scholarship, and the Black-White Binary." *Texas Law Review* 75 (1997): 1181.

———. "Alternative Dispute Resolution Conflict as Pathology: An Essay for Trina Grillo." *Minnesota Law Review* 81 (1997): 1391.

———, ed. *Critical Race Theory: The Cutting Edge.* Philadelphia: Temple University Press, 1995.

Delgado, Richard, and Victoria Palacios. "Mexican Americans as a Legally Cognizable Class Under Rule 23 and the Equal Protection Clause." *Notre Dame Law Review* 50 (1975): 393.

Delgado, Richard, and Jean Stefancic, eds. *Failed Revolutions: Social Reform and the Limits of Legal Imagination.* Boulder: Westview, 1994.

———. *The Latino/a Condition: A Critical Reader.* New York: New York University Press, 1998.

Edley, Christopher, Jr. *Not All Black and White.* New York: Hill and Wang, 1996.

Edmonston, Barry and Jeffrey S. Passel, eds. *Immigration and Ethnicity.* Washington, D.C.: Urban Institute, 1994.

Edwards, Harry. *The Revolt of the Black Athlete.* New York: Free Press, 1969.

Espinoza, Leslie G. "Masks and Other Disguises: Exposing Legal Academia." *Harvard Law Review* 103 (1990): 1878.

———. "The LSAT: Narratives and Bias." *American University Journal of Gender and the Law* 1 (1993): 121.

———. "Multi-Identity: Community and Culture." *Virginia Journal of Social Policy Law* 2 (1994): 23.

Espinoza, Leslie G., and Angela P. Harris. "Afterword: Embracing the Tar-Baby—LatCrit Theory and the Sticky Mess of Race." *California Law Review* 85 (1997): 1585; *La Raza Law Journal* 10 (1998): 499.

Farber, Daniel A. "The Outmoded Debate Over Affirmative Action." *California Law Review* 82 (1994): 893.

Farber, Daniel A., and Suzanna Sherry. *Beyond All Reason*. New York: Oxford University Press, 1997.

———. "Telling Stories Out of School: An Essay on Legal Narratives." *Stanford Law Review* 45 (1993): 807.

Federal Register 62 (July 9, 1997), 36,874.

Farnham, T. J. *Life, Adventures, and Travels in California*. New York: Cornish, Lamport, and Co., 1840.

Fernández, Carlos A. "La Raza and the Melting Pot: A Comparative Look at Multiethnicity." In *Racially Mixed People in America*, edited by Maria P.P. Root. Newbury Park: Calif.: Sage, 1992.

Fernández, Gastón, ed. *Hispanic Migration and the United States*. Bristol, Ind.: Wyndham Hall, 1987.

Fisch, Louise Ann. *All Rise: Reynaldo G. Garza, The First Mexican American Federal Judge*. College Station: Texas A&M University Press, 1996.

Flagg, Barbara J. "'Was Blind, But Now I See': White Race Consciousness and the Requirement of Discriminatory Intent." *Michigan Law Review* 91 (1993): 953.

Foley, Neil. *The White Scourge: Mexicans, Blacks, and Poor Whites in Texas Cotton Culture*. Berkeley: University of California Press, 1997.

Ford, Christopher A. "Administering Identity: The Determination of 'Race' in Race-Conscious Law." *California Law Review* 82 (1994): 1231.

Frankenberg, Ruth. *White Women, Race Matters*. Minneapolis: University of Minnesota Press, 1993.

Funderburg, Lise. *Black, White, Other: Biracial Americans Talk About Race and Identity*. New York: William Morrow (1994).

García, María Cristina. *Havana USA*. Berkeley: University of California Press, 1996.

Gey, Fredric C. et al. *California Latina/Latino Demographic Data Book*. Berkeley: California Policy Seminar, 1993.

Gilanshah, Bijan. "Multiracial Minorities: Erasing the Color Line." *Law and Inequality Journal* 12 (1993): 183.

Glazer, Nathan. *We Are All Multiculturalists Now*. Cambridge: Harvard University Press, 1997.

Glazer, Nathan, and Daniel P. Moynihan. *Beyond the Melting Pot*. 2d ed. Cambridge: M.I.T. Press, 1970.

Gold, George W. "The Racial Prerequisite in the Naturalization Law." *Boston University Law Review* 15 (1935): 462.

Gonzalez-Rivera v. INS, 22 F.3d 1441 (9th Cir. 1994).
Gooding-Williams, Robert, ed. *Reading Rodney King/Reading Urban Uprising*. New York: Routledge, 1993.
Gordon, James W. "Did the First Justice Harlan Have a Black Brother?" *Western New England Law Review* 15 (1993): 159.
Gordon, Lewis R. "Critical 'Mixed Race.'" *Social Identities* 1 (1995): 381.
Gordon, Milton M. *Assimilation in American Life*. New York: Oxford University Press, 1964.
Gotanda, Neil. "A Critique of 'Our Constitution is Color-Blind.'" *Stanford Law Review* 44 (1991): 1.
Grillo, Trina. "Anti-Essentialism and Intersectionality: Tools to Dismantle the Master's House." *Berkeley Women's Law Journal* 10 (1995): 16.
Gutíerrez, David G. *Walls and Mirrors: Mexican Americans, Mexican Immigrants, and the Politics of Ethnicity*. Berkeley: University of California Press, 1995.
Handlin, Oscar. *The Uprooted*. 2d ed. Boston: Little, Brown, 1973.
Haney López, Ian Fidencio. "Community Ties, Race, and Faculty Hiring: The Case for Professors Who Don't Think White." *Reconstruction* (Winter 1991), p. 46.
———. "The Social Construction of Race: Some Observations on Illusion, Fabrication, and Choice." *Harvard Civil Rights-Civil Liberties Law Review* 29 (1994): 1.
———. *White by Law*. New York: New York University Press, 1996.
———. "Race, Ethnicity, Erasure: The Salience of Race to LatCrit Theory." *California Law Review* 85 (1997): 1143; *La Raza Law Journal* 10 (1998): 57.
Harris, Angela P. "Race and Essentialism in Feminist Legal Theory." *Stanford Law Review* 42 (1990): 581.
———. "Foreword: The Jurisprudence of Reconstruction." *California Law Review* 82 (1994): 741.
Harris, Cheryl I. "Whiteness as Property." *Harvard Law Review* 106 (1993): 1707.
Harrison, Melissa and Margaret E. Montoya. "Voices/Voces in the Borderlands: A Colloquy on Re-Constructing Identities in Re/Constructed Legal Spaces." *Columbia Journal of Gender and Law* 6 (1996): 387.
Harvard Law Review, Centennial Album (1987).
Hayes-Bautista, David E. et al. *No Longer a Minority: Latinos and Social Policy in California*. Los Angeles: UCLA Chicano Studies Research Center, 1992.

Hayman, Jr. Robert L., and Nancy Levit. "The Tales of White Folk: Doctrine, Narrative, and the Reconstruction of Racial Reality." *California Law Review* 84 (1996): 377.

Hernández, Tanya Katerí. "'Multiracial' Discourse: Racial Classifications in an Era of Color-Blind Jurisprudence." *Maryland Law Review* 57 (1998): 97.

Hernández-Truyol, Berta Esperanza. "Building Bridges—Latinas and Latinos at the Crossroads: Realities, Rhetoric, and Replacement." *Columbia Human Rights Law Review* 25 (1994): 369.

———. "Building Bridges: Bringing International Human Rights Home." *La Raza Law Journal* 9 (1996): 69.

———. "Borders (En)Gendered: Normativities, Latinas, and a LatCrit Paradigm." *New York University Law Review,* 72 (1997): 882.

Herrnstein, Richard J., and Charles Murray. *The Bell Curve: Intelligence and Class Structure in American Life.* New York: Free Press, 1994.

Hicke, Carole. *Heller Ehrman White & McAuliffe: A Century of Service to Clients and Community.* San Francisco: Heller Ehrman White & McAuliffe, 1991.

Hickman, Christine B. "The Devil and the One Drop Rule: Racial Categories, African Americans, and the U.S. Census." *Michigan Law Review* 95 (1997): 1161.

Higham, John. *Strangers in the Land: Patterns of American Nativism, 1860–1925.* 2d ed. New Brunswick, N.J.: Rutgers University Press, 1988.

Hing, Bill Ong. "Beyond the Rhetoric of Assimilation and Cultural Pluralism: Separatism and Conflict in an Immigration-Driven Society." *California Law Review* 81 (1993): 863.

———. *Making and Remaking Asian America Through Immigration Policy, 1850–1990.* Stanford: Stanford University Press, 1993.

———. *To Be an American.* New York: New York University Press, 1997.

Hirabayashi v. United States, 320 U.S. 81 (1943).

Hollinger, David A. *Postethnic America.* New York: Basic Books, 1995.

Hopwood v. Texas, 78 F.3d 932 (5th Cir.), *cert. denied, sub nom.* 518 U.S. 1033 (1996).

Horsman, Reginald. *Race and Manifest Destiny: The Origins of American Racial Anglo-Saxonism.* Cambridge: Harvard University Press, 1981.

Hovenkamp, Herbert. "Social Science and Segregation Before *Brown.*" *Duke Law Journal* 1985 (1985): 624.

Iglesias, Elizabeth M. "Rape, Race, and Representation: The Power of Discourse, Discourses of Power, and the Reconstruction of Heterosexuality." *Vanderbilt Law Review* 49 (1996): 869.

———. "International Law, Human Rights, and LatCrit Theory." *University of Miami Inter-American Law Review* 28(1996–97): 177.

Ignatiev, Noel. *How the Irish Became White.* New York: Routledge, 1995.

Johnson, Alex M. "Destabilizing Racial Classifications Based on Insights Gleaned from Trademark Law." *California Law Review* 84 (1996): 887.

Johnson, Kevin R. "*Los Olvidados:* Images of the Immigrant, Political Power of Noncitizens, and Immigration Law and Enforcement." *Brigham Young University Law Review* 1993 (1993): 1139.

———. "Free Trade and Closed Borders: NAFTA and Mexican Immigration to the United States." *U.C. Davis Law Review* 27 (1994): 937.

———. "Civil Rights and Immigration: Challenges for the Latino Community in the Twenty-First Century." *La Raza Law Journal* 8 (1995): 42.

———. "An Essay on Immigration Politics, Popular Democracy, and California's Proposition 187: The Political Relevance and Legal Irrelevance of Race." *Washington Law Review* 70 (1995): 629.

———. "Public Benefits and Immigration: The Intersection of Immigration Status, Ethnicity, Gender, and Class." *UCLA Law Review* 42 (1995): 1509.

———. "Fear of an 'Alien Nation': Race, Immigration, and Immigrants." *Stanford Law and Policy Review* 7 (1996): 111.

———. "Racial Restrictions on Naturalization: The Recurring Intersection of Race and Gender in Immigration and Citizenship Law." *Berkeley Women's Law Journal* 11 (1996): 142.

———. "'Aliens' and the U.S. Immigration Laws: The Social and Legal Construction of Nonpersons." *University of Miami Inter-American Law Review* 28 (1996–97): 263.

———. "Some Thoughts on the Future of Latino Legal Scholarship." *Harvard Latino Law Review* 2 (1997): 101.

———. "Racial Hierarchy, Asian Americans and Latinos as 'Foreigners,' and Social Change: Is Law the Way to Go?" *Oregon Law Review* 76 (1997): 347.

———. "The New Nativism: Something Old, Something New, Something Borrowed, Something Blue." In *Immigrants Out! The New Nativism and the Anti-Immigrant Impulse in the United States,* edited by Juan F. Perea, p. 165. New York: New York University Press, 1997.

———. "Race, the Immigration Laws, and Domestic Race Relations: A 'Magic Mirror' into the Heart of Darkness." *Indiana Law Journal* 73 (1998).

Kahlenberg, Richard D. *Broken Contract: A Memoir of Harvard Law School.* New York: Hill and Wang, 1992.

———. *The Remedy.* New York: Basic Books, 1996.

Kanellos, Nicolás. *The Hispanic Almanac.* Detroit: Visible Ink, 1994.

Karst, Kenneth L. *Belonging to America.* New Haven: Yale University Press, 1989.

———. "Myths of Identity: Individual and Group Portraits of Race and Sexual Orientation." *UCLA Law Review* 43 (1995): 263.

Kennedy, Duncan. "Legal Education as Training for Hierarchy." In *The Politics of Law,* edited by David Kairys, p. 38. 2d ed. New York: Pantheon, 1990.

Kennedy, Randall L. "Racial Critiques of Legal Academia." *Harvard Law Review* 102 (1989): 1745.

Kerlow, Eleanor. *Poisoned Ivy: How Egos, Ideology, and Power Politics Almost Ruined Harvard Law School.* New York: St. Martin's, 1994.

Klor de Alva, J. Jorge. "Telling Hispanics Apart: Latino Sociocultural Diversity." In *The Hispanic Experience in the United States,* edited by Edna Acosta-Belén and Barbara R. Sjostrom, p. 106. New York: Praeger, 1988.

Knight, *In re,* 171 F. 299 (E.D.N.Y. 1909).

Kreiger, Linda Hamilton. "The Content of Our Categories: A Cognitive Bias Approach to Discrimination and Equal Employment Opportunity." *Stanford Law Review* 47 (1995): 1161.

Kwan, Peter. "Unconvincing." *Iowa Law Review* 81 (1996): 1557.

Laing, R. D. *The Politics of Experience.* New York: Pantheon, 1967.

Lamm, Richard D., and Gary Imhoff. *The Immigration Time Bomb.* New York: Truman Talley, 1985.

Larson, Jane E. "Free Markets in the Heart of Texas." *Georgetown Law Journal* 84 (1995): 179.

Lawrence, Charles R., III. "The Id, the Ego, and Equal Protection: Reckoning With Unconscious Racism." *Stanford Law Review* 39 (1987): 317.

———. "Foreword: Race, Multiculturalism, and the Jurisprudence of Transformation." *Stanford Law Review* 47 (1995): 819.

Lawrence, Charles R., III, and Mari J. Matsuda. *We Won't Go Back.* Boston: Houghton Mifflin, 1997.

Lazarre, Jane. *Beyond the Whiteness of Whiteness: Memoir of a White Mother of Black Sons.* Durham: Duke University Press (1996).

Lazos Vargas, Sylvia R. "Deconstructing Homo[geneous] Americanus: The

White Ethnic Immigrant and Its Exclusonary Effect." *Tulane Law Review* 71 (1998): 1493.

Lee, Cynthia Kwei Yung. "Race and Self-Defense: Toward a Normative Conception of Reasonableness." *Minnesota Law Review* 81 (1996): 367.

Legomsky, Stephen H. "Immigration, Equality, and Diversity." *Columbia Journal of Transnational Law* 31 (1993): 319.

Lind, Michael. *The Next American Nation*. New York: Free Press, 1995.

López, Gerald P. *Rebellious Lawyering: One Chicano's Vision of Progressive Law Practice*. Boulder: Westview, 1992.

Lukas, J. Anthony. *Common Ground: A Turbulent Decade in the Lives of Three American Families*. New York: Knopf, 1985.

Luna, Guadalupe T. "'Agricultural Underdogs' and International Agreements: The Legal Context of Agricultural Workers within the Rural Economy." *New Mexico Law Review* 26 (1996): 9.

Lux, Guillermo, and Maurilio E. Vigil. "Return to Aztlán: The Chicano Rediscovers His Indian Past." In *Aztlán,* edited by Rudolfo A. Anaya and Francisco A. Lomelí. Albuquerque, N.M.: Academia/El Norte, 1989.

Lythcott-Haims, Julie C. "Where Do Mixed Babies Belong? Racial Classifications in America and Its Implications for Transracial Adoption." *Harvard Civil Rights-Civil Liberties Law Review* 29 (1994): 531.

Martínez, George A. "Legal Indeterminacy, Judicial Discretion and the Mexican-American Litigation Experience." *U.C. Davis Law Review* 27 (1994): 555.

———. "The Legal Construction of Race: Mexican-Americans and Whiteness." *Harvard Latino Law Review* 2 (1997): 321.

———. "Latinos, Assimilation, and the Law: A Philosophical Perspective." Unpublished manuscript.

———. "African-Americans, Latinos, and the Construction of Race: Toward an Epistemic Coalition." *Chicano Latino Law Review* 19 (1998).

Martínez, John. "Trivializing Diversity: The Problem of Overinclusion in Affirmative Action Programs." *Harvard BlackLetter Law Review* 12 (1995): 49.

Martínez, Oscar. *Border People*. Tucson: University of Arizona Press, 1994.

Matsuda, Mari J. "Public Response to Racist Speech: Considering the Victim's Story." *Michigan Law Review* 87 (1989): 2320.

Matsuda, Mari J. et al. *Words That Wound: Critical Race Theory, Assaultive Speech, and the First Amendment*. Boulder: Westview, 1993.

McBride, James. *The Color of Water: A Black Man's Tribute to His White Mother.* New York: Riverhead, 1996.

McWilliams, Carey. *North from Mexico,* rev. ed. New York: Greenwood, 1990.

Menchaca, Martha. "Chicano Indianism: A Historical Account of Racial Repression in the United States." *American Ethnologist* 20 (1993): 583.

Mirandé, Alfredo. *Gringo Justice.* Notre Dame: Notre Dame University Press, 1987.

———. *Hombres y Machos: Masculinity and Latino Culture.* Boulder: Westview, 1997.

Montejano, David. *Anglos and Mexicans in the Making of Texas, 1836–1986.* Austin: University of Texas Press, 1987.

Montoya, Margaret E. "Mascaras, Trenzas, y Greñas: Un/Masking the Self While Un/Braiding Latina Stories and Legal Discourse." *Harvard Women's Law Journal* 17 (1994): 185; *Chicano-Latino Law Review* 15 (1994): 1.

———. "Lines of Demarcation in a Town Called Frontera: A Review of John Sayles' Movie 'Lone Star.'" *New Mexico Law Review* 27 (1997): 223.

Moraga, Cherríe. *Loving in the War Years.* Boston: South End, 1983.

———. *The Last Generation.* Boston: South End, 1993.

Moran, Rachel F. "Foreword—Demography and Distrust: The Latino Challenge to Civil Rights and Immigration Policy in the 1990s and Beyond." *La Raza Law Journal* 8 (1995): 1.

———. "Full Circle." In *Critical Race Feminism: A Reader,* edited by Adrien Katherine Wing, p. 113. New York: New York University Press, 1997.

———. "Neither Black Nor White." *Harvard Latino Law Review* 2 (1997): 61.

———. "What if Latinos Really Mattered in the Public Policy Debate?" *California Law Review* 85 (1997): 1315; *La Raza Law Journal* 10 (1998): 229.

Mörner, Magnus. *Race Mixture in the History of Latin America.* Boston: Little, Brown, 1967.

Murray, Yxta Maya. "Merit-Teaching." *Hastings Constitutional Law Quarterly* 23 (1996): 1073.

———. "The Latino-American Crisis of Citizenship." *U.C. Davis Law Review* 31 (1998): 503.

Nash, Philip Tajitsu. "Multicultural Identity and the Death of Stereotypes." In *Racially Mixed People in America,* edited by Maria P. P. Root, p. 330. Newbury Park, Calif.: Sage, 1992.

National Board of Changing Relations Project. *Changing Relations: Newcomers and Established Residents in U.S. Communities.* New York: Ford Foundation, 1993.

Navarette, Ruben. *A Darker Shade of Crimson*. New York: Bantam, 1993.

Newman, William M. *American Pluralism*. New York: Harper and Row, 1973.

North, David S. *The Long Gray Welcome*. Washington, D.C.: NALEO Education Fund, 1985.

Nunn, Kenneth B. "Law as a Eurocentric Enterprise." *Law and Inequality Journal* 15 (1997): 323.

Obama, Barack. *Dreams From My Father: A Story of Race and Inheritance*. New York: Random House, 1995.

Oboler, Suzanne. *Ethnic Labels, Latino Lives: Identity and the Politics of (Re)-Presentation in the United States*. Minneapolis: University of Minnesota Press, 1995.

Olivas, Michael A. "The Chronicles, My Grandfather's Stories, and Immigration Law: The Slave Traders Chronicle as Racial History." *St. Louis University Law Journal* 34 (1990): 425.

———. "'Breaking the Law' on Principle: An Essay on Lawyers' Dilemmas, Unpopular Causes, and Legal Regimes." *University of Pittsburgh Law Review* 52 (1991): 815.

———. "Torching Zozobra: The Problem with Linda Chávez." *Reconstruction* 2 (1993): 48.

———. "The Education of Latino Lawyers: An Essay on Crop Cultivation." *Chicano-Latino Law Review* 14 (1994): 117.

Omi, Michael, and Howard Winant. *Racial Formation in the United States*. 2d ed. New York: Routledge and Kegan Paul, 1994.

Oppenheimer, David Benjamin. "Understanding Affirmative Action." *Hastings Constitutional Law Quarterly* 23 (1996): 921.

Oquendo, Angel R. "Re-Imagining the Latino/a Race." *Harvard BlackLetter Law Journal* 12 (1995): 93.

Orantes-Hernandez v. Thornburgh, 919 F.2d 549 (9th Cir. 1990).

Padilla, Laura M. "Intersectionality and Positionality: Situating Women of Color in the Affirmative Action Dialogue." *Fordham Law Review* 66 (1997): 843.

Passel, Jeffrey S., and Barry Edmonston. "Immigration and Race: Recent Trends in Immigration to the United States." In *Immigration and Ethnicity*, edited by Barry Edmonston and Jeffrey S. Passel, p. 31. Washington, D.C.: Urban Institute, 1994.

Payson, Kenneth E. "Check the Box: Reconsidering Directive No. 15 and the Classification of Mixed-Race People." *California Law Review* 84 (1996): 1233.

Paz, Octavio. *The Labyrinth of Solitude.* New York: Grove, 1961.

Pedraza-Bailey, Silvia. "Cuban Political Immigrants and Mexican Economic Immigrants: The Role of Government Policy in Their Assimilation." In *Hispanic Migration and the United States* edited by Gastón Fernández et al., p. 68. Bristol, Ind.: Wyndham Hall, 1987.

Penn, William S., ed. *As We Are Now: Mixblood Essays on Race and Identity.* Berkeley: University of California Press, 1997.

Perea, Juan F. "*Los Olvidados:* On the Making of Invisible People." *New York University Law Review* 70 (1995): 965.

———, ed. *Immigrants Out! The New Nativism and the Anti-Immigrant Impulse in the United States.* New York: New York University Press, 1997.

Piatt, Bill. *Black and Brown in America.* New York: New York University Press, 1997.

Piper, Adrian. "Passing for White, Passing for Black." *Transition* 58 (1992): 4.

Plessy v. Ferguson, 163 U.S. 537 (1896).

Ponce, Mary Helen. *Hoyt Street.* Albuquerque: University of New Mexico Press, 1993.

Plunkett, Jim, and Dave Newhouse. *The Jim Plunkett Story.* New York: Arbor House, 1981.

Portes, Alejandro. "From South of the Border: Hispanic Minorities in the United States." In *Immigration Reconsidered,* edited by Virginia Yans-McLaughlin, p. 160. New York: Oxford University Press, 1990.

Rainof, Alexander. "How to Best Use an Interpreter in Court." *California State Bar Journal* 55 (1980): 196.

Ramirez, Deborah. "Multicultural Empowerment: It's Not Just Black and White Anymore." *Stanford Law Review* 47 (1995): 957.

Regents of the University of California v. Bakke, 438 U.S. 265 (1977).

Rivera, Rick P. *A Fabricated Mexican.* Houston: Arte Publico, 1995.

Rodriguez, *In re,* 81 F. 337 (W.D. Tex. 1897).

Rodríguez, Clara E., ed. *Latin Looks: Images of Latinas and Latinos in the U.S. Media.* Boulder: Westview, 1997.

Rodriguez, Richard. *Hunger of Memory.* Boston: Godine, 1981.

———. *Days of Obligation.* New York: Viking, 1992.

Roediger, David. *Towards the Abolition of Whiteness.* London, New York: Verso, 1994.

Roitmayr, Daria. "Deconstructing the Distinction Between Bias and Merit." *California Law Review* 85 (1997): 1449; *La Raza Law Journal* 10 (1998): 363.

Román, Ediberto. "Common Ground: Perspectives on Latino-Latina Diversity." *Harvard Latino Law Review* 2 (1997): 483.

Romero, Mary. *Maid in the U.S.A.* New York: Routledge, 1992.

Root, Maria P.P., ed. *Racially Mixed People in America.* Newbury Park, Calif.: Sage, 1992.

Ruiz, Vicki. *From Out of the Shadows: Mexican Women in Twentieth-Century America.* New York: Oxford University Press, 1998.

Russell, Jennifer M. "On Being a Gorilla in Your Midst, or, The Life of One Blackwoman in the Legal Academy." *Harvard Civil Rights-Civil Liberties Law Review* 28 (1993): 259.

Saito, Natsu Taylor. "Alien and Non-Alien Alike: Citizenship, 'Foreignness' and Racial Hierarchy in American Law." *Oregon Law Review* 76 (1997): 261.

Salins, Peter D. *Assimilation, American Style.* New York: Basic Books, 1997.

Samora, Julian. *Mestizaje: The Formation of Chicanos.* Stanford: Stanford Center for Chicano Research, 1996.

Samora, Julian and Patricia Vandel Simon. *A History of the Mexican-American People,* rev. ed. Notre Dame: Notre Dame University Press, 1993.

Sánchez, George I. *Forgotten People,* rev. ed. Albuquerque, N.M.: C. Horn, 1967.

Sánchez, George J. *Becoming Mexican American.* New York: Oxford University Press, 1993.

Sándor, Gabrielle. "The 'Other' Americans." *American Demographics,* June 1994, p. 36.

Sandrino-Glasser, Gloria. "Los Confundidos: De-Conflating Latinos/as' Race and Ethnicity." Unpublished manuscript.

Saragoza, Alex M., et al. "History and Public Policy: Title VII and the Use of the Hispanic Classification." *La Raza Law Journal* 5 (1992): 1.

Scales-Trent, Judy. *Notes of a White Black Woman.* University Park, Pa.: Pennsylvania State University Press, 1995.

Scaperlanda, Michael. "Who is My Neighbor? An Essay on Immigrants, Welfare Reform, and the Constitution." *Connecticut Law Review* 29 (1997): 1587.

Schlesinger, Arthur M., Jr. *The Disuniting of America.* New York: Norton, 1992.

Schuck, Peter H. "Alien Rumination." *Yale Law Journal* 105 (1996): 1963.

———. "The Transformation of Immigration Law." *Columbia Law Review* 84 (1984): 1.

Seligman, Joel. *The High Citadel*. Boston: Houghton Mifflin, 1978.

Shorris, Earl. *Latinos*. New York: Norton, 1992.

Skerry, Peter. *Mexican Americans: The Ambivalent Minority*. New York: Free Press, 1993.

Spickard, Paul. *Mixed Blood*. Madison: University of Wisconsin Press, 1989.

Stefancic, Jean. "Multiracialism: A Bibliographic Essay and Critique in Memory of Trina Grillo." *Minnesota Law Review* 81 (1997): 1521.

———. "Latino and Latina Critical Theory: An Annotated Bibliography." *California Law Review* 85 (1997):1509; *La Raza Law Journal* 10 (1998): 423.

Stoddard, Lothrop. *Re-Forging America: The Story of Our Nationhood*. New York: C. Scribner's Sons, 1927.

Stonequist, Everett V. *The Marginal Man*. New York: C. Scribner's Sons, 1937.

Sturm, Susan, and Lani Guinier. "The Future of Affirmative Action: Reclaiming the Innovative Ideal." *California Law Review* 84 (1996): 953.

Suleiman, Susan Rubin. *Risking Who One Is*. Cambridge: Harvard University Press, 1994.

Suro, Roberto. *Strangers Among Us: How Latino Immigration is Transforming America*. New York: Knopf, 1998.

Symposium, "LatCrit Theory: Naming and Launching a New Discourse of Critical Legal Scholarship." *Harvard Latino Law Review* 2 (1997): 1.

Symposium, "Difference, Solidarity and Law: Building Latina/o Communities Through LatCrit Theory." *Chicano Latino Law Review* 19 (1998).

Symposium, "LatCrit: Latinas/os and the Law." *California Law Review* 85 (1997): 1087; *La Raza Law Journal* 10 (1998): 1.

Symposium, "The Meanings of Merit: Affirmative Action and the California Civil Rights Initiative." *Hastings Constitutional Law Quarterly* 23 (1996): 1115.

Takaki, Ronald. *Strangers from a Different Shore*. Boston: Little, Brown, 1989.

Telles, Edward E., and Edward Murguia. "Phenotypic Discrimination and Income Differences Among Mexican Americans." *Social Science Quarterly* 71 (1990): 682.

Thomas, Piri. *Down These Mean Streets*. New York: Knopf, 1967.

Toro, Luis Angel. "'A People Distinct from Others': Race and Identity in Federal Indian Law and the Hispanic Classification in OMB Directive No. 15." *Texas Tech Law Review* 26 (1995): 1219.

Trucios-Haynes, Enid. "LatCrit Theory and International Civil and Political Rights: The Role of Transnational Identity and Migration." *University of Miami Inter-American Law Review* 28 (1996–97): 293.

———. "The Legacy of Racially Restrictive Immigration Laws and Policies and the Construction of the American National Identity." *Oregon Law Review* 76 (1997): 369.

Tsuang, Grace W. "Assuring Equal Access of Asian Americans to Highly Selective Universities." *Yale Law Journal* 98 (1989): 659.

Turow, Scott. *One L: An Inside Account in the Life in the First Year at Harvard Law School.* New York: Putnam, 1977.

Unterburger, Amy L. et al. *Who's Who Among Hispanic Americans.* 2d ed. Detroit: Gale Research, 1992.

U.S. Commission on Immigration Reform. *Legal Immigration: Setting Priorities.* Washington, D.C.: U.S. Government Printing Office, 1995.

U.S. Department of Justice. *1994 Statistical Yearbook of the Immigration and Naturalization Service.* Washington, D.C.: U.S. Government Printing Office, 1996.

United States v. Changco, 1 F.3d 837 (9th Cir.), *cert. denied,* 510 U.S. 1019 (1993).

Valdes, Francisco. "Foreword: Poised at the Cusp: Lat Crit Theory, Outsider Jurisprudence and Latina/o Self-Empowerment." *Harvard Latino Law Review* 2 (1998): 1.

———. "Foreword: Under Construction—LatCrit Consciousness, Community, and Theory." *California Law Review* 85 (1997): 1087; *La Raza Law Journal* 10 (1998): 1.

Vasconcelos, José. *The Cosmic Race: A Bilingual Education.* Baltimore: John Hopkins University Press, 1997.

Villarreal, Carlos. "Culture in Lawmaking: A Chicano Perspective." *U.C. Davis Law Review* 24 (1991): 1193.

Viramontes, Helena María. *Under the Feet of Jesus.* New York: Dutton, 1995.

Waters, Mary C. *Ethnic Options: Choosing Identities in America.* Berkeley: University of California Press, 1990.

West, Martha S. "Gender Bias in Academic Robes: The Law's Failure to Protect Women Faculty." *Temple Law Review* 67 (1994): 67.

White, Lucie E. "Mobilization on the Margins of the Lawsuit: Making Space for Clients to Speak." *New York University Review of Law and Social Change* 16 (1987–1988): 535.

Wildman, Stephanie. *Privilege Revealed.* New York: New York University Press, 1996.

Williams, Gregory Howard. *Life on the Color Line.* New York: Dutton, 1995.

Williams, Patricia J. *The Alchemy of Race and Rights.* Cambridge: Harvard University Press, 1991.

Willie, Charles V. et al., eds. *Mental Health, Racism, and Sexism.* Pittsburgh: University of Pittsburgh Press, 1995.

Wolff, Jeffrey B. "Affirmative Action in College and Graduate Admissions." *SMU Law Review* 50 (1997): 627.

Woodward, C. Vann. *The Strange Career of Jim Crow.* 2d rev. ed. New York: Oxford University Press, 1966.

Wright, Lawrence. "One Drop of Blood." *New Yorker,* July 25, 1994, p. 46.

Wright, Luther, Jr. "Who's Black, Who's White, and Who Cares: Reconceptualizing the United State's Definition of Race and Racial Classifications." *Vanderbilt Law Review* 48 (1995): 513.

Wu, Frank H. "The Future of the American Mosiac: Issues in Immigration Reform." *Stanford Law and Policy Review* 7 (1996): 35.

———. "From Black to White and Back Again." *Asian Law Journal* 3 (1996): 185.

Yans-McLaughlin, Virginia, ed. *Immigration Reconsidered: History, Sociology, and Politics.* New York: Oxford University Press, 1990.

Zack, Naomi. *Race and Mixed Race.* Philadelphia: Temple University Press, 1993.

Index

Acuña, Rodolfo F., 191n
Affirmative Action, ix, 186–87n; benefits alleged from identifying as Latino, 90, 159–60, 172–73; box checkers and, 31–32, 172–73, 188n, 193n; benefits to educational institutions, 31–32, 188n; and importance of community ties, 188n (*see also* "Check-the-Box" minority); at educational and other institutions, 12; at Harvard Law School, 27–29 (*see also* Harvard Law School); immigrant eligibility for, 166–67, 208n; lawfulness of, 89, 195–6n, 208n; in legal academia, 110–11, 121–27, 128–31, 195n, 213–14n; overinclusion of minorities, 31–32, 188n; purposes, 31, 166–67; racial identification, impact on admission to universities, 12, 90–91, 188n (*see also* Racial Identity); end of, at University of California, 89, 128, 195n
African Americans, 27–29, 84, 112–13, 118, 129, 154, 158, 166, 169, 171, 175, 177, 199n, 207n, 212–13n; diversity among, ix, 204n; racism directed at, 32–33, 48, 81–83, 97, 127, 162, 197n, 210n, 210–11n; as exceptional, 215n; and legacy of slavery, 176–77, 180. *See also* Racism
Alianza, La (*Alliance, The*), 23, 29, 30; meeting with president about *Harvard Law Review* affirmative action, 45
Alien Nation (book), 167
Alvarez, Julia (author), 191n
American Civil Liberties Union, 35
"Americanization" programs, 153, 200n
Anaya, Herbert (human rights activist in El Salvador), 116
Anaya, Jim, 23
Arreola, Juan Sanchez, 141
Arriola, Elvia, 162
Asian Americans, 48, 137, 169, 176, 190n; assimilation of, 153, 154, 180–81; confusion about my identity as, 24–25, 82, 137; discrimination against, 48, 153, 176 (*see also* Racism); diversity among, 204n; friends in college, 93–94; as "model minority," 177; stereotypes of, 199n; at U.C. Berkeley, 93–94. *See also* University of California at Berkeley

Assimilation: "Americanization" programs to promote, 153, 200n; through Anglicizing Spanish surname, 56–57, 144, 191n (*see also* Surname, Spanish); Asian immigrants and Asian Americans 153, 176 (*see also* Asian Americans); historical analysis of, 198n; of immigrants, 152–54, 179–80, 198n; learning English, 139–40, 152, 191–92n, 198n; Latino, 1–9, 60–61, 152–74, 191n, 198n; of Latinos at Harvard Law School, 10–51, 29–32; limits on, 6, 9, 86, 88, 152–53, 154, 155–58, 180–81, 187n, 199n, 200n (*see also* Latinos and Latinas); and multiculturalism, 62, 152–53, 180, 198n; through marriage (*see* Intermarriage); deficiencies of "melting pot" or "tossed salad" metaphor, 62, 152–53; of minorities, 9, 155–56, 175–82, 198n; experiences of women, 9, 52–63; pain and suffering caused by, 52–63, 199n, 202n; changing physical appearance to further, 203n; adoption of society's racial attitudes, 58, 84–85, 86–87, 192n; "ring of fire" metaphor, 62–63; white ethnics, 6, 153–54, 179–80

Association of American Law Schools, 121, 122, 123–24, 132

Autobiography: difficulty in writing, xii–xiii; error in Stephen Carter's, 183n; legal scholarship in, 6, 184–85n; and race relations, ix, xii–xiii; and untold stories of Mexican Americans, xiii, 6

Azusa, California, 54, 69, 73, 74, 77, 78, 81, 139, 140, 142

Ballet Folklorico, 145

Barrera, Mario, 96

Bator, Paul, 49

Bell, Derrick, 34, 195n, 196n

Berkeley (California), 89, 91, 98; Telegraph Avenue, 91. *See also* University of California at Berkeley

Borton, Bob, x, 113

Boston, Massachusetts, racism in, 32–33. *See also* Racism

Bracero (guest worker) Program, 141–42

Brawley, California, 5, 53, 76, 114

Brimelow, Peter (*Alien Nation*), 167

Burger, Chief Justice Warren, 41

Burke, Yvonne Braithwaite, 112

Bush, George, 146, 186n

California "Civil Rights" Initiative, 89, 128

California Club, 36–37

California International Marathon (Sacramento), 3–4

California Rural Legal Assistance, 131

Cameron, Christopher David Ruiz, xi, 30, 42, 43–44, 46

Carr, Vikki (entertainer), 164

Carter, President Jimmy, 17–18

Carter, Stephen, 122, 183n

Castañeda, Jorge (Mexican intellectual), 162

Catholic Church, 53, 58–59, 68; in Azusa, 76; baptism of children in, 149–50; Catechism, 75; in El Salvador, 116; family relationship with, 148–50; immigration, 149, 198n; importance to Latino identity, 148–50, 166; liberation theology, 116; marriage in, 53, 67–68, 148

Census, U.S., classification of multiracial people, 8–9, 169, 179, 211n. *See also* Mixed-race people

Chambers, J. LeVonne, controversy over civil rights course at Harvard, 33–36

Chang, Robert S., xi, 190n
Chávez, César 47, 149
Chávez, Linda, views about "Hispanic" assimilation, 6, 154, 155, 179; classification as Latina, 172, 213n; mixed-race background, 207n; "Check-the-Box" minority, 172–73, 193n. *See also* Affirmative Action
Christmas, 14, 22, 99
Clifford, Charlie, x, 112
Clinton, President Bill, 34, 41, 177
Coleman, William T., 43
College, 89–100; academics, 92–93, 96–97; assimilation and Mexican Americans in, 95–96; assimilation and working class in, 98; education about status of Chicanos and minorities in United States, 96–97; graduation, 99; jobs during, 12, 97–99; interactions with Latinos during, 95–96; mixed-race student, 94–95; racial identification in, 90, 99–100; racial uncertainty during, 94–97
Conspicuous consumption, 36–38
Coombs, Mary, 184n
Cortez, Eddie, 161
Crenshaw, Kimberlé, 35
Critical Latino (LatCrit) theory, 132, 187n, 196n
Critical Legal Studies, 132
Critical "Mixed Race" Theory, 173, 214n
Critical Race Theory, 132, 189n; intersectionality concept, 192n
Culver City Star News (California), 53

Davis, Adrienne D., 212n
Davis, California, 125, 142. *See also* University of California at Davis
Davis Enterprise (Davis, California), 125
Delgado, Richard, x, xi, 35, 195n, 205n
Divorce, 53–54, 58–59, 74–75, 80–81. *See also* Gallardo, Angela (Angie [mother])
Donovan Leisure Newton & Irvine, 36–38. *See also* Law firms
Donovan, "Wild" Bill, 37
Dorsen, Norman, 35
Duarte, Lisa, xi
Dukakis, Michael, 42

East Los Angeles, 7, 69
East Side Journal (Los Angeles, California), 69
Edley, Chris, 34
Edwards, Harry, 96, 192–93n
Elena (daughter), xii, 3, 8, 63, 145, 146, 150–51, 159. *See also* Johnson, Elena (daughter).
El Salvador, 113, 115, 116
Enrich, Peter, 44
Ermer, Mike, 33
Estrich, Susan, 41–42

Farnham, T. J., racist views about persons of Mexican ancestry, 168–69, 211n
Farrakhan, Louis, 47
Fernandez, Anne, 95
Flagg, Barbara, on transparency of whiteness, 184n
Fong, Paul, 93
Frankenberg, Ruth, 146
Frug, Mary Jo, attack on, in *Harvard Law Revue,* 50, 190n

Gallardo, Angela (Angie [mother]), xii, 2, 5, 52–63, 144; Anglicizing Spanish surname, 56–57; assimilation experiences of, 52–63; and Catholic Church, 58–59, 149–50 (*see also* Catholic Church); Christmas Day

Gallardo (*continued*)
with, 22, 99; college (Los Angeles City College), 53; divorce, 53–54, 58–59, 74–75; and Harvard Law School plaque, 21–22; health problems, 62; marriage to Anglo men, 53, 59, 78–79; "passing" as Spanish, 55–57 (*see also* "Passing" as white); poverty, 59, 62; psychological problems, 21, 59, 60–63; racial attitudes, 58; and use of Spanish language, 7, 57, 61–62; unemployment and welfare, 59, 77–78
Gallardo, Tommy (Great Uncle), 76
Gándara, Arturo, x, xi, 117, 125, 127
Garcia-Rodriguez, Sergio, x, 117, 120
Garcia v. Hilton Hotels, 20–21, 25
Garza, Judge Reynaldo, 172
Gonzales, Josephine (great grandmother), 76–77
Gotanda, Neil, 35
Grandfather. *See* Johnson, Raymond (grandfather)
Grandmother. *See* Johnson, Mary (grandmother) and Moran, Hortense (Julia [grandmother]).
Greenberg, Jack, controversy over civil rights course, 33–36
Greene, Linda, 35
Guatemala, 113, 115
Güeros (white ones), 7, 186n
Guerrero, José Francisco (President, Supreme Court of El Salvador), 116
Guinier, Lani, 34, 110, 196n

Haar, Professor Charles, Socratic questioning of, 20
Harris, Cheryl, 171
Harvard Club (Boston), 46
Harvard Law Review, 18, 37, 38–51, 119; affirmative action controversy, 18–19, 35, 42–46; increased minorities as result of, 45; experiences with, my, 38–50; Gannett House, 39, 43, 49, 51; minority editors, lack of, 41–46; publications, my, 40–41. See also *Harvard Law Revue*
Harvard Law Revue, 46–50, 51; description of tradition, 46; horrible parody of Mary Jo Frug in, 50, 190n; racism in, 46–50
Harvard Law School, 10–51, 92, 109, 118, 119; admissions criteria, 27–29; affirmative action at, 27–29, 42–46; alcohol use by student body, 26; my anti-Harvard persona, 19, 22–27; first year anxiety, 19–20; Back Bench Pub, 26; stereotypes of Californian students, 17, 23; controversy over civil rights course, 33–36, 188n; class tensions, 16, 18–19, 50; competitive nature of students, 38–39; conservatives at, 17–18; Cuban Americans at, 23–24; my experiences at, 10–51; "face book," 16–17; financial aid, 13, 37–38, 50; grades, 21, 39; graduation, 50; Hemingway Gym, 40; Holmes Hall, 10; jobs during, 37–38; my Latino identity at, 22–27; Latinos at, 13, 22–27, 29–32 (*see also* Latinos and Latinas); "Law 4 Sale" graffiti, 10, 36–38; Legal Aid Bureau, 24; lack of minority professors, 25–26, 188n; mixed Anglo/Latinos at, 29–32, 35–36 (*see also* Mixed-race people); mother's psychological problems during my studies at, 21–22; Socratic method, 20–21; student body at, 15–16; TGIF ("Thank God It's Friday"), 26; Third World Coalition, 24, 33–36; tuition, 13. See also *Harvard Law Review; Harvard Law Revue*

Hastings College of the Law (San Francisco, California), 110–11, 123
Hawaiian Gardens, California, 81
Hawk, Robert, x, 120
Hearst, Patty, 91
Heller, Ehrman, White & McAuliffe, x, 109–20, 121, 123, 131; affirmative action at, 117–19; class issues, 120; my experiences at, 111–21; Latinos at, 117; *pro bono publico* work, 112–17, 120; my racial classification at, 118–19
Helm, Mark, 38
Hernández-Truyol, Berta Esperanza, 195n
Hinchberger, Bill, 14
Hing, Bill Ong, 87, 194n
Hispanics: allegation of false identity for purposes of affirmative action, 167, 209n; terminology, controversy over, 44, 184n
Hispanic National Bar Association, "Dirty Dozen," 125
Hopwood, Cheryl, affirmative action litigation, 128
Houck, Darcie, xi
Hylton, Maria, controversy over racial classification of, 173, 213–14n

I Love Lucy (television show), 12
Imperial Valley (California), 5, 53, 56, 76, 114
Immigration and immigrants, 175–76; "alien" terminology, 194n; Asian immigrants, 153, 154, 180–81; assimilation, 152–55, 179–81, 198n; *Bracero* (guest worker) program, 141–42; Central Americans, representation of, 113–16, 194n; eligibility for affirmative action, 166–67, 208n; Immigration and Naturalization Service (INS), 86, 113–14, 127, 194n, 203n; *Migra, La* (INS), 86; naturalization, 157; racial minorities, increased immigration of, 201n; restrictionist laws and proposals, 153–54, 198n, 200n, 201n; based on alleged failure of immigrants to assimilate, 154, 200n; stereotypes, inaccuracy of, 87; transnational identity of Mexican immigrants, 157, 199n; undocumented immigrants, 86–87. *See also* Assimilation; Nativism; Naturalization; Racism
Inter-ethnic conflict, 175, 177–78. *See also* Riots, Race
Intermarriage, 8, 164, 214n; African American and white marriages, 8, 210n, 210–11n; increasing rates of, 167, 186n, 209n; Mexican-American and Anglo marriages, 4–5, 53, 191n (*see* Gallardo, Angela (Angie [mother]); as route toward racial justice, 153–54, 169–70, 179, 212n. *See also* Mixed-race people
Irell & Manella (law firm), 24

Johnson, Brown-eyes (Kennard), 4–5, 66, 68, 170
Johnson, Carl, x, 120
Johnson, Elena (daughter), 3, 8, 63, 145, 146, 150–51, 159
Johnson, Eric (brother), 72, 74
Johnson, Kenneth (father), 2, 5–6, 64–72; racial sensibilities, 57, 58, 66–67, 70–72
Johnson, Marilyn (aunt), 71–72
Johnson, Mary (grandmother), 66
Johnson, Michael (brother), 7, 72, 73–74, 160
Johnson, Ralph, 40
Johnson, Raymond (grandfather), 65–68

Johnson, Rosie (great aunt), 4–5, 66, 68, 170
Johnson, Teresa (daughter), xii, 3, 7, 63, 64, 139, 142, 145, 146, 147, 149–50, 151, 159
Johnson, Tomás (son), xii, 3, 7, 63, 142, 145, 146, 147, 150, 151, 159
Johnson family, 139–51; exemplifying Latino diversity, 161. *See also under individual names*

Karst, Ken, 157–58
Kellogg, Mike, 90
Kennedy, Justice Anthony, 166
Kennedy, President John F., importance to Mexican-American community, 11–12
Kennedy, Randall, 185 n
King, Rodney, 139, 176, 182
King (Martin Luther King Jr.) Hall, 1
Ku Klux Klan, 210–11 n

LatCrit theory. *See* Critical Latino (LatCrit) theory
Latinos and Latinas: and affirmative action, 159–60, 166–67 (*see also* "Check-the-Box" minority); Anglicizing Spanish surname, 56–57, 83, 144, 191 n; assimilate, alleged failure to, 154, 200 n; assimilation, limits of, 6, 9, 86, 88, 155–57, 180–81, 187 n, 200 n; assimilation experiences of, 52–63, 152–74, 191 n, 198 n, 200 n, 200–201 n, 206 n; resistance to assimilation, 157; and Catholicism as part of identity, 148–50; conflict among, 161–62, 166–67, 206 n; changing demographics of, 8; discrimination against (*see* Racism); diversity among, ix, 6–9, 134–35, 150–51, 156, 160–67, 173–74, 178–79, 186–87 n, 203–4 n, 204 n, 205 n; electoral participation, 202 n; importance of family, 166; classification as "foreigners," 9, 144, 154, 155, 166, 187 n, 200 n; forgotten in civil rights scholarship, 181–82, 185 n; *gabacho,* 161, 205 n; at Harvard Law School, 22–27; mixed Anglo/Latino students at Harvard, 29–32; Hylton, Maria, 173, 213–14 n; identification as, 6–7, 166, 172–73, 178–79, 184 n; immigrants, 86–87, 156–57, 166–67, 206 n (*see also* Immigration and immigrants); alleged inferiority of, 168–69 (*see also* Racism); law to achieve social change for, limits of, 115, 207–8 n; law professors, 122, 131–32, 203 n (*see also* Law professor); *mestizaje,* 212 n; Mexican immigrants, 86–87, 156–57, 199 n, 202 n; mixed-race Latinos, 83, 85–86, 121–25, 155–56, 167–74, 186 n, 211 n, 212 n; as monolithic group, 160; national origin difference, 156, 158–59, 160–61, 162–63, 202 n, 203 n, 203–4 n, 206 n, 215 n; naturalization, 157, 202 n, 210 n; efforts at and pains of "passing," 55–57, 156, 171, 191 n, 213 n (*see also* "Passing" as white); physical appearance, 24–25, 82, 137, 145, 156, 158–59, 161–62, 186 n, 204–5 n, 212 n; *pocho,* 205 n; poverty, 6, 181, 185 n, 216 n; racial mixture, attitudes toward, 170 (*see also* Mixed-race people); *raza cosmica* (cosmic race), 170, 212 n; religion, 148–50, 166; "Spanish" heritage, 55–57, 191 n, 213 n (*see also* "Passing" as White); Spanish language, use of, 7, 57, 147, 163–64, 166, 191–92 n, 200 n, 206 n; Spanish surname, 4, 89, 126–27, 138,

164–65, 191 n, 206 n; stereotypes about Latinos, 142, 161, 162, 206 n; storytelling by, importance of, 190–91 n; at U.C. Berkeley, 94–97; at U.C. Davis, 134–38; middle class values, 154. *See also* Hispanics; Mixed-race people; Racial identity; Racism; Surname, Spanish

Law firms: Donovan Leisure Newton & Irvine, extravagance of, 36–38; Heller Ehrman White & McAuliffe, experiences at, 109–20; *Pro bono publico* work, 112–17, 120

Law professor: affirmative action, 128–31, 195 n; Association of American Law Schools, 121–24, 195 n; class tensions, 127; committee assignments, 128–29; Distinguished Teaching Award, 137; my experiences as, 121–38; Latinos as, 122, 131–32, 137, 196–97 n, 203 n; other minorities as, 125–26, 195 n, 197 n; my racial classification as, 121, 122–23, 124–25, 137; student admissions, 128–30, 134; tenure reviews, 133–34. *See also* University of California at Davis

Lawrence, Charles, 35

Law School Admissions, 12, 196 n

Law School Aptitude Test (LSAT), 11–12; negative impact on minority admissions, 129–30; my racial classification for, 12. *See also* Affirmative Action

Lewis, Evelyn, 125–26

Lopez, Gerald (Jerry), 25

Lopez, Ian Haney, 117

Los Angeles, 2, 4, 6, 47, 53, 55, 65, 110, 140, 150, 175

Los Angeles City College, 53, 68

Loyola Marymount University, 140

Mackey, Dave, xi, 25

MacKinnon, Catherine, 47

MacMillan, Bruce, x, 120

McBride, James, experiences as mixed African American/white person, 8

McGinnis, John, comments on affirmative action, 42–43

McNab, Cecil, 32

Marquez, Rosanna, 23

Martínez, George A., xi, 210 n, 212 n

Matsuda, Mari, 35

Mayeda, Mari, 24

Medina, Judge Harold, 172

Medina, Mike, and "Rat Race" comics, 6

Mexican American. *See* Latinos and Latinas

Michigan State University, Julian Samora Research Institute, 52

Microaggressions; as reflecting limits of assimilation, 5, 183 n; negative comments, jokes, and stories, 2–3, 4–5, 24–25, 33, 46–50, 57, 59, 78, 87, 109, 114–15, 118–19, 122, 124–25, 126, 134, 135–36, 137, 141–42, 142, 145, 146–47, 155–56, 161–62, 183–84 n, 196 n, 196–97 n, 200 n, 201 n. See also *Harvard Law Revue*; Racism

Migra, La (Immigration & Naturalization Service), 86

Miller, Professor Arthur, Socratic questioning of, 20–21.

Mixed-race people, ix, 167–74, 209 n, 210 n, 211 n; adoption of racial identity by, 6–8, 157–60; affirmative action, classification for purposes of, 130, 159–60 (*see also* Affirmative Action); African American/white persons, 8, 74, 155, 169, 170–73, 210 n, 210–11 n, 213 n, 213–14 n (*see also* "Passing" as white)

—Anglo/Latino persons: 2–5, 173; adoption of racial identity, 157–60; animus toward, 170 (*see also* Racism); assimilation of, 155–56 (*see also* Assimilation); Chávez, Linda, 172, 207 n (*see also* Chávez, Linda); classification difficulties of, 8–9, 90, 121, 167–74; on *Harvard Law Review*, 38–46; ridicule in *Harvard Law Revue,* 46–50; at Harvard Law School, 29–32; in high school, 85–86; Medina, Judge Harold, 172; microaggressions, 161–62 (*see also* Microaggressions); Moraga, Cherríe, 35–36, 186 n; benefits of "passing" as white, 138, 171–72 (*see also* "Passing" as white); Plunkett, Jim (professional football player), 164; Quinn, Anthony (actor), 164; Richardson, Bill, U.S. Ambassador to the United Nations, 164; Samora, Julian, 164; Spanish surname, 89, 126–27, 138, 164–65; at U.C. Berkeley, 94–95; at U.C. Davis, 94–95, 134–35; uncertainty of racial identity, 9, 80–85, 160; whites treated as, 171, 172–74; Williams, Ted (professional baseball player), 164. *See also* Latinos and Latinas

—Anglo/Latino marriages, 4–5, 53; classification difficulties, 8–9, 22, 168–71, 172–73, 186 n, 211 n (*see also* Census, U.S.); classification for college and law school applications, 12; benefits of overinclusion of minorities, 31–32; demographics, changing, 8, 167, 169–70, 174, 186 n, 209 n; "half breed," 168; as inferior, 168–69, 210 n, 210–11 n (*see also* Racism); invisibility of, 48, 168–70; as multicultural, 185 n; ambiguity of racial identity, 9 (*see also* Racial Identity); Thomas, Piri, 213 n. *See also* Multiracialism; "One drop" rule; Racial identity

Montejano, David, 96, 193 n

Montoya, Margaret, xi, 31, 155, 197 n

Moraga, Cherríe, 35–36, 186 n

Moran, Hortense (Julia [grandmother]) 10–11, 52, 54; abused by husband, 55, 57; assimilation experiences of, 52–63; "passing" as Spanish, 55–56; racial attitudes of, 58; search for status, 10–11; storytelling of, 55–56

Morena, La (*The Dark One*), 8

Morris, Glenn, 41

Mother. See Gallardo, Angela (Angie [mother])

Multiculturalism, ix, 152–53, 178, 198 n

Multiracialism, 167–74. *See also* Mixed-race people

Munger Tolles & Olson (law firm), 40

Muríeta, Joaquin, 193 n

Nativism, ix, 6, 85–86, 153–54, 167, 176, 185 n, 198 n, 200 n, 215 n. *See also* Racism

Naturalization: process and rates of, 202–3 n; racial prerequisites for, 168, 210 n

Navarette, Ruben, 95

Nelson, Alan (former Commissioner, Immigration & Naturalization service), 127

New York Times, 44–45, 45, 141

Noblin, Rob, 46

Northwestern University School of Law, Maria Hylton controversy, 173

Obama, Barack, 42, 189 n

O'Cadiz, Sergio, xi, 89

O'Farrell, Leo, 93

Oki, Jeff, 94
Olivas, Michael, x, 131–32
Olympic Games (1968), 70
"One drop" rule, 168, 209–10 n. *See also* Racial identity
Ontiveros, Maria, 117

Paper Chase, The (movie), 10, 187 n
"Passing" as white, 55–57, 138, 171–72, 191 n, 212–13 n. *See also* Racial identity
Patiño, Judge Lorenzo, 135
Patrick, Deval, 110, 194 n
Paz, Octavio, 140
Piatt, Bill, xi, 213 n
Piper, Adrian, experiences as "white looking" African American, 171
Placita, La (Los Angeles), 150
Plunkett, Jim (professional football player), 164
Pro bono publico work: economic pressures to reduce, 120; at Heller Ehrman White & McAuliffe, 112–17. *See also* Heller Ehrman White & McAuliffe; Law firms
Proposition 227 (anti-bilingual education initiative), 147, 163

Quinn, Anthony (actor), 164

Race as Social Construction, 6, 177–79; examples (Irish and Jewish immigrants), 215 n; formation of "new" races by society, 179
Race Relations, 175–82; beyond black and white, 167; complexity of, in multiracial population, 174; racial hierarchy, 176, 212 n
Racial identity, 173–74; consistency of, and variation among groups, 158–59, 203 n; of mixed-race people, 2–5, 8–9, 167–74, 186 n, 209–10 n (*see also* Mixed-race people); naturalization laws and classification of, 168, 209–10 n; "one drop" rule, 168, 209–10 n; voluntary adoption of, 6–8, 157–60, 173–74, 178, 203 n
Racial Minorities, increased numbers, 167, 209 n
Racism, 109, 171, 175–82, 186 n; toward African Americans, 32–33, 78, 81–82, 84, 97, 127, 169, 176–77, 197 n, 210 n, 210–11 n; as exceptional, 215 n; in Boston, 32–33; in Los Angeles, 73–88; toward Asian Americans, 24–25, 153, 176 (*see also* Asian Americans); toward immigrants, 215 n; toward Latinos, 152–74, 176, 177 (*see also* Latinos and Latinas); Mexican Americans and Mexican immigrants, 59, 78, 81, 82–88, 96, 114–15, 141–42, 144, 158–59, 168–69, 183 n, 185 n, 191 n, 205 n, 211 n; toward mixed-race people, 168–71 (*see also* Mixed-race people); relationship between, and subordination of various racial minorities, 176–77, 215 n; "white flight," 81–82. See also *Harvard Law Revue;* Microaggressions; Nativism
Ramirez, Deborah, 167
Ramirez, Richard ("Night Stalker"), 162
Razo, Joe, incident as student at Harvard College, 155
Reagan, President Ronald, 17–18
Regents of the University of California v. Bakke, 28, 128
Reinhardt, Judge Stephen, x, 109–11, 123; my clerkship with, 109–11
Reynoso, Justice Cruz, 130–31
Richardson, Bill (U.S. Ambassador of the United Nations), 164

Riots, race, 70, 96, 139, 175
Robby (brother), 21, 74, 99, 160
Rochin, Refugio, 52
Rodriguez, Richard, 140, 205n; naturalization of father, 157; views about affirmative action, 193n; "Hispanic" assimilation, 6, 154
Roscow, Steve, 3, 93
Roth, Jerry, 38

Saito, Natsu Taylor, 212n
Salazar, Joe, Jr., 142, 143
Salazar, Joe, Sr., 143–44
Salazar, Mary Helen, 4, 142, 144
Salazar, Virginia (Ginger), xii, 7, 51, 87, 110, 121, 139–42; and Catholicism, 148–50; children, 145–48 (*see also individual names*); family, 141–45; racial sensibilities, 141–42
Samora, Julian, 164
San Gabriel Valley (California), 54, 56, 69, 73, 74, 81, 139, 190n
Sandrino-Glasser, Gloria, 214n
Scales-Trent, Judy, experiences as mixed African American/white person, 8, 155, 183–84n, 212n
Schenker, Marty, 17
Serrano, Jose, 86–87
Sheen, Martin (actor), 164, 207n
Smith, Jim, 87, 127
Sobrino, Jon (Jesuit priest), 116
Sotomayor, Vic, 23
South Bay Daily Breeze (Torrance, California), 69
Spanish immersion program, 147–48
Spanish Language. *See* Latinos and Latinas
Spanish Surname. *See* Surname, Spanish
Stanford Law School, 117, 196n
Stefancic, Jean, 214n
Steinem, Gloria, 47
Surname, Spanish, 158, 206n; Anglicizing, 31, 56–57, 191n; lack of, among some mixed Latinos, 4, 48, 89, 126–27, 138, 164–65

Teaching. *See* Law professor; University of California at Davis
Teresa (daughter). *See* Johnson, Teresa (daughter)
Thomas, Justice Clarence, 11
Tomás (son). *See* Johnson, Tomás (son)
Torrance, California, 69, 73, 74, 81, 82, 83, 85, 86, 109
Torres, Dan, 23
Torres, Gerald, 192n
Toro, Luis Angel, 193n

United States, as multiracial society, 175–76
University of California at Berkeley, 11, 13, 15, 22, 31, 32; Boalt Hall, 117, 130; Ehrman Hall, 92; my experiences at, 89–100; fees (in 1980s), 99; Latinos at, 95–96; Moffitt Library, 15, 94; Muríeta, Joaquin House, 94, 96
University of California at Davis, 1–2, 117; affirmative action, 128–31; faculty appointments, 130–31; student admissions, 128–30; dean selection, 130–31; my experiences at, 1–2, 125–38; La Raza Law Students Association, 135; Lorenzo Patiño banquet, 135; students at, 134–38; Latino students, 134–35, 138; questioning of my racial identity at, 137
U.S. Commission on Immigration Reform, 200n
U.S. News & World Report, 129

Valdavinos, Miguel, xi, 135
Valdes, Frank, 132
Valencia, Rey, 117
Vasconcelos, José (philosopher), 212n
Vazquez, Carlos Manuel, 110
Virginia. *See* Salazar, Virginia (Ginger)
Vorenberg, Dean James, 49; on affirmative action, 18–19, 43; on Third World Coalition boycott, 34

Waters, Mary C., 157
Watson, Tom, 65, 192n
Welfare, 77–78
West High School (Torrance, California), 83, 87–88, 109
Whiteness, privilege of, 7–8, 32, 71, 156, 172, 184n, 202n, 213n
Wildman, Stephanie, 213n
Williams, Greg, experiences as mixed African American/white person, 8, 155, 203n, 210–11n
Williams, Patricia, 212–13n
Williams, Ted (professional baseball player), 164
Wilson, Pete (California Governor), 131
Wisdom, Judge John Minor, 49
Woods, Tiger (professional golfer), 169, 211–12n

Yale Law School, 32, 117
Yoneda, Mary, 93–94
Youth, my, 73–88, mistaken as Asian American, 82; assimilation efforts during, 84–88; Catechism, 75; classmates, 75, 83–84; impact of divorce on, 74–75, 80–81; elementary school, 75–76; Mexican American culture, influence of 75–76; trips to Mexico during, 76; racial uncertainty, 80–85, 87–88; racial tensions, 81–86; study of Spanish, 85; welfare and poverty, 77–79; working with undocumented persons, 86–87
Yu, Peter, 42

Zeitlin, Cary, 93
Zellhart, Lynne, xi